Shadow Warriors

Shadow Warriors

The Untold Stories of American
Special Operations During WWII

Dick Camp

ZENITH PRESS

First published in 2013 by Zenith Press, an imprint of MBI Publishing Company, 400 First Avenue North, Suite 400, Minneapolis, MN 55401 USA

Zenith Press titles are also available at discounts in bulk quantity for industrial or sales-promotional use. For details write to Special Sales Manager at MBI Publishing Company, 400 First Avenue North, Suite 400, Minneapolis, MN 55401 USA.

To find out more about our books, join us online at www.zenithpress.com.

Library of Congress Cataloging-in-Publication Data

Camp, Richard D.

Shadow warriors : the untold stories of American special operations during WWII / Dick Camp.

pages cm

Includes bibliographical references and index.

ISBN 978-0-7603-4429-3 (hardcover)

1. World War, 1939-1945--Secret service--United States. 2. World War, 1939-1945--Commando operations--United States. 3. United States. Marine Corps--History--World War, 1939-1945. 4. United States. Office of Strategic Services. I. Title.

D810.S7C328 2013

940.54'8673--dc23

Editor: Scott Pearson
Design Manager: James Kegley
Layout: Helena Schimizu
Cover designer: Simon Larkin

On the front cover: Raiders or Paramarines bring their rubber boats ashore to conceal in the jungle. *USMC Photo*

On the back cover: Capt. Frank Farrell, 1st Marines intelligence officer, and two unknown Marines in the Guadalcanal jungle in 1942. *USMC Photo*

Printed in the United States of America

10 9 8 7 6 5 4 3 2 1

To all those warriors who remain in the shadows.

Contents

Preface

During my formative years in the Marine Corps, I volunteered and I was accepted as a platoon commander in a reconnaissance company. It was an exciting peacetime assignment because of the many and varied training opportunities, one of which was to make clandestine raids from submarines using seven-man rubber boats—heady stuff for a brand new first lieutenant with less than two years' service.

On one exercise, I led my twenty-man platoon to Pearl Harbor where we loaded our three two-hundred-pound rubber boats aboard the USS *Tunny* SS-282, a World War II attack submarine. After securing the boats and seeing that my men were "bedded down," I ventured to the bridge to discuss the day's activities with the boat's skipper, a young lieutenant commander. I reported in the approved Marine Corps manner—formal salute, body rigidly at attention—"Sir, First Lieutenant Camp reporting for training."

The commander gave me a wave that I took to be a return salute, stuck out his hand and said pleasantly, "Hi, Lieutenant, I'm Jack, what would you like to do today?" To say that I was caught off guard would be an understatement. I was tongue-tied. He was in essence giving me carte blanche to use his multimillion dollar submarine for whatever I wanted to do—*wow*! I found out later "Jack's" informal manner was his way of having a little harmless fun with the Marines.

The boat got under way to the assigned training area off Fort Hasse beach on the windward side of Oahu. Later that day, after carrying out several practice launches, I was informed that the regimental commander, Col. Ed Dupras, was on the way to observe our training. Shortly afterward, he arrived in a launch, pulled alongside, and climbed aboard. Needless to say I was unnerved by his sudden appearance but the colonel went out of his way to make me feel relaxed. Now comfortable, I proceeded to explain, in great boring detail how to conduct a raid from a submarine. After fifteen minutes of mind-numbing "how-to" minutia about rubber boats, launch procedures, and insertion tactics, I finally wound down. I expected questions galore, because, after all he was just a senior officer who commanded a desk. Instead, he just nodded and casually mentioned that "things hadn't changed much since my days as a Raider!" Damn, I felt two inches high! He had "been there, done that" in actual combat, and here I was prattling on about "how to do" when he had "done it." I found out later that Colonel Dupras had been a platoon commander in the 1st Raider Battalion in World War II, under the famous Col. "Red Mike" Edson. The World War II raiders and their brethren in the ParaMarines, and Office of Strategic Services were held in the highest regard by my generation of reconnaissance men. We considered them real life "tough guys," the bravest of the brave, who blazed the trail for our current day Special Operations Forces.

Shadow Warriors is a tribute to the accomplishments of those early unconventional warriors.

PART I

European Theater

CHAPTER 1

Spy Master

Colonel William A. "Bill" Eddy, the recently assigned naval attaché in Tangier, was ordered to London to brief Maj. Gen. George S. Patton Jr. and other high ranking generals on the situation in North Africa. The officers were gathered in a hotel room, when Eddy, wearing his Marine Corps uniform with its two rows of World War I ribbons, limped through the doorway. Among the ribbons on Eddy's blouse were the Navy Cross and the U.S. Army's Distinguished Service Cross (both the second-highest decorations for bravery in action within their respective services), the Silver Star with Gold Star indicating a second award, and the Purple Heart for being wounded in action—the cause for his limp—with Gold Star.

Taking care of introductions, Col. Edward Buxton asked Patton, "Do you know Bill Eddy?"

Patton looked at all the ribbons on Eddy's chest. "Never saw him before in my life, but the son of a bitch's been shot at enough, hasn't he?"

William Alfred Eddy was born in 1896 in Sidon, Syria (present day Lebanon). His parents were American Presbyterian missionaries, who insisted their son immerse himself in the local culture, a decision that would have important consequences in his later life. Young Eddy took advantage of the local traditions and customs and was soon comfortable in the bazaars and souks, sampling the local cuisine of sheep's eyes and couscous. He spoke colloquial Arabic like a native, enabling him to make friends with the tribal chieftains and move among them like few Westerners of the time could do. A 6 November 2008, article in *The Economist* titled "An Earlier Envoy" noted that, "If anyone could have been America's Lawrence of Arabia it was Colonel William Eddy." Anthony Cave Brown in *Wild Bill Donovan: The Last Hero* wrote of Eddy, "As a personality, Eddy was difficult, a man of pronounced likes and dislikes, trusts and distrusts . . . extremely clannish . . . who had powerful vocal cords and was a large, tall football player type, rarely minced words."

After completing middle school Eddy was sent to the United States in 1908 to complete his schooling. He attended the College of Wooster, a Presbyterian school in Ohio, until his sophomore year when he transferred to Princeton. Upon graduation, Eddy surprised his family by applying to become a Marine officer. On 6 June 1917, he was notified that "he had successfully passed the examination for appointment as a temporary second lieutenant" and was ordered to report to the new Marine Corps base at Quantico, Virginia. Three months later, he sailed for France with the 6th Marine Regiment as intelligence officer.

Devil Dog

Second Lieutenant Bill Eddy and the two enlisted Marines of his reconnaissance patrol lay concealed in the uncut field, heavy with the smell of clover, just a few feet from a gravel road. The crunch of hobnail boots, guttural commands, and the muffled sound of engineer tools drowned out the night sounds. Eddy carefully recorded the activity and then the three silently withdrew into the darkness. They slipped back through the German lines and reported their observations to the regimental commander, Col. Albertus W. Catlin. "The Germans are organizing in the woods and consolidating their machine-gun positions," Eddy said, before describing his observations in more detail. The report impressed Catlin. "Eddy did some remarkable work with the patrols," he noted. "He was a daredevil, who loved nothing better than to stalk German sentries in Indian fashion and steal close to their lines. The Marine service has always attracted men of this type."

Eddy's actions that night earned him both the Navy Cross and Army Distinguished Service Cross. The citation read in part: "Near Torcy, France, on the night of June 4, 1918, at a great personal risk, he led a reconnoitering patrol of two men into the enemy's lines and established the location of those lines. At one time he and his patrol were between two bodies of the enemy, remaining there for more than an hour. The information which he brought back proved of great value in determining the disposition of the enemy, and he was in imminent risk of capture during the greater part of his journey."

The Marine Brigade, consisting of the 5th and 6th regiments and 6th Machine Gun Battalion, moved into attack positions, and at 1700 on 6 June 1918 assaulted the heavily defended "Bois de Belleau," wrestling it from the German defenders in a horrific month-long battle and earning the nickname "Devil Dogs" from their enemies. Thereafter, the wood was known as the "Bois de la Brigade de Marine." During the action, Eddy and Sgt. Gerald C. Thomas (later General) made a personal reconnaissance in front of the lines to judge the effects of Allied artillery. Thomas recalled: "We worked forward slowly through the dense wood. Eddy climbed a tree to get a better look. He had no more gotten up there when he came down with a thump. 'My God,' he whispered, 'I was looking square at a German in a machine-gun nest!' " After several more close personal observations, they returned to friendly lines. Both Marines were awarded the Silver Star for their actions, the first of two for Eddy.

Catlin noted, "Eddy's conduct was distinguished to a degree by unerring judgment, immediate action, and a remarkable sangfroid." His luck finally ran out on 25 June, when he was wounded in the leg by a high-explosive shell. After recuperating, he rejoined the brigade as its intelligence officer and aide-de-camp to Brig. Gen. Wendell C. "Buck" Neville. Three months later Eddy was evacuated to the U.S. Naval Hospital, Brooklyn after contracting a near-fatal case of pneumonia. In his weakened condition, he contracted a severe infection in his right hip, which resulted in complete loss of motion in the joint that caused him to walk with a limp for the rest of his life. The Marine Retiring Board found that he was "unfit for active service" and placed him on the retired list with the grade of captain. In a letter to his mother, Eddy expressed concern for the future. "It is a real question what [I] will do after I leave the hospital. As you know, I will be a cripple all my life. There will be something I can do, I know."

"A profession with which I am definitely out of love"

Eddy decided to pursue his education by entering the Princeton graduate program, earning an MA in 1921 and a PhD in philosophy the following year. In 1923, he took a position with the American University in Cairo, a private institution that offered him an opportunity to return to the Arab world. His old commander General Neville gave Eddy a ringing endorsement. "I know of no man whose personal qualifications so appeal to me as did those of Captain Eddy in the short time we were together. Captain Eddy's personal character is all that could be desired. His capacity for leadership, his influence upon others, and his ability for efficient administration are beyond praise. To me he showed intelligence, energy, judgment, and knowledge far beyond that warranted by his age and length of service." Neville's commendation highlighted the character and ability of the man and, seen in hindsight, offered a remarkable insight into Eddy's future influence in the Middle East.

In 1928, he returned to the United States as a professor of English at Dartmouth, and in 1936 he became the first non-clerical president of both Hobart College and its sister institution, William Smith College, on Seneca Lake in upper New York State. Major General John H. Russell sent a letter of congratulations. "As Commandant of the Marine Corps, and speaking for your friends, it gives me distinct pleasure to offer you congratulations and best wishes for every success in your new assignment." One of his first official acts as president of the colleges was to ask that Hobart be included in providing candidates for the Corps' Platoon Leaders Class. In 1936 Eddy was promoted to major on the retired list. At a chance meeting with the commandant, Lt. Gen. Thomas Holcomb, Eddy volunteered for active duty "if his services could be profitably utilized." He wrote a friend, "I shall welcome active service with the Marines if that comes next summer, and, if not, I shall ask for it a year later if the world emergency continues to be acute." He applied for a leave of absence from Hobart but told the friend that he was unwilling to return to the school because it was "a profession with which I am definitely out of love." In view of Eddy's impressive background in the Middle East, Holcomb discussed his request to return to active duty with the director of Naval Intelligence. A short time later, he sent a personal note to Eddy. "I am writing to find out how quickly you can report for duty, should your services be required, which I am inclined to think will be the case." In mid-May, Eddy received the orders: at the end of the college year, he would report for active duty.

Naval Attaché, Cairo

"All U.S. Naval Attaches were involved in counterintelligence in various forms."
—Marine Corps Counter Intelligence Association

On 23 June 1941, Eddy was formally designated as Naval Attaché and Naval Attaché for Air in Cairo. The Unites States would not officially enter the war until the attack on Pearl Harbor later that year, but U.S. support for its allies was steadily building behind the scenes. The embassy's Chief of Mission was informed that, "Major Eddy, you will find, is more than a Naval Attaché. The Navy Department envisages using [him] not only in Egypt but in nearby Arabic speaking countries such as Saudi Arabia, Palestine, Syria, and Iraq. From our own point of view we not only see no objection to such an arrangement, but heartily approve of it. Major Eddy has many close friends among high-placed Arab officials and Arab families throughout these territories, and I believe he can make contact with these groups that would be impossible for almost any other American. We should like to have him have as much opportunity as possible to travel around freely, make contacts and observations and submit reports." A month later Eddy, now a lieutenant colonel, reached Cairo and immediately got to work. In a letter to his wife, he wrote about his duties. "The nature of the information on naval matters which I seek (and sometimes find) concerns the enemy more than the allies and covers: naval operations, trade, merchant marine, suspects and agents, technical devices and inventions . . . bases, mine fields, mutinies or disaffection among personnel in ports, contraband being shipped to enemy by or thru neutrals, arrivals and departures of all vessels, volume of supply going to for example Dardanelles or North Africa, sailing routes."

There was another part of his job that he was particularly suited to because of his many Arab connections. "[A]s you know, I am charged with political errands too, counter-espionage, study of Axis propaganda, personnel, organization, sabotage, blacklists . . . I have developed sources of information in several cities." He went on to caution his wife about the danger inherent in the assignment. "Nothing on this sheet should ever appear in print unless you are in a hurry to become a widow." The chief of mission disapproved of his counter-espionage function, saying "it would end diplomatic immunity, but I had other instructions from my primary

COORDINATOR OF INFORMATION

The Office of the Coordinator of Information (COI) was founded 11 July 1941 by President Franklin D. Roosevelt at the prompting of William J. Donovan. The COI was the U.S. government's first central-ized propaganda and espionage agency. In 1940 and 1941, Roosevelt had sent Donovan to Britain to assess the country's ability to fight Germany, and Donovan's experience with British military intelligence convinced him the United States needed a similar organization.

Donovan's proposal created a bureaucratic firestorm, particu-larly with the FBI's J. Edgar Hoover and the U.S. Army's Gen. George C. Marshall. Both looked upon the COI as a naked ploy to usurp their power. Despite their heated opposition, Roosevelt approved its formation. Initially the agency had the "authority to collect and analyze all information and date, which may bear upon the national security . . . correlate such information and data . . . [and make it] available to the President and to such departments and officials of the Government as the President may determine. " However, Donovan soon expanded the agency into a worldwide fiefdom that not only collected intelligence but organized a force of agents who conducted espionage activities behind enemy lines.

boss, the director of Naval Intelligence, and I went on my own way." Many of Eddy's intelligence and political reports were read at the highest levels of government, including the newly assigned coordinator of information, William J. "Wild Bill" Donovan, World War I hero and prominent New York City lawyer.

Spies and Lies in Tangier

"[Tangier] might have inspired a chapter from a . . . spy novel, with its walled Arab quarter and narrow streets where veiled women, camels, smugglers, and spies plied their trade. . . . It was Bill Eddy's kind of place . . ."

—Hal Vaughan

In late fall 1941, the president approved a plan Donovan had proposed to conduct undercover intelligence activities in North Africa. A principal feature of the plan was the designation of a coordinator of information (COI) representative to coordinate and direct the clandestine operations. Donovan selected Eddy based on his knowledge of the area, his language capability, and his high level contacts among the Arabs. The appointment as naval attaché in Tangier became official in December 1941. In a letter to his wife, Eddy wrote, "I returned from my two weeks observation cruise with the Navy to find a bombshell in the form of telegraphic orders awaiting me: 'Immediate return to Washington for instructions regarding other foreign duty.' . . . " In early December, he met with Donovan at the new COI headquarters in the Apex Building in downtown Washington and was given his marching orders. "That the aid of native chiefs be obtained, the loyalty of the inhabitants be cultivated; fifth columnists organized and placed, demolition materials cached; and guerrilla bands and daring men organized and installed . . . [and] to maintain a line of demarcation in so far as practicable, between operations and intelligence."

Eddy arrived in Tangier in late January 1942 with a two-fold mandate: "Prepare a network of agents and seven clandestine radio stations to (a) leave behind in case the Axis occupies North Africa (b) to prepare intelligence and sabotage in case the Allies should land an expeditionary force."

Eddy was well aware that Tangier's reputation as a spying and smuggling center made it a unique destination for many European and American diplomats and spies. Eddy wrote that the city "was full of persons who had been, or ought to be, in jail. As Lisbon was for Europe, Tangier was for Africa—the escape hatch from prison, banking laws, justice, persecution, morality (there was no neighborhood without sin fit to cast the first stone)." The city, located on the North African coast at the western entrance to the Strait of Gibraltar, broiled with intrigue, swarming with Allied and Axis agents, spy vs. spy, who rubbed shoulders in its watering holes and bistros.

By the time of Eddy's assignment the situation in North Africa had deteriorated. With the entry of the United States into the war after Pearl Harbor, the collaborating French Vichy government imposed severe restrictions on Americans and carried out reprisals against any Frenchman who associated with them. Americans were denied access to docks, airfields, and other militarily significant installations. Gestapo agents who had previously maintained a hands-off policy now began to apply political and strong-arm methods against them. Journalist Thomas Lippman noted, "Eddy and his agents were engaged in serious and sometimes deadly business. Smuggled weapons blew up. People disappeared. At one point Eddy began to carry a pistol . . . against the possibility of an attack on the street." Unscrupulous double agents thrived by passing information to the highest bidder. "Dirty work" abounded: car bombings, sabotage, assassinations, and intimidations. One night Eddy's assistant, 1st Lt. Franklin P. Holcomb, USMC, son of the commandant, was accosted by a group of Italian thugs. In the ensuing brawl, Holcomb upheld the highest traditions of the Corps. President Roosevelt learned of the Marine "victory" and directed that Holcomb be immediately promoted to captain.

Eddy was concerned that the Axis powers, assisted by the Vichy government, might act before he could carry out his mission. The Vichy government had changed hands, the new prime minister, Pierre Laval, was friendlier toward Nazi Germany than in the past. This cozy relationship offered advantages to the German and Italian agents in the duel of intrigue that was playing out. The two Axis powers enjoyed a near-monopoly on intelligence and propaganda because of the wave of anti-British sentiment as a result of their attack on the French fleet at Mers-el-Kebir and Dakar in July and September 1940. Vichy then severed diplomatic ties and ejected the British from North Africa. Two powerful collaborationist organizations, the *Service d'ordre legionnaire* (SOL) and the *Parti Populaire Français* (PPF) supported the Axis and made Eddy's undercover work even more difficult. The United States continued to have diplomatic relations with the Vichy government and maintained a consulate in the Tangier International Zone of the old city, where it enjoyed extra-territorial rights under a 1786 agreement with Sultan Sidi Mohammed (which remained in effect until 1956, when Moroccan independence was attained).

One important factor was in Eddy's favor. An economic pact between the United States and Vichy France, known as the Murphy-Weygand Agreement, had been signed allowing twelve U.S. vice-consuls, dubbed the "Twelve Apostles," to oversee the allocation of humanitarian aid. The twelve men were in actuality undercover intelligence agents that Eddy "was to be given appropriate authority over . . ." As Kermit Roosevelt wrote in *War Report of the OSS (Office of Strategic Services)*, "The agents were recruited from all walks of life, principally for their knowledge of the French language and their experience abroad. Most of them had seen service in World War I; several had served with the French Army prior to the entry of the United States into that conflict." They were stationed in the port cities of Tunis, Oran, Algiers, and Casablanca. In *Cloak & Gown: Scholars in the Secret War, 1939–1961* Robin W. Winks wrote, " . . . the group was dismissed by the Germans as representing 'a perfect picture of the mixture of races and characters in that savage conglomeration called the United States' . . . The group proved quite effective . . . because they were wisely chosen and because Colonel Eddy was extraordinarily competent." Eddy immediately began the process of setting up a coordinated intelligence and special operations system to meet the possibility of an Axis invasion. One of his first steps was to route all the agents' intelligence reports through his office to ensure proper dissemination. The vice-consuls, with their diplomatic immunity, were able to routinely make courier trips to Tangier to deliver their reports to him without raising too much suspicion.

Eddy was particularly anxious to establish a clandestine radio network in the event of a diplomatic rupture or Axis military action. He tasked the vice-consuls to recruit pro-Allied locals to man the stations. The "recruits" were secretly transported to Gibraltar for training by British radiomen. By the summer of 1942, the secret network was up and running. Washington was given the code name VICTOR, the base station in Tangier was MIDWAY, with YANKEE at Algiers, FRANKLIN at Oran, PILGRIM at Tunis, and LINCOLN at Casablanca, which had to be mobile because the Germans had a triangulation unit that could zero in on the station's location. The base station in Tangier was in the naval attaché's office, across a narrow street from the Consulate. Carleton Coon, who considered Eddy "one of the greatest men he had ever met," noted in *Adventures and Discoveries*, "Soon Mrs. Childs, a White Russian lady who had no knowledge of what we were doing, complained that the bussing and crackling of our radio transmitter spoiled her sleep, and it had to go. It is idle to point out that the success of the invasion was more important than Mrs. Child's sleep. Colonel Eddy moved the set to a small rented villa on the mountain."

With the agents and the radio network in place, Eddy concentrated on developing an agent network, which was not without its risks. "We are followed everywhere we go," Eddy wrote to his son, "so we have to be very careful about meeting our confidential agents. I know the men who follow me because I have photographs of the fifty-five Axis agents in Tangier and Spanish Morocco. It is lots of fun to turn on them and stare them in the face. They dare no overt action because the Germans are most unpopular here. The people of Tangier want only to be left alone, they do not want anybody bringing violence to the town. Our telephones are all tapped. We never say anything confidential over the phone so it is lots of fun to say, 'I'll meet you for lunch at the El Minzah Hotel [Eddy and other Allied agents lived in the hotel, while Axis agents lived in the Riff Hotel] but we will not invite the damned German who is listening to this conversation!' " In a letter to his daughter, Eddy wrote, "We have quite a time with counterespionage. The head telephone operator in the El Minzah Hotel (a very well educated man on our side who prepared for months to disguise himself as a mere telephone operator) has just been offered five thousand francs a month by the Germans to report to them . . . he promptly told us. We are taking the francs and composing faked conversations for him to report to them, conversations which should give the Germans plenty of phony information."

Eddy established contact with the leader of the most powerful religious brotherhood in northern Morocco, codenamed "Strings." Kermit Roosevelt noted, "Members of the 'Strings' group numbered tens of thousands of Moors from every walk of life, ready to obey unquestioningly the will of their divine leader. 'Strings' reports to [Eddy] came from sheiks and holy men who penetrated areas forbidden by the French authorities to the general populace and from farmers and shepherds who relayed pertinent items of intelligence in comparative anonymity." Eddy also bankrolled one of the most influential Berber tribesmen, designated "Tassels," to smuggle arms and equipment. Roosevelt wrote, "The Riffs [a Berber tribe] under 'Tassels,' on the other hand were Berber adventurers, willing to carry out any job regardless of the danger involved, and highly adept at avoiding detection by Spanish or French police. These men knew how to handle arms and conduct guerrilla warfare in difficult terrain." Eddy kept the two groups separate, never letting the other know about the other. He conducted secret meetings where detailed combat intelligence was passed—such as battle order, troop movements, or fortifications—and significant political events.

Axis agents kept close watch on Eddy and his confederates. "Bars and restaurants and lodgings were staffed by double agents who took money with both hands impartially," Eddy noted. "Our hotel bureau drawers were ransacked regularly, as we proved many times by placing 'confidential papers' in marked positions . . ." Meetings with agents had to be carefully planned so as not to give their identity away. On one occasion Eddy waited on a roof while a subordinate, Carleton Coon, "lay in the bushes next to a reed fence, and spiders and ants crawled over me and spun webs over me. Meanwhile, a pair of Spanish lovers lay down on the other side of the fence; I was treated to all their physiological noises as well as their periodic inane conversation . . . After what seemed to me a distinguished effort, they left, and I was able to move and brush off a few cobwebs. I retired to the roof and Gordon [Browne, another agent] made a sortie, finally picking Tassels, who was wondering about lost several blocks away." Coon related that, "Tassels gave us much combat intelligence . . . in great detail . . . [I]t was seldom that Tassels was inaccurate."

The agent network also included individuals with occupational covers. A fisherman provided the location of antiaircraft guns and the movement of German submarines; herdsmen located hidden fortifications; two coding clerks turned over all decoded copies of German cables; an airline chief technician passed on the blueprints of all airfields, their defenses, and recognition signals, etc., providing a treasure trove of intelligence. Roosevelt noted, "To meet a possible German attack or to support an Allied sea and airborne assault, the Riff and Moslem groups were directed by [Eddy] to plan for an organized revolt . . . This planned uprising involved some 80,000 natives . . . [S]imilar preparations were being made in ports where landings might be attempted. In Oran, combat groups totaled more than 2,500 men." These groups needed weapons and equipment, which Eddy pleaded with Donovan to provide. "We have days before us, not weeks," he told the spy master. "We will not find such leaders elsewhere, and we dare not lose them. . . . They are taking all the risk; they will receive, distribute, and use the supplies, every step being taken with the threat of execution as traitors if they are uncovered. The least we can do is to help supply them on their own terms, which are generous and gallant."

Eddy's request for massive amounts of supplies was turned down. "If I cannot be trusted with a few million francs in an emergency then I should be called back and someone who can be trusted sent," he responded petulantly. What he did not realize at the time was that the equipment and weapons were simply not available, given the limited U.S. production capability at this stage of the war. Eddy continued to rely on the British Special Operations Executive (SOE), formed in July 1940 to conduct reconnaissance, espionage, and sabotage against the Axis powers in occupied Europe and to support local resistance movements. Prime Minister Winston Churchill's charge to the SOE was to "set Europe ablaze!" The SOE had a cache of weapons in Gibraltar to help supply Eddy's agents. Roosevelt wrote that, "Sten guns, .45 pistols, ammunition, flares, explosives and other needed items were loaded in British diplomatic pouches in Gibraltar and shipped across on a Portuguese tugboat to the British Legation at Tangier. Here they were shifted to the U.S. Legation where they were reloaded into U.S. Navy or State Department pouches and smuggled through the Spanish Zone to Casablanca." Hand grenades were a different story. They could not be shipped in the diplomatic pouches so they were obtained from "Tassels." The grenades were left over from the Spanish Civil War and were of dubious value.

Eddy selected Carleton Coon as one of the couriers. "During late August, September, and early October, I became the commuter between Gibraltar and Tangier," Coon related. "My business was to load [the weapons] into British diplomatic pouches . . . and see that they got to Legation." On one occasion, Coon was separated from his "goods." "When I arrived in Tangier empty-handed, I saw Colonel Eddy on the dock waiting for me, with a number of armed men to take custody of the pouches." Eddy was extremely disappointed that Coon did not have the weapons. He approached his trusted confederate and, in a voice that brooked no discussion, ordered, "Go back tomorrow, and come back with your shield or on it!" Coon "took this literally and came back with the pouches."

Operation Torch

Operation Torch, the landing in North Africa in November 1942, was the first major British-American operation in World War II. Under the command of Gen. Dwight D. Eisenhower, it was a dress rehearsal for subsequent landings in Italy and southern France two years later.

In late July 1942, Eddy was in London to pitch his requirements when he was invited to a dinner party with several high ranking officers, including General Patton and the director military intelligence Gen. George Strong. After meeting Patton (the "SOB's been shot at enough" meeting), Eddy was invited to brief the officers on his views of North Africa. Stewart Alsop and Thomas Braden wrote in *Sub Rosa: The O.S.S. and American Espionage* that, "They took chairs in the room, and Eddy began to talk about Africa. Before he could get fairly underway, Strong interrupted him. 'Now wait a minute, Eddy,' Strong said, 'I'm G-2 [intelligence chief] of this army and I'm going to tell you something. If you're going to tell us what you think instead of what you know, you might find yourself contributing to the murder of thousands of your own countrymen. Now for God's sake, tell us the facts!' " Eddy was unshaken by Strong's remark and proceeded to lay out the situation in North Africa. "He named the groups he had trained outside the Army and his plans for them," Alsop and Braden wrote. "He told of his own organization and of the intelligence on ship movements and defenses which his group had already assembled."

Harris Smith noted in his book, OSS: The Secret History of America's First Central Intelligence Agency, "Even General Strong was impressed by Eddy's seemingly factual, detailed account of the French underground— its strength, organization, leadership, and potential. And all three took particular note of Eddy's conclusion: 'If we sent an expeditionary force to North Africa, there would be only token resistance.' " Strong was indeed impressed. "You seem to know what you're talking about," he conceded. The successful briefing earned Eddy an audience with General Eisenhower (Allied supreme commander) the next afternoon. After the briefing Ike telegrammed the Army chief of staff, Gen. George C. Marshall, "Colonel Eddy of the Marines will arrive in Washington this week. He possesses much information which will be valuable to the Chiefs of Staff." Before leaving Washington, Eddy learned that an operation in North Africa was going to be approved, although he was not given its scope, its timing, or its objectives.

During this time, the COI was undergoing a radical organizational change. Donovan proposed that the COI be placed under the military Joint Chiefs of Staff (which itself was first formed for World War II) to improve trust and gain access to military resources. On 13 June 1942, Roosevelt established the Office of Strategic Services to collect and analyze strategic information required by the Joint Chiefs of Staff and to conduct special operations not assigned to other agencies.

Throughout the fall of 1942, rumors persisted of an Allied invasion of Africa. "Both sides originated and encouraged these: the Axis in order to smoke out denials; the Allies for the purpose of misleading German opposition," Kermit Roosevelt noted. "COI agents spread the word that Americans would land at Dakar." Eddy found out later that the Germans fell for the disinformation. He also learned that the Nazis were planning their own landing, but at a later date than Torch. On 14 October he received the long awaited Special Operations Instructions outlining the plan for Operation Torch. Eddy was one of a very few who knew the landings were scheduled for 8 November. "The Allied Force is divided into three task forces, Eastern Task Force, landing at Algiers, Center Task Force at Oran, Western Task Force at Port Lyautey, Fedala, and Safi, at a date and hour that will be communicated to you separately," it noted. "From Algiers, Eastern Task Force (1st Army) is to advance with all speed into Tunisia with the object of forestalling any German or Italian counter mover." The directive appointed Eddy as Eisenhower's staff officer, dual-hatted him as the head of the joint OSS/SOE organization in French North Africa, and directed him "to carry out subversive activities prior to the landing." In a subsequent directive, Eddy was assigned to the Civil Affairs Section under Robert D. Murphy, the civil affairs officer of Allied Forces.

With the Torch plan and tasking order in hand, Eddy ordered the final arrangements made at each of the ports and beaches where the landings were to take place. "Strong-arm squads were appointed to guard all important public buildings and to make arrests if the order not to resist were ignored," Kermit Roosevelt wrote. "Others were instructed to cut telegraph and telephone lines. . . . obstruct public utilities . . . detonate mines on roads and beaches. . . . Groups were assigned to beach-heads and parachute fields with flares to signal in troops . . . . [G]uides and interpreters were assigned to meet them. . . . [A]n OSS representative led an armed group with a 'Rebecca' radio beacon to guide paratroopers. . . . " The Rebecca navigation system consisted of an airborne receiver (Rebecca) and a ground-based transponder, which was actually called Eureka. Rebecca determined the range to Eureka by the time difference of signals between the units, and its highly directional antenna yielded relative position. Obviously, the correct positioning of the ground-based component was critical. Coon described the challenges of placing the beacon: "Gordon [Browne] posted himself in a slight depression in a field where the paratroopers were supposed to land. . . . Vichy troops appeared and began shooting at Gordon. He killed several and kept Rebecca-signaling until the planes came in sight." Browne was awarded the Silver Star for this brave act.

OFFICE OF STRATEGIC SERVICES

The Office of Strategic Services (OSS) was created on 13 June 1942 and placed under the Joint Chiefs of Staff (JCS), with Donovan as its director, reporting directly to President Roosevelt. Donovan told the president when the OSS was created that the Germans were the "big league professionals" of warfare, and America the "bush league club." The only way to quickly get up to speed against Germany was to "play a bush league game, stealing the ball and killing the umpire." The OSS quickly grew in size and became America's primary espionage and unconventional warfare agency during World War II. It focused on special intelligence, psychological warfare, and special operations— espionage, counter-intelligence, disinformation, and guerrilla leadership. At its peak in 1945, the OSS reached thirteen thousand personnel, nearly three-quarters; some nine thousand were uniformed members of the Armed Forces.

At one time or another, four thousand women served in its ranks, most in the United States but seven hundred females went overseas. The few who served behind enemy lines were the heroines of the OSS. Often they were indigenous agents. Helene Deschamps, code named "Anick," joined the French Resistance as a teenager. After joining the OSS, she reported on German mines and camouflaged weapons and helped downed fliers and persecuted Jews to escape. At one point she was arrested, interrogated, and beaten but survived the war. American socialite Virginia Hall was perhaps the most famous woman spy, known to the Gestapo as the "Limping Lady," because of her wooden leg. She served as a volunteer ambulance driver until France surrendered and then fled to London where she was recruited by the British SOE. They sent her to Lyons, where she organized and worked with an operational resistance unit until it was betrayed. After escaping back to England, she joined the OSS when the SOE refused to send her back to France. She became a major resistance leader, directing espionage and guerrilla operations under the code name "Diane." For her exploits, Hall was awarded the French Croix de Guerre, the Order of the British Empire, and the

U.S. Army's Distinguished Service Cross, the first woman to receive the award.

The major operational branches within the OSS were:

- Secret Intelligence (SI)—These men and some women were the "cloak and dagger operatives who ran intelligence operations and rings of indigenous spies primarily in enemy-occupied countries.
- Special Operations (SO)—Its members were trained to blow up bridges and railroad lines and to lead guerrilla attacks on enemy outposts and lines of communications and supply.
- Operational Groups (OG)—Highly trained foreign-language specialists were recruited for commando teams to operate behind enemy lines with indigenous resistance groups.
- Maritime Units (MU)—Specialist seaborne raiders whose mission was to infiltrate enemy harbors to destroy ships and facilities and perform reconnaissance of landing beaches to identify obstacles.
- Morale Operations (MO)—Its mission was to use "black" propaganda to spread confusion, dissension, and disorder among enemy troops and civilians.
- Research and Analysis (R&A)—Its job was to collect and analyze economic, political, social, and military information about Axis or Axis-occupied nations or countries.
- Communications Branch (CB or "Commo")—A global network designed to provide secure and effective communications.
- Research and Development (R&D)—The OSS workshop and laboratories that produced specialized weapons, explosives and other deadly devices.
- X-2 Branch—Its mission was to collect information on espionage and subversive activities of the enemy; analyze, process and exchange this information; maintain operational security and prevent infiltration by enemy intelligence services; and create foreign area subversive personality lists.

In a major coup, Eddy was able to exfiltrate two harbor pilots who knew "every rock and buoy and wreck, as well as . . . the very treacherous swell which is perhaps the chief hazard for any landing party." One of the men was smuggled out of Morocco in a trailer where he was almost asphyxiated by exhaust fumes from the car that pulled it—*"Tout va bien, pas trop de monoxide,"* he gasped at one point (All is well, not too much monoxide)—before reaching the coast where he was hustled aboard a motorboat for the trip to Gibraltar. Not all of Eddy's recommendations were accepted. General Mark W. Clark, Eisenhower's deputy, wrote in *Calculated Risk* that he received a memorandum from Eddy recommending "that on D-day, when the landing operations actually begin, I be authorized to arrange the assassination of the members of the German Armistice Commission at Casablanca . . . and for any members of the German or Italian Commissions who may then be in the city of Oran." Clark scrawled in the margin, "O.K. Looks good to me" and forwarded it up the chain of command, where it was disapproved.

As D-day approached, no one was quite sure how the French would react. Eddy wrote that, "We can count on the submission or active support of the French Army as we must also count upon the determined resistance of the French Navy and of the aircraft under the Navy's control." Eddy's agents were also able to convince some, but not all, of the French coastal battery commanders to withhold resistance. "Before the Allied landing on the coast of North Africa on November 8, 1942, the handful of us who knew the date and place of the landings were terrified lest we might talk in our sleep," Eddy wrote in *F.D.R. Meets Ibn Saud.* "In those days before the landings it was imperative that one neither cancel nor increase normal engagements of any kind lest he give the alert. One must plan to go to the tailor as usual to be measured for a suit, or to a barber for a haircut, or to invite Spanish friends in for a cocktail party which will never come off, just as though nothing were to happen."

In accordance with the Special Operations instructions, Eddy shifted his headquarters from Tangier to Gibraltar. Coon noted the relocation " . . . required considerable planning not to give the show away. He [Eddy] kept his room in the Minzah, and left most of his clothing there; he told them that he would be gone for a few days." On the night of 7 November,

Eddy anxiously waited for the code word announcing the landing—
"Robert has arrived"—that was to be broadcast on the BBC's French
language program. He was elated when the message came through and
cabled Donovan—"Thank God, all well . . . '*Le Jour De Gloire, C'est Arrive*
[The day of glory has arrived].' " Donovan wired back, "You are a superb
soldier." Coon recalled that afterward, "We ate ham sandwiches and
drank beer, and soon came this historic broadcast in several languages—
I remember most clearly the German, *Achtung, Achtung*—and then,
Franklin Roosevelt in his Grotonian French, making his announcement
to the French people. Then the Marseillaise and the Star Spangled Banner.
Eddy and I, groggy with excitement and lack of sleep, went back to the
office and made out a message to General Donovan. And then we slept."

Operation Torch was a success, thanks in no small measure to Eddy's
agent organization, secret intelligence and campaign of subversion.
An OSS assessment found that " . . . [I]ntelligence networks operated
smoothly and completely in all strategically important parts of North
Africa; the clandestine radio stations were able to funnel information
efficiently; resistance groups were organized, ready to take over the
government long enough to allow the landing forces in with a minimum
of opposition; and special agents were ready to guide and advise
the landing force commanders." The effectiveness of the OSS support for
the landing helped the organization gain support in Washington and
dampen opposition to Donovan's power. Two weeks after the landing,
Donovan wrote the commandant of the Marine Corps recommending
Eddy's promotion. Holcomb responded, "I have thought for some time
that he should be promoted. I will send his name in at once for spot
promotion to the temporary rank of colonel." Donovan also increased
Eddy's span of authority by designating him chief of the OSS in the
Mediterranean Theater. His responsibilities encompassed secret intel-
ligence, special operations, and counterespionage for Italy, southern
France, Spain, Tunisia, and Spanish Morocco.

Special Assignment

In November 1943, the State Department wrote Donovan requesting the
loan of "a senior officer expert in the Arabic language and political matters

in the Arabic speaking countries of the Levant" and requested Eddy by name, saying, "[he] is ideally suited for the functions that the Department has in mind." Donovan concurred, and in a letter to Cordell Hull, the Secretary of State, confirmed that the OSS and the State Department would share Eddy's intelligence reports while on this "special temporary duty." Eddy's official title was "Special Assistant to the American Minister" at the American Legation in Jeddah, Saudi Arabia. The secretary of state gave him carte blanche to visit the Arab countries anytime he desired and assigned him to "establish contact with both official and nonofficial persons . . . acquaint yourself with local personalities, problems, currents of thought, wants, needs, and aspirations . . . with particular reference to American interests, friendly and helpful relations between the United States and the local governments and peoples, and the attitude of their governments and their respective nationals. . . ." The secretary's instructions were amazingly broad and showed that Eddy was held in high regard in Washington.

Eight months later Eddy's assignment was cut short. The U.S. representative to Saudi Arabia was recalled and who better to replace him than Bill Eddy. In August 1944, President Roosevelt confirmed Eddy as "Envoy Extraordinary and Minister Plenipotentiary" to the Kingdom of Saudi Arabia. FDR's letter to King Ibn Saud stated, "My knowledge of Colonel William A. Eddy [is as] a distinguished citizen of high character and ability." Eddy officially "resigned" from the OSS and was placed on the retired list of the Marine Corps to accept the assignment. At the time of his assignment, the U.S. was trying to establish a closer relationship with Saudi Arabia. In early February 1945, Eddy was notified that President Roosevelt wanted to meet with Ibn Saud in one week's time, an unprecedented undertaking considering that the Arab leader was a semiliterate desert potentate who knew little about the world beyond his dealings with the British.

Eddy worked literally night and day on the trip arrangements. His plan called for the king and his entourage to travel overland from Riyadh to Jeddah and board the destroyer USS *Murphy* for the voyage up the Red Sea to Egypt where he would meet the president on the cruiser USS *Quincy* at the Great Bitter Lake in the Suez Canal. "We were still at war with Germany, bombs were still being dropped on Cairo and on the Suez Canal, and a target more attractive to German bombers could hardly be imagined than a cruiser with the American President and the Arabian King on board," Eddy recalled. At 1630, 12 February 1945, the *Murphy* weighed anchor with the king and a party of forty-eight, as well as live sheep to provide fresh mutton on board the overcrowded ship. For two-thirds of the party, there were no accommodations and they were forced to sleep wherever they could find space—gun turrets, on the deck, in the scuppers. A tent was erected on the forecastle for the king. Bosun's Mate Thomas Hilliard recalled the Saudis provided twenty-five to thirty "great big rolls." "We hand-sewed the canvas together with four-inch needles. I started in the morning and worked all night, and the next morning before the king arrived, we were just finishing up." Eddy noted that, "At prayer times the ship's navigator would give him the exact compass bearing for Mecca, which the King would verify with his astrologer. Facing the holy city he would lead the entire company of Arabs in their prayers."

The trip took two nights and one day and from all accounts, it was a success. "The Arabs and the sailors fraternized without words with friendliness which was really astonishing," Eddy said. The sailors showed the Arabs how they did their jobs and even permitted the Arabs to help them; in return the Arabs would permit the sailors to examine their garb and their daggers, and demonstrated by gestures how they are made and for what purposes." At precisely 1000 the *Murphy* tied up alongside the *Quincy*. Sailors manned the rails as the king and his ministers crossed the gangplank to meet the president who was sitting in his wheelchair on the quarterdeck. Later, after lunch, Eddy joined the president and the king to interpret for " . . . five very intense hours." Eddy said the two heads of state "got along famously together." He described the president as being "in top form as a charming host, witty conver-sationalist, with the spark and light in his eyes and that gracious smile which won people over to him. . . . [H]owever, every now and then I would catch him off guard and see his face in repose. It was ashen in color; the lines were deep; the eyes would fade in helpless fatigue. . . . [E]ight weeks later he was dead." Eddy remained ambassador, serving as a key figure in the development of the United States' relationship with Saudi Arabia and other Arab countries, until resigning in July 1946.

The following month, Eddy was appointed as special assistant to the secretary of state for research and intelligence, becoming an instrumental figure in passing the National Security Act of 1947, which created the CIA. During the late 1940s and 1950s, he was a consultant for the Arabian American Oil Company (Aramco) while living in Beirut, Lebanon. He died in 1962 and is buried in Sidon.

CHAPTER 2

Carrying the Torch

In September 1942, the London, England, and Londonderry, Northern Ireland, Marine detachments received a classified message ordering them to send men to the naval base at Rosneath, Scotland, to conduct marksmanship training. London sent fifteen enlisted men, under the command of 1st Lt. Fenton J. Mee, and Londonderry sent Lt. Col. Louis C. Plain, Capt. William E. Davis, and twenty-five enlisted men. Upon arrival at Rosneath, the Marines found out that they had been assigned to conduct a three-week weapons training course for U.S. Navy landing craft crewmen involved in a highly classified joint American-British amphibious landing in North Africa. The landing, codenamed Operation Torch, was slated for early November 1942, allowing just enough time to train the sailors in the rudiments of weapons handling and marksmanship. In typical Marine fashion the detachment quickly designed a training schedule, and set up rifle and machine gun ranges that safely and expeditiously passed the neophyte marksmen through the program. F. O. Cooke wrote in *They Took Thirty Marines*, ". . .[F]or the next three weeks [the detachment] put the bluejackets through an intensive series of secret maneuvers, equivalent to two months of advanced boot camp training." At the end of the training period, the Marines were surprised to learn that they had been "volunteered" to join the operation.

OPERATION TORCH

Operation Torch, the joint American-British invasion of French North Africa, was designed to wrest control of North Africa—Morocco, Algeria, and Tunisia—from the Axis Powers (Nazi Germany and Fascist Italy) and improve Allied naval control of the Mediterranean Sea. The operation was to be conducted by three amphibious task forces, which were assigned to seize the key installations and airfields at Casablanca, Oran, and Algiers from the Vichy Regime, the French government which was collaborating with the Axis Powers. The Western Task Force—some 35,000 Americans of the U.S. 2nd Armored Division and the 3rd and 9th Infantry Divisions—under the command of Maj. Gen. George Patton, was aimed at Casablanca. The Centre Task Force—18,500 men of the 509th Parachute Infantry Regiment, the 1st Ranger Battalion, 1st Infantry Division, and the 1st Armored Division—was tasked with Oran. The Eastern Task Force—20,000 men of the British 78th and the U.S. 34th Infantry Divisions, and two British Commandos (No.1 and No. 6 Commando)—was slated for Algiers. The operation was to commence on 8 November 1942.

In early October, Eisenhower decided to incorporate into the general plan a direct frontal attack on the ports of Algiers and Oran in an attempt to prevent the Vichy French from blocking the two vital ports and sabotaging shipping and harbor installations. The plan envisioned the Royal Navy forcing the entrance of both ports by two small warships and to discharge joint Allied military landing parties to secure the ports intact.

The three officers and thirty of the enlisted men were divided into six teams and assigned to six different ships (the other ten enlisted men returned to the Londonderry base). Their "commando" style missions involved a landing at the port city of Arzeu, Algeria, by three officers and twenty-four enlisted men, and a direct assault into the harbor of Oran, code named Operation Reservist, by the remaining six Marines.

Arzeu Landing

The landing at Arzeu was scheduled for 0100 on 8 November by two companies of the 1st Ranger Battalion. Their mission was to capture the town and the two coastal artillery batteries so the port could be used to land supplies and equipment to support the North African campaign. Lieutenant Colonel Plain and eleven men of the Londonderry detachment were assigned to support the U.S. Navy Advance Base Unit, which was to take over the port as soon as the Rangers had completed their mission. *U.S. Army in World War II: The Technical Services* noted that, "The first landing craft to go ashore at Arzeu were equipped with loudspeakers through which men especially chosen for their American-accented French were to shout, *'Ne tirez pas! Vive la France!'* One of the combat teams carried a mortar that would shoot an egg-shaped bomb about two hundred feet in the air, where it would burst into a magnificent pyrotechnic display of an American flag in color. There were four such sets of fireworks, each capable of flinging the star-spangled banner a hundred feet across the sky."

Shortly after 0100, Plain and his eleven-man force boarded a British LCA assault boat, which they lightheartedly described as "about three times as big as a bathtub." The heavily armed Marines were keyed up, expecting a fight to get ashore. As they approached the harbor, it was as quiet as a church. The navigation lights were still functioning, the floating barrier blocking the entrance had not been deployed: indications that the French were unaware of the operation. Plain's boat sailed unopposed into the inner harbor and tied up alongside the Grand Quay. The Marines piled out of the landing craft and took up firing positions, somewhat dismayed by the lack of opposition. Private First Class Robert Marsh broke the tension by whispering, "Run for your lives girls. There is a man on the beach!"

F. O. Cooke, a sailor on board the assault boat, reported, "We beached very quietly indeed: there was hardly a sound. The Americans went off excellently and very quietly, so quietly in fact that once they were on the beach, the sound of their feet on the sand woke one of the inhabitants of a cabana who opened his door letting out a flood of light and who was completely bewildered by soldiers running past him on either side.

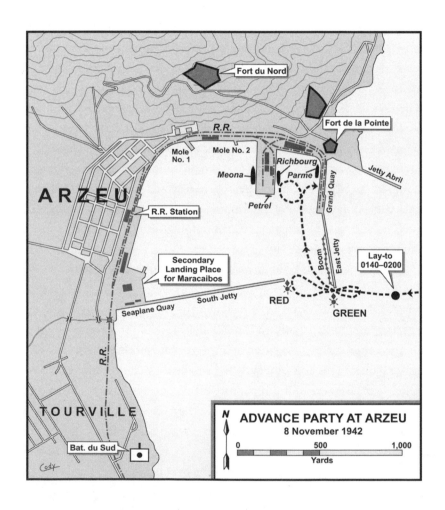

Fort du Nord

Fort de la Pointe

R.R.

Mole No. 1

Mole No. 2

Richbourg

Meona

Parme

Jetty Abril

A R Z E U

Petrel

Grand Quay

R.R. Station

Secondary
Landing Place
for Maracaibos

Boom

East Jetty

Lay-to
0140–0200

Seaplane Quay

South Jetty

RED

GREEN

R.R.

T O U R V I L L E

Bat. du Sud

Cody

N

ADVANCE PARTY AT ARZEU
8 November 1942

0   500   1,000

Yards

He stood there in trousers and shirt scratching his head and wondering what was happening."

Once the advance party had arrived, Plain's men assisted in seizing three small steamers and a patrol boat lying in the harbor. Cooke wrote, "So many ships were lying peacefully at anchor that not enough officers could be found to take them over. So the job was given to the Marines— one Marine for each ship, complete with crew." The first ship to be boarded was the SS *Richebourg*, of about three thousand tons; the second was the SS *Parme*, of about the same size. The crew of the first ship was largely Arab, the crew of the second mainly French. "The captain was roused from his cabin, the crew ordered to stand by, and a lone Marine assumed temporary command of each of four vessels in the name of the U.S. Navy," Cooke noted. "They maintained order over their sections of the harbor until relieved by the newly formed Naval Command." Other Marines were assigned to guard the five hundred foot South Jetty, which commanded the harbor entrance. They held the position all night, until relieved by the Rangers. The 22 March 1949 *London Gazette* noted, "At 0300, searchlights and gun flashes from the direction of Oran were seen in the sky over the hills above Cape Carbon. This, as it later transpired and was at the time suspected, was the French reception of HMS *Walney* and *Hartland*, which were due to enter Oran harbor at that hour. . . ."

After daybreak in Arzeu, several French snipers started shooting from the southern breakwater and adjoining seaplane base but were quickly silenced by the small Marine detachment. Cooke noted, "Corporal George C. Brown deployed a detail to clean out a nest of snipers in a garage on the waterfront. Some snipers were hiding in a drain, while others had a machine gun inside the garage. The Marines advanced, using extended order tactics, and to fire their first shots of the landing." Private First Class Anthony Damato said his team killed three snipers, including one woman. After the fire fight, the captives were marched off to the POW compound.

On the Way to Oran

The American-British planning staff considered the commando-style raid to be a high risk operation because the defenses in the Oran harbor

OPERATION RESERVIST

As part of the Center Task Force amphibious assault, a direct assault on the Oran harbor was planned by two small shiploads of American troops and naval personnel under Royal Naval Command, with the mission of forestalling sabotage, eliminating the coastal artillery threat, and taking charge of Vichy French ships moored in the harbor. The assault force consisted of 17 officers and 376 enlisted men of the 3rd Battalion, 6th Armored Infantry, 1st Armored Division; 4 officers and 22 seamen of the U.S. Navy; 52 Royal Navy commandos; and 6 Marines from the Londonderry Northern Ireland detachment. The plan called for the force to be lifted in two British *Branff*-class sloops, HMS *Hartland* (Y-00) and HMS *Walney* (Y-04), which were the former U.S. Coast Guard cutters *Ponchartrain* and *Sebago* that had been given to the British under the lend-lease program. The ships were chosen because of their "American" appearance, although no one questioned how the French could determine their registry in the darkness. The cutters were fitted with iron plating around the wheelhouse and lower bridge for additional protection. "The armor plate was clearly for an ominous purpose," British Leading Seaman J. H. Finch surmised. Each cutter was manned by 200 sailors.

The plan called for *Walney* to smash through the floating barrier at the harbor entrance, land its troops on the Middle Pier (Mole Centre), and capture the batteries in Fort Lamoune. *Hartland* was tasked to land its troops ashore on the first pier, Mole du Ravin Blanc, and knock out the gun battery of the same name. Crewmen from both ships were trained on how to board and seize French ships, if possible. "We spent a great deal of time practicing coming alongside and boarding vessels in the dark," Finch recalled. Stoker Les Elder said, "I was detailed to boarding parties. . . . [W]e were sent aboard merchant vessels to famil-iarize ourselves with the engine-room and boiler room layout. We had no idea why at the time." Two armed motor launches, HMML-483 and HMML-480, were assigned to lay down a smoke screen to cover the sloops' passage through the harbor entrance.

were formidable. The French had deployed numerous searchlights and coastal gun batteries in the hills surrounding the harbor. Many of the guns could be turned inland to fire on invading troops. In addition, there were the deck guns of two submarines (*Ceres* and *Pallas*) and three destroyers (*Tramontane*, *Typhon*, and *Epervier*). Rear Admiral A. C. Bennett, USN, commander Advance Group Amphibious Force Atlantic Fleet, was sharply critical of the planned operation. "An entry into the port by these cutters, with additional objectives of seizing batteries fully manned, prior to the capitulation of the town . . . is suicidal. If determined resistance is met from the French Navy . . . it is believed that this small force will be wiped out. . . ." Despite Bennett's objections, the planners thought the risk was acceptable if French defenders could be taken by surprise. There was also a chance that the French would cooperate with the landing forces, although the North African spymaster, Col. William A. Eddy, thought otherwise. The planning came a cropper, as he predicted, when the French put up a spirited resistance—they were neither surprised nor cooperative. Admiral Sir Andrew Cunningham, Allied naval commander later admitted, "The moment chosen could hardly have been less fortunate, since the French alarm to arms was in its full flush of Gallic fervor and they had not yet been intimidated by bombing or bombardment."

On 25 October 1942, Marine 1st Sgt. Fred Whittaker led his six-man Londonderry commando detachment aboard the *Hartland* moored alongside her sister ship *Walney* in the harbor of Tail of the Clyde, Scotland. Whittaker's Marines were part of a small U.S. Navy contingent (five officers, twenty-two sailors) under the command of U.S. Navy Lt. Cmdr. G. D. Dickey. The ships sailed the next day in convoy with the Center Naval Task Force, an imposing array of thirty-nine British and American warships and transports. There was great concern at the highest levels of the military and among the embarked troops because of the German U-boat threat. The British naval staff estimated that, if the enemy got wind of the convoy, fifty U-boats could be deployed against, "the most valuable convoys ever to leave these shores." In all about a hundred escort vessels were allocated to the convoys. Correspondent Drew Middleton wrote, "Patrolling the perimeter of the convoys were destroyers of the

British escort. Tiny out there on the gray waters, but loaded with depth charges, they searched for U-boats everyone expected."

Aboard the *Hartland*, F. O. Cooke wrote in a July 1943 *Leatherneck* magazine article, "During the slow voyage south through the U-boat danger zone, the Marines spent most of their time learning to operate with the British sailors and commandos who accompanied them. Weapons classes were held in the use of the Tommy-gun [sub-machine gun] and service pistol—which caused quite some excitement as the British Tommies cut loose with the unfamiliar weapons on the transports' heaving decks." The overloaded cutters wallowed in the heavy seas. Middleton noted that, "Seasickness was a far greater worry to the troops than enemy attack. For two days fairly rough weather made many of them extremely unhappy." On 6 November, the Eastern and Center naval task forces split off from the main convoy and proceeded independently through the Strait of Gibraltar. During an at-sea refueling, Captain Davis aboard the SS *Orbita* was able to communicate with First Sergeant Whittaker's commandos. Cooke wrote that, "The seven Marines on the *Orbita* and the six on the *Hartland* exchanged semaphore greetings . . . and wished each other good luck." Thirty hours remained before the assault landing.

United Press staff writer Leo S. Disher was on board the *Walney*. "In the dead of the deep black night of November 7, two U.S. Coast Guard cutters and two trailing motor launches turned away from an Allied convoy off the North African coast," he wrote. "It was midnight when we left the convoy, steaming without lights." The night was so clear that the Marines on deck could see the navigation lights in Oran's harbor. The French appeared blissfully ignorant of their approach—but was it a ruse? "Would the French fight," they wondered, as the ship went to action station. Author Michael G. Walling noted, "All-close range ammunition for the .50-caliber machine guns, rifles, automatic weapons, pistols, and other small arms, was brought to the upper deck and placed either at the guns, in the fo'csle lockers or in the gun shelter or laundry."

Oran Harbor

A stone breakwater three thousand yards long separated Oran Harbor from the sea. An entrance about 160 yards wide on the eastern end was protected by a boom, but it was uncertain how substantial an obstruction the boom would be for the incoming ships. The long, narrow harbor within was further divided into four large subsections (or basins) by wide stone moles extending northward from shore toward the breakwater. There were two smaller subsections on the western end divided by the Mole Centre, which ran parallel to the breakwater. Traveling westward through the harbor, ships first encountered Avant Port, the largest of the basins, then continued past Mole Ravin Blanc; followed by the second basin, Mole Millerand; Bassin du Maroc; Mole J. Giraud; Bassin Aucer; and Mole St. Marie. At the end were the two small basins; the larger one, on the breakwater side near the French naval barracks, berthed naval vessels, while the smaller, inner basin was for small vessels.

Shortly before 0300, two hours after the Arzeu assault, the sloops began creeping in along the twenty-five-fathom line toward the harbor with *Walney* in the lead and *Hartland* five hundred yards astern. "A British cruiser, lying offshore, sent up rockets to divert attention from our entrance to the harbor," Disher noted. Lieutenant Wallace Moseley RN recalled, "We ran up to the outer boom where we carried out a complete circle whilst Lt. Paul E. A. Duncan RN announced in American accented French over the Ardente loud hailer, '*Ne tirez pas* (don't shoot)!' *Nous sommes vos amis*. '*Nous sommes vos amis* (we are your allies).' *Ne tirez pas*". '*Ne tirez pas* (don't shoot)!' This appeared to rouse the batteries which had been silent up to then . . . principally at *Harland* as [we] were well covered by smoke laid by the two ML in company, one of which, ML 483, came into collision with us when coming out of the smoke screen." The motor launch survived the collision and was able to proceed out of the harbor for repairs. Marine Corporal Norman Boike said, "It was something out of one of those pirate pictures that Errol Flynn and Tyrone Power are always playing in, only more fireworks."

The sound of air raid sirens warbled across the harbor as Cmdr. Emile Abgrall, *capitaine de corvette* of the Vichy *Bourrasque*-class destroyer *Typhon* (T-72), breathlessly stepped onto the bridge. The officer of the watch informed him that enemy ships were approaching the harbor. "Sound, '*Aux postes de combat*' ("to combat stations")," Abgrall ordered

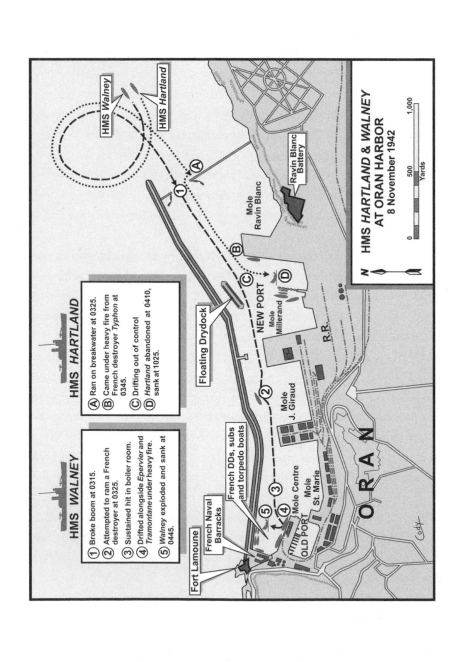

HMS WALNEY

1. Broke boom at 0315.
2. Attempted to ram a French destroyer at 0325.
3. Sustained hit in boiler room.
4. Drifted alongside *Epervier* and *Tramontane* under heavy fire.
5. *Walney* exploded and sank at 0445.

HMS HARTLAND

A. Ran on breakwater at 0325.
B. Came under heavy fire from French destroyer *Typhon* at 0345.
C. Drifting out of control
D. *Hartland* abandoned at 0410, sank at 1025.

Fort Lamoune

French Naval Barracks

French DDs, subs and torpedo boats

Floating Drydock

HMS *Walney*

HMS *Hartland*

Ravin Blanc Battery

Mole Ravin Blanc

NEW PORT

Mole Millerand

Mole J. Giraud

R.R.

Mole Centre

Mole St. Marie

OLD PORT

O R A N

Cody

N

HMS *HARTLAND* & *WALNEY* AT ORAN HARBOR
8 November 1942

0   500   1,000
Yards

without hesitation. The strident blare of the klaxon roused the French sailors from their bunks and sent them racing to their battle stations. Within minutes the ship was "manned and ready." Commander Abgrall ordered the *Typhon*'s main and secondary batteries trained out to cover the harbor entrance and to make emergency preparation for getting under way. Suddenly a searchlight from Fort Lamoune at the far end of the harbor stabbed into the smoke shrouded darkness, illuminating two ships emerging from the murkiness. Abgrall immediately recognized the hated British White Ensign flying from the mast. There had been bad blood between the two navies ever since July 1940, when the British launched an unprovoked attack on the French fleet at anchor in Algeria, killing almost 1,300 French seamen and sinking a battleship; the British felt the pre-emptive attack was justified because they feared the French fleet would be turned over to the Germans after France signed an armistice with Germany at the beginning of World War II. In addition to their own White Ensigns, the *Hartland* and the *Walney* had also been given permission "to wear the largest size American Ensigns they could carry," and Abgrall was momentarily taken aback by the bed sheet-sized stars and stripes waving from the stern. "American flag," he mumbled and gave the order to fire.

One of *Hartland*'s officers, Lt. V. A. Hickson recalled, " [W]e were caught in the glare of a searchlight and became an easy target. We were hit several times. . . ." The gunfire put short shrift to a message *Walney* had received from the higher headquarters that there was "No shooting thus far; landings unopposed. Don't start a fight unless you have to." Corporal Boike, stationed by the captain's cabin, reported "four-inch shells streaking through *Hartland*'s thin sides like blue flame." Heavy machine guns from the mole and the Ravin Blanc Battery opened a devastating barrage at point blank range. First Sergeant Whittaker, Pfcs. James Earhart and Richard K. Spencer, Pvts. Robert F. Horn and William L. Dickinson, and the British commandos waited below on the mess decks for the signal to come topside. Cooke described the effects of the shelling. "The first six-inch shell came through about four feet from Whittaker's head and exploded far back in the hold, wounding several men. The men were picked up and laid on a table in the officer's wardroom, converted into a temporary hospital. Just as a British doctor was bending over the first patient to probe for shrapnel, three more shells scored direct hits, and turned the entire below-decks into a shambles." Private First Class Horn was swept away and killed by this salvo.

HMS *Walney*

At this point in the action, the ships were less than a half mile from the entrance. Captain Frederic Peters aboard the *Walney*, a retired Royal Navy officer who was brought back on active duty and placed in charge of the operation, ordered the engines to flank speed in order to hit the boom with full force to smash their way through. "All men below decks lie flat," Peters ordered, "we are approaching the boom." *Walney* sliced through it, "with barely a noticeable tremor," according to Moseley. A moment later she broke through the second boom, a row of coal barges, "like a wire through cheese." As the ship crept farther into the smoke enshrouded harbor, she endured heavy but inaccurate close-range fire. Rear Admiral Samuel Eliot Morison wrote in *History of U.S. Naval Operations in World War II* that *Walney* "boldly steamed right up the three hundred-yard-wide harbor past Mole Revin Blanc, drawing fire from two submarines (*Ceres* and *Pallas*) docked between it and the next quay, Mole Millerand. Having passed this mole, she was about to turn and ram a French destroyer standing out of the harbor when her bridge was shot away." Survivors estimate that the destroyer opened fire from a distance of two hundred feet.

The *Walney* continued until within six hundred yards of her objective, the Mole Centre at the furthermost end of the harbor when the French torpedo boat *Tramontane* and the destroyer *Epervier* opened fire at almost muzzle-end range. One shell exploded in the engine room, killing most of the crew, and destroying the lubricating tanks. With the oil supply cut off, the automatic stop valve closed and the engine shuddered to a stop. Another shell detonated in the boiler room, wiping out the two main boilers. No one escaped from the compartment. Author Jack McIntyre described the action in the 14 December 1943 *London Gazette*: "The toll in death and destruction was mounting. . . . The bridge exploded in flame from another [direct hit], blowing Peters off the bridge, the only survivor of eighteen officers and men . . . [T]he devastation above and below decks was indescribable. . . . *Walney*'s situation was hopeless." The ship was a floating heap of jagged, twisted metal, with bodies piled two- and three-feet deep on her decks. Peters ordered abandon ship. At 0445, *Walney* capsized and sank only a few yards from the head of the harbor. Only one officer and thirteen ratings survived, while eighty-one of her crew and most of the soldiers went down with the ship.

HMS *Hartland*

HMS *Hartland* was a sitting duck. A searchlight from Fort Lamoune held her in its beam and the French destroyer *Typhon* pounded the ship from only one hundred feet away with its two 4.7-inch guns. The salvoes were devastating and within minutes most of her gun crews were casualties. Fires raged fore and aft. She lost all control and power, and drifted several hundred yards while absorbing a merciless shelling from the destroyer and the two submarines that had fired on *Walney*. Within minutes of the first shells hitting the ship, Corporal Boike was knocked unconscious and severely wounded. Cooke noted, " . . . [S]hrapnel tore away the muscle of his left arm. When he came to, only dead men were below decks. He climbed painfully topside and found most of the ship ablaze still under direct fire from the destroyers. . . . " An officer bound up Boike's arm, gave him a shot of morphine, then the two jumped over the side and swam through a mass of floating wreckage to a life raft holding six British sailors. The men turned to and after 150 yards of furious paddling they reached a floating dry dock manned by a squad of French soldiers, who quickly took them prisoner. After spending several hours on the dock, Boike was taken to a French naval hospital and treated for his wounds. He was liberated the next day by U.S. soldiers.

First Sergeant Whittaker was trapped below decks with "the smoke getting thicker by the minute." The compartment was filled with dead and wounded men, all the hatches were still battened down and, unknown to them, all the men on the main deck had been cut down. "The situation looked grim for the trapped men," Cooke wrote. "Escape forward was barred by a wall of flame. The hold was rapidly filling with deadly carbon dioxide gas from the blasted refrigeration plant . . . one of the British seaman remembered an emergency hatch far aft." The men had to clamber over debris, bodies, and piled-up equipment to get to the escape hatch that was blocked by a wooden block that had not been removed in years. Cooke noted that, "Four rifle stocks were broken on it before the hatch cover finally gave way, and a path was cleared out of the deathtrap below decks to the dubious safety of the open deck, which was still being swept by machine gun fire."

Enemy fire swept the bridge, killing and wounding most of the men and leaving the *Hartland* drifting, out of control. Lt. Cmdr. Godfrey Philip Billot, RN, *Hartland*'s commander, was severely wounded in both legs and a shoulder. He saw there was no alternative but to abandon ship. The word was passed from man to man. First Sergeant Whittaker remained behind, directing the evacuation of the wounded, even though he was close to unconsciousness from the soaring heat and smoke. Finally he was told that everyone was out and had just started climbing the ladder when he heard a faint voice calling for help. He turned around immediately and was able to locate the man. "By this time the Marine sergeant was too weak to lift him," Cooke wrote, "and conditions in the after-hold were all but unbearable. Whittaker directed the wounded man to hold onto his legs and keep his nose close to the deck where there was an inch or two of breathable air. Then he crawled toward the emergency exit, dragging the man after him. The sailor was too weak to climb and fell at the foot of the ladder. Whittaker kept climbing, made the open deck and gave directions for another man to make the final rescue . . . then he passed out."

By the time the fresh air revived Whittaker, fires raged in several locations close to crates of ammunition and mortar shells. He realized the ship could blow up at any moment, so he gathered the two surviving Marines and went over the side. They reached the seawall only fifty yards away but could not climb it. Cooke wrote, "By luck, an old tire was hanging over the side. This Whittaker hung onto, but was too exhausted to get to the top. The man behind him used Whittaker's body as a ladder and climbed up. Whittaker then was boosted by the man behind him, and so by a kind of human chain, the Marines and a few comrades reached the beach at Oran." The handful of survivors took shelter in a shallow trench at the base of a cliff and took stock of their situation. Several men were wounded and needed medical treatment, they only had two .45-caliber pistols, a half dozen hand grenades for defense, and their position was open to attack from three sides. Nevertheless, Whittaker organized a defense and when several small French patrols stumbled into their position, they were taken prisoner.

By 0410 the *Hartland*'s superstructure was engulfed in flames and she was completely abandoned. Lieutenant Commander Dickey had high praise for the men in his command. "They had action stations in the captain's cabin in the after part of the ship. Fire and smoke from enemy hits made conditions almost unbearable, yet not one attempted to leave his station. Upon abandoning ship officers and men again showed the highest kind of leadership and spirit in helping to save the lives of many United States soldiers who were unfamiliar with the ship and the use of the life jackets . . . and at the wharf, although physically exhausted, they continued to save lives by pulling men out of the water." Private First Class Earheart, according to his Silver Star citation, "volunteered in the face of continuous Vichy French shelling, to swim to a harbor tug whose movements were endangering the men abandoning the warship. He was killed in this effort." At 0525, the *Hartland* exploded, damaging a number of buildings around the Mole Ravin Blanc, and sank. One officer recalled, "The American flag still flew, readily visible in the light from the flames before the explosion."

For five hours the group managed to hold out, waiting for the outcome of the battle. They now numbered three Marines, six unwounded and fourteen wounded British seamen, and two dozen French prisoners. Sometime around 0900, a large group of heavily armed French soldiers surrounded their position and demanded their surrender. The men had no other choice and came out with their hands up. The wounded were taken to the local hospital, while the three Marines were taken to an air raid shelter where prisoners were being assembled and later that day to a French fortress overlooking the city. The next morning they were transferred to a former barracks where they stayed until being liberated on the following day. Cooke wrote that the "[f]irst direct bearer of the news was a U.S. Army half-track, mounting a .30-caliber machine gun which drove into the prison past several open-mouthed French sentries, pulled up at the entrance with a flourish, and took over the fort." Operation Reservist was a deadly failure, a waste of gallantry and men. Of the 17 officers and 376 men of the 6th Armored Regiment, 9 officers and 180 men were killed in action, and 5 officers and 153 wounded. The U.S. Navy lost five killed and seven wounded (including two Marines—Earhart's body was recovered but not Horn's remains) and the Royal Navy suffered 113 killed and 86 wounded. Rick Atkinson noted in *An Army at Dawn, The War in North Africa, 1942-1943* that, "Eisenhower eventually accepted blame for the debacle. . . . [N]o consequence attended the gesture . . . but Andrew Bennett . . . persisted in his criticism; he infuriated both the British and Eisenhower, who declared he was 'going to get that fellow out of there immediately.' Unrepentant, Bennett soon found himself in Iceland."

The commanding officer of the Londonderry Marines in an Order of the Day dated 23 February 1943 stated, "[The Marines] were called upon and were found not wanting. Their names will go down in the history of our organization as a symbol of courage and self-sacrifice."

CHAPTER 3

Marine with the Chetniks

The matte-black Royal Air Force (RAF) four-engine Halifax bomber from No. 138 (Special Duties) Squadron winged its way across the Mediterranean and western Greece toward the clandestine drop zone in the mountains of Yugoslavia. The single passenger in the fuselage was bundled up against the cold. At eight thousand feet, the temperature was not the scorching heat he was used to in the Sahara desert of Libya where the flight had originated. The experienced bomber crew had warned him about the cold, having conducted many agent insertions and supply drops along this same route. The British Special Operations Executive (SOE) used this special "Moon Squadron" for the heavy duty work of dropping containers, packages, and agents into German occupied Europe because of its ability to carry heavy loads of supplies over long distances. Their mission this night was to drop the agent and three tons of arms, ammunition, and explosives to the Yugoslav resistance fighters.

The aircrew anxiously scanned the ground looking for the signal fire. They were near the end of the scheduled five-hour flight and should be approaching the drop zone (DZ) at any moment. "There it is," the co-pilot called out, pointing to the bonfires in the shape of a square cross.

The passenger, Marine Capt. Walter R. Mansfield recalled, "A tiny light blinked 'dit-dah-dit' from the ground near the fires. Then it repeated. These were the signals we had been briefed to accept. We flashed a coded response back from an Aldis lamp. Then the lights passed beyond the hole and I could not see them. We came downstairs to about a thousand feet. After two passes over the target, the bombardier leaned over and yelled in my ear, 'Get yourself ready—this is it!' " Mansfield slid over to the "Joe hole," a hatch in the deck of the aircraft named for the agents ("Joes") that parachuted from it. "The light directly over the bole went red—my warning signal!" he explained. "I threw my legs over the side of the hole and suspended myself over it, hands supporting on the edges, eyes facing the light directly above me. One-two-three-four-five—'Green light!' I shoved off."

Walter Mansfield

Prior to World War II, Walter R. Mansfield was a successful anti-trust lawyer in William J. "Bill" Donovan's New York City firm. When Donovan was appointed as the head of OSS, Mansfield volunteered for the secret organization and then applied for commission in the Marine Corps Reserve. After receiving a commission, he received orders to the Marine Parachute Training School at New River, North Carolina, which he downplayed—"All they do is throw you out of a plane. Do five jumps and you're a parachutist." In 1942 he was commissioned in the Marine Corps Reserve. He underwent special operations training at areas "A" and "C," located adjacent to the Marine Corps Base at Quantico, Virginia; Area "B" in the vicinity of Catoctin Mountain in Maryland; and London, England. The training included hand-to-hand combat techniques, marksmanship and physical conditioning. The OSS developed several unique training facilities—the "House of Horrors," designed to teach close shooting techniques; the "Tranizaium," a twenty-foot by twenty-foot structure where recruits learned to maneuver and walk in narrow spaces—and "hired" the renowned hand-to-hand combat instructor Maj. William "Fearless Dan" Fairbairn to teach "gutter fighting." In England Mansfield said he "trained with French and Norwegian parachutists."

Upon completion of training and a period of indoctrination, Mansfield was sent to the Middle East in the latter part of July 1943 where he was briefed and trained for the Yugoslav mission. "We conferred with the British representative of the MO-4 [Military Operations Directorate], the corresponding British unit similar to the OSS. We were given long lectures on the latest intelligence in Yugoslavia, both on the side of Mihailovich [General Draza, leader of the monarchist Chetnik movement] and on the side of Tito [Josip B., leader of the Communist partisans]." Within days, Mansfield was assigned a comprehensive multi-faceted fact-finding mission. "I was to be the preliminary American liaison representative directly to General Draza Mihailovich; that I was to report general military intelligence, including disposition of his forces as well as those of the enemy; that I was to find out what operations he had been conducting as well as those planned for the future; that I was to see what his manpower and supply situation was, and to report any suggestions and plans for operations in the future."

At the time of Mansfield's assignment, there were two factions vying for power in Yugoslavia—the Partisans under Communist Party leader Tito, a Croatian, with their core area in the mountains and forests of northern Bosnia; and the Royalist Chetniks under Yugoslavian Mihailovich, a Serb, who operated out of their base in the wooded mountains of Montenegro in the south. They were bitter enemies who fought each other as much as the Germans. Britain initially favored the former resistance leader but they were increasingly supporting Tito because they thought Mihailovich was not doing enough to fight the Germans and there were indications that he was collaborating with the enemy. In late summer 1943, Donovan was able to break the British monopoly on undercover operations in the Balkans, despite SOE objections, and send in his own fact-finding agents. President Roosevelt spelled out this policy in a letter to Donovan saying in part, "In order that there should be no misunderstanding, it should be made clear to the British that, in accordance with the established policy and practice, we intend to exercise this freedom of action for obtaining independent American secret intelligence." Mansfield explained, "At the time the

American policy in Yugoslavia . . . was that we backed all resistance leaders who would fight against the Germans."

"Zdravo, Purvi Americanec" (Greetings, First American)

Mansfield leaped into space. "The chute blossomed easily," he said, "and I suddenly found myself in a contrasting world of silence, with no more roar of motors. I gained my bearings and saw that I had been dropped too far to one side of the fires, which were several hundred yards distant." As the ground rapidly came up, he frantically tried to maneuver closer to the signal fires "but realized that I would never make it. I landed in a pile of rocks on a hillside." Fortune was with him and he was just bruised, not injured. "I got out of my harness, drew my .45 and waited in the cold. Within ten minutes I heard voices, yelling out in Serbian. *'Zdravo! Zdravo! Piatelj!'* (Greetings! Greetings! Friend!). I answered and soon was surrounded by a small group of weird, ragged-looking men, most of whom had black beards and hats bearing a skull and bones emblem. I told their leader that I was an American, whereupon they all began to whoop, holler and kiss me (black beards and all) yelling *'Zdravo, Purvi Americanec'* (Greetings, First American). I mustered my Serbian to reply, *'Zdravo! Chetnici!'*—the first American had landed."

The drop zone seemed to be covered with members of Mihailovich's fighters. "There were about three hundred guerrillas; some tending fires, others standing guard around the little hillocks near the field or waiting to gather up the containers and put them in oxen carts," Mansfield said. "All cheered loudly as I marched with my little escort to the middle of the field where a group was waiting." He was introduced to the group—SOE representatives Col. William Bailey and Maj. Kenneth Greenlees, and Mihailovich's emissary, a Serb named Slepcovich. "Just then the bomber roared in over our heads and dropped fifteen parachute containers . . . approximately three tons of arms . . . mostly [German] material that had been captured in North Africa . . . three or four heavy machine guns, explosives with primer cords, time fuses, percussion caps, and the necessary paraphernalia to do the demolition work. Each cylindrical container weighed about three hundred pounds . . . and each container of the rhomboid type somewhat less."

The experienced Halifax crew dropped the bundles on target and the guerrillas wasted little time in gathering the containers and loading them on carts. British Capt. Michael Lees noted:

> In the dropping zone there was hectic activity. Peasants dressed in broadly cut jodhpur-style breeches and square-waisted jackets, all of heavy homespun material, were carrying in the twelve or so containers dropped from our Halifax and loading them onto bullock carts. These were driven by their womenfolk, and as soon as they had their load up, they rumbled off into the darkness. My first impression was one of remarkable organization. No one stood around. Everyone seemed to know his task and to get on with it, although they all had time to greet us, embrace us, and make us feel welcome. The relatively few mobile troops guarding the dropping zone were dressed for the most part in peasant gear, though some of them wore battle-dress jackets. The officers mostly wore Yugoslav military clothing and equipment, and most of them carried Schmeisser submachine guns; I learned that the possession of one of these was a sign of considerable prestige. In all, the Loyalists were a motley lot in their clothing and equipment. What struck me most was the integration of the peasantry and these Loyalist Chetniks. The peasants, a proportion of whom were carrying long, ancient rifles slung across their backs, acted as runners, supplied the bullock carts and transport, and brought food and drink.

Mansfield said that the "air was cool and the soil rocky in the mountains, a wonderful contrast to the burning sands of Africa." With a simple wave of his hand, the Serbian emissary led the group off the drop zone along a rough path into the wooded hillside. Mansfield recalled:

> After two miles of walking, we penetrated a little woods on the top of one of the hills and there found a big log fire, with rough-hewn benches lying about. Big bearded guards stood about under the trees . . . all were dressed in homespun peasant breeches in rather ragged condition, with white hats bearing the Yugoslav emblem. Nearby there were two or three Serbian mountain peasant houses

called 'kolibas,' a few captured pup tents . . . and a group of tents made from camouflaged parachutes which housed the British contingent— Col. Bailey, his second in command, Lt. Col. Duane Hudson, [Capt.] Michael Lees and three noncommissioned officers, including two Royal Marine sergeants who had been captured on Crete, escaped, and ended up in the camp.

General Mihailovich

Colonel Bailey spoke up. "This is for the present the general staff head-quarters. I think the General will be along shortly because I know he has been waiting and is anxious to see you." Mansfield was somewhat disappointed as he expected "something a little more pretentious," for the headquarters of a guerrilla leader who supposedly commanded thousands of fighters. "I was soon to learn, however, that appearances were deceiving," Mansfield said. "The surrounding woods were full of guerrillas, fully equipped with radio communications to all parts of Serbia, and their power could not be measured by the size of their headquarters." He learned later that over four hundred men were deployed in the hills surrounding the headquarters. About a half mile away, Mihailovich had set up his central communication stations, which consisted of five portable suitcase radios that maintained contact with thirty-eight field commanders throughout the country. Within minutes, "a dark figure emerged from one side of the woods, with several others following," Mansfield said.

Colonel Bailey stepped forward and introduced the Chetnik leader. "The General and I saluted and shook hands," Mansfield said before describing Mihailovich. "Before me stood a man of perhaps forty-five years, stocky-medium build, heavy iron-gray beard, wearing a black cap, leather jacket, peasant britches, and a well-polished cartridge belt from which a Luger protruded at a cocky angle. He smiled broadly. 'Greetings, Captain. Welcome to our free mountains of Yugoslavia,' he said quietly, in perfect French. 'Thank God you landed safely. We were all worried. We don't want anything to happen to the American officer who had been sent in to us.' I thanked him." Mansfield soon discovered that the British officers were not keen on any private discussions with Mihailovich in French—they wanted to be present to interpret and thus aware of all that was going on. The SOE headquarters was still not happy with the American presence. Later on Mansfield received hints from the British officers that their government was considering cutting off aid to Mihailovich.

Mihailovich invited the group to sit around the fire. "Yanko, the General's orderly, appeared with a bottle of 'Rakia,' a strong peasant-made vodka distilled from plums," Mansfield recalled. "This loosened our tongues and in a short while I was telling them about various Yugoslav staff officers who had escaped in 1941 [when the country was overrun by the German Army] and were now working for their country's liberation in Cairo and London. . . . I could not help noticing the sharp contrast in appearance between these ragged men and the neat well-dressed officers I had met in Cairo. Here it was the man, not the cut of his uniform that mattered. Here were the fighters!" During the conversation, Mansfield learned that the Germans patrolled the roads but seldom came up into the woods, and then only with a sizable force, "which would be detected well enough in advance," Mihailovich assured him. "[But], always be ready for a quick move, or '*pocred*,' on a moment's notice."

Wrong Assumption

The general's assurance proved to be wrong. "At about 0530 one morning a guerrilla guard came to the parachute tent where Bailey and I were sleeping and said, '*Nemsi su blizu*,' (Germans are close)," Mansfield said. "Not taking any chances, however, we had our guards pack all radio and other equipment on the horses, saw that everything was squared away, then went back up to the mountainside." The two officers had no sooner reached their tent when "All hell broke loose!"

"Heavy machine gun and small arms fire [broke out] on all sides right around us. We grabbed our rifles and jumped into the bushes. The fog was just lifting and we could spot some figures dodging behind trees and bushes and firing at intervals. Machine guns at higher elevations were blazing away down the other side of the hill." The fire fight was confusing; neither officer could determine where the guerrillas were. "Bailey finally spotted two or three Jerries [German soldiers] off to the left, running from tree to tree. Their uniforms were a solid green-gray color. We opened up on them, but it was impossible to tell whether we connected because of the thick brush."

The firing died down and the two officers worked their way back to Mihailovich's headquarters. "The General hurriedly advised us that about two hundred German soldiers had come by truck before day-break to a spot on the road nearest our camp. Then, under cover of fog, they had successfully slipped through our outer defenses before being detected. By that time they were so spread out that confusion reigned. Mihailovich himself was directing operations, dispatching groups here and there." The Germans were forced to retreat after losing twenty dead and wounded. The Chetniks captured five prisoners but lost about the same number of casualties. With their location pinpointed, "[t]he General ordered that we move at once," Mansfield said. "We started with many others in single file up over a trail to the rear through the mountains."

The withdrawal proved to be a test of endurance, as Mansfield recalled.

I shall never forget the '*pocred*'. In all there must have been about five hundred of us, including old and young, stretcher cases, cooks, camp followers, and rugged little heavily-laden pack horses. Hour after hour, we slowly wound our way up and down steep, almost impassable, mountain trails, through a cold, penetrating rain. The march started around noon and continued all day and night until 0300 the following morning, with frequent rests while we waited for patrols to report. . . . I became weary and stiff. Whenever I asked, 'How much longer?' I would always receive the same reply, 'Only two hours.' This would stretch into three, then four more hours. We finally camped in a little village. The endurance of these men amazed me. Despite their ragged condition and the tiring, steady, endless pace, there was only cheerfulness and no complaints.

As Michael Lees observed:

In that country of gentle mountains and woodland, which stretched mile after mile with only an occasional track and no paved roads at all, the peasant holdings were often separated by one or two ravines and usually a mile or so as the crow flies. This distance could entail two or three hours' march on foot with one, two, or maybe more ascents and descents of hundreds of feet each time. Each holding was independent and virtually self-supporting. There was usually barley or wheat corn and grazing for livestock. There were cattle, sometimes sheep, bullocks for transport, small sturdy horses, but very few mules. Pigs and chickens ran around the homesteads, and the warm summer climate favoured peppers and other semi exotic vegetables. Beans formed the main item of the staple diet. No holding was without plum trees for making the potent *rakiya* or *shlivovica* (plum brandy), and many had pear and apple trees as well. The women worked with the men on the land, and after cooking the food, they wove all the material they needed on their own looms; they also made all of the clothing, some of which was of fine quality, design, and appearance. The footwear was formed from rectangles of rawhide wrapped around the foot and known as *opanke*.

Lees described the peasant houses, which were built of mud with home-fired tiled roofs.

In the mountains they were universally single-storied. A two-storied house was regarded as a sign of enormous prestige and fortune, and was to be found only in the foothills and plains. But even in the mountains, most of the houses had a cellar, or *podrum*, which served the vital purpose of storing the *rakiya*. Chimneys were a rarity; the smoke from the open fire in the center of the floor filtered through a hole in the peak of the roof. There was usually just one bed in the house, reserved for the mating couple. Grandparents, children, and others slept on mats on the floor, where we would join them in due course. There would be a low, round table and a few small stools and, apart from the looms, no other furniture. The reserves of food, mostly dried, hung from hooks in the ceiling. The homesteads were simple. The holdings seemed limited only by the amount of land the members of the family were physically able to cultivate; there were large areas of unexploited woodland between each settlement. The families were almost entirely self-supporting. Some produce was carried was carried up to ten, fifteen, or more hours' journey—an average difference to the nearest village or township—and sold in order to purchase needles, sugar, or salt, which were the articles most in demand. The mountain peasants the life was rugged and hard. They were proud and fiercely individualistic, and they loved their *svoyna*—their home and land.

Field Operations

After several weeks of observing the headquarters and getting the lay of the land, Mansfield requested to be allowed to go on an operation. "I spoke to the General about this and after considerable reluctance he agreed to let me go on a job to be jointly planned by ourselves and the British." The target was the main railroad line running from Belgrade to the Adriatic Sea. "It was an important German supply link to the coast," he pointed out. "The local guerrilla chieftain, Captain Radovich, told us there were three or four unguarded tunnels and a river bridge near the town of Vardiste." The information was almost too good to be true because usually they were heavily guarded and fortified with pillboxes, barbed wire, and mines. Mansfield and Lieutenant Colonel Hudson decided on a personal reconnaissance, along with a large detachment of guerrillas. "We marched three days over the mountains to the vicinity of the bridge and tunnels," Mansfield explained. "There were several tunnels in the mountain where the railroad skirted around the side of it, on two different levels." He was able to get to a good vantage point within a couple hundred yards of the bridge. "Through my binoculars I saw only a few Bulgarian puppet troops hanging around." He waited until a train passed by. "It was a medium-sized engine drawing eight cars, three of which were full of soldiers," a lucrative target.

The detachment returned to the base camp and started planning for the operation. They estimated that it would take about two hundred pounds of explosive to drop the span. "The bridge was a modern, single-track, steel girder type, about one hundred feet long, supported by concrete abutments and two concrete piers," Mansfield explained. "We estimated that by using ring-mounted charges set on all girders and beams about five feet in from both piers we could cut it clean and drop it into the river." They wanted to deny the Germans the use of the railroad for at least a month, so they planned on wrecking the train inside the tunnel. "The only railroad wrecking yard was located east of the bridge, which lay between it and the tunnel. By blowing the bridge, the Jerries would have to replace it before getting to the wrecked train." The plan called for Mansfield to plant the derailing charges in the tunnel, while Hudson took down the bridge. "We spent the next two days preparing the charges and briefing the men on their assignments. The explosives were packed on four horses and we started out for the target area."

The three-day trip was uneventful. "At the railroad we found the situation to be the same. No one was guarding either bridge or railroad," Mansfield explained, "but we were concerned about a detachment of five hundred Bulgars in a town about three miles away." The men quickly set up security. "Machine guns were placed on two hills near the bridge, which gave us good enfilade fire. Two hundred men took up positions, spread out in the edge of the woods, under Captain Radovich's command. The prepared explosive charges were unloaded and made ready for carriage by small three-man groups to the bridge. Hudson busied himself cutting the time fuses. Everything was secure." Mansfield and a security force left to place the explosives in the tunnel, which was about a mile away.

The group took cover in the woods at the west end of the tunnel until a reconnaissance patrol reported that the coast was clear. "I entered the tunnel with five men, leaving one group at each end," Mansfield said. The track rested on very short ties, supported by rocks and cinders. We walked about two hundred feet when my eyes became accustomed to the darkness and I could see the other entrance about three hundred feet away. I put two half-pound blocks of TNT under the rail, connected up the prima cord and snapped the detonator on the tracks—a simple job." Mansfield was a graduate of the OSS demolitions school where he had been taught how to blow up railroad tracks and other interesting things. "I had just crossed the track and was kneeling down to place a staggered charge on the other side when cries came from the west end of the tunnel. We all looked up, and simultaneously heard the 'chug-chug' of an engine! A train was coming, even though none was due for about an hour. Panic seized us! Someone cried 'Idemo' (Let's go) and all six of us bounded down the tracks toward the east entrance away from the train. It seemed as if we would never reach the exit, but we finally made it, turned off at the end and kept right on running up into the woods where we hit the trail leading down toward the bridge." The train roared out the tunnel right on their heels and squealed to a stop—undamaged. "I could not understand it," Mansfield murmured, "Why hadn't it derailed?"

At that moment, a terrific explosion shook the ground. "Hudson had blown the bridge," Mansfield explained, "a beautiful job in which he succeeded in cutting it completely at both ends, dropping it into the river and ruining the piers." Mansfield and his security element continued on the trail to the rendezvous point. "I met Hudson and got the story . . . After I had started out for the tunnel, he had decided that the situation was safe enough to place the charges on the bridge. With a dozen men he had tied them on . . . and was about to retire to the hills when he heard the train in the distance. . . . [H]e had pulled the fuse igniters and, retiring to his post in the hills, watched the bridge go up in the air." As the two talked, shooting broke out near the destroyed bridge. "Apparently some Jerries or Bulgars had arrived," Mansfield said. "Captain Radovich dispatched a hundred men under Lieutenant Medenovich to go back to the tunnel, while we withdrew about three miles up into the hills."

Lieutenant Medenovich returned that night and told Mansfield what happened inside the tunnel. "[The] charge had exploded and blown about four or five feet of rail out of the track," he related, "but the train's large wheels still continued to pass over the gap without derailment. The engineer, hearing the explosion, realized something was wrong and stopped the train after exiting the tunnel." Medenovich's force surrounded the train and succeeded in capturing three Bulgar soldiers. They tried to destroy the train but only succeeded in damaging it. Despite his failure to block the tunnel, Mansfield considered the raid a success because they were able to destroy the bridge. Before they could mount another foray, news reached them that the Italian Army had surrendered to the Allies, only six days after the invasion of Italy proper. Mansfield recalled that, "General Mihailovich sent out orders to all his field commanders to attack German and Italian occupation forces everywhere. . . . I personally saw and had translated a good many orders which were sent by radio from his central headquarters." At the same time, SOE headquarters in Cairo radioed them to do "everything possible to effectuate peaceable surrender of Italian forces in Yugoslavia."

At the time of the surrender, there were five Italian occupation divisions and two German divisions in and around the area where Mansfield was located. It was doubtful that the Italians, even if they wanted to, would be allowed to surrender by the Germans. Furthermore Mansfield noted, "What would we do with all the Italians, if they surrendered . . . we could not feed and house them in the woods and mountains." However, orders were orders and, "After a quick conference with the General, we decided to make a stab at it." They decided on a two prong; Bailey and eight hundred guerrillas would march on the headquarters of the Italian "Venezzia" Division and try to entice it to surrender, while Mansfield and a smaller force of 300 men would try to affect the surrender of the 1,800-man Italian garrison at Priboj. "We used the General's typewriter to type up a surrender demand—a pompous document which made us both blush when we read it," Mansfield recalled. "It called upon the Italian CO to send out a delegation which would meet us in the woods and work out terms of surrender, and guaranteed their safe conduct; otherwise we would attack."

The following night, Mansfield and his guerrilla force marched over the mountains for over eight hours to get into position overlooking the Italian fort, a formidable structure stretching along the crests of several small hills. "It was pitch black and movement through the woods was most difficult," Mansfield said regretfully. "We realized that our timing was poor and that daylight would have provided more suitable conditions, but decided to go through with it." The guerrillas crept forward to the edge of the woods, about four hundred yards from the garrison's position and gave the surrender demand to a local man to deliver. "About fifteen minutes after the peasant departed, the silence was broken by a burst of heavy machine gun fire . . . then the Italian hit us with everything they had," Mansfield exclaimed. "[M]ortars and machine guns fired wildly into the side of the mountain. . . . [P]anic apparently seized the Italians and they mowed down our emissary before he even reached the gate." The guerrillas withdrew and assembled on top of the mountain where they spent the night.

The next day, Mansfield sent the Italian commanding officer another demand. He responded that he had did not have any orders to surrender and therefore would not do so. "One remark in the note, however, made us determined to wait another day," Mansfield recalled. "The writer, half-pleading, stated that he was 'only a soldier, and must obey his orders.' Through the peasant grape-vine we learned that there was trouble inside the garrison. The commander wanted to surrender but there were about a hundred Fascist 'Black Shirts' who demanded to fight it out to the bitter end and threatened rebellion." The next morning an emissary brought a note from the commander stating that he would, in fact, enter surrender negotiations. "Within three hours, we were discussing preliminary plans . . . with a cocky little Italian major dressed in fancy blue-gray peg pants, high boots, and a tight-waisted, almost feminine-looking blouse. Six hours later we walked with a heavy guerrilla guard through the streets of the town to the garrison commander's headquarters, cheered by laughing Serbs, saluted at every turn by cheerful little Italian soldiers."

The Italian surrender brought forth an embarrassment of riches for the ill-equipped and poorly supplied guerrillas—shoes, blankets, small arms and ammunition, and mortars. For three days they enjoyed "the good life" before word reached them that a large force of Germans were coming. "We decided to evacuate rather than rely on the Italians to join in making a stand against their recent allies," Mansfield related. "We got our guerrillas started on a quick exodus up through the mountains. Before leaving, however, our men loaded fifteen of the mortars with several hundred rounds on the horses and carried out a large number of rifles, machine guns, and ammo. By nightfall we were camped up in the mountains." Mansfield learned that the Germans used large numbers of the Italian garrison as labor troops, while hundreds of others fled into the woods. "We were plagued with stray Italian soldiers wanting to join us," he said. "Most of them were far too soft for guerrilla life and ended up working on peasant farms for their keep. . . . [W]hatever became of them we never learned."

Blood Feud

The animosity between Tito and Mihailovich was reaching a critical stage. A bloody civil war was raging throughout Herzegovina and south Bosnia, threatening to involve both the United States and Britain in the feud. "Both Tito and Mihailovich were jockeying for Allied support," Mansfield explained. "Allied missions and supplies were parachuted to both guerrilla groups. With Britain as well as Russia appearing to side with Tito, those of us with Mihailovich were in the middle of a chaotic situation. Mihailovich, ignoring the British, turned to me in his anger and pleaded for more American support as well as additional teams to come in and see for themselves what his guerrillas were doing." Mansfield radioed headquarters for instructions. "I felt it would be a sorry situation if Allied missions on both sides found themselves using Allied equipment to destroy each other rather than the Germans."

In late September 1943, OSS headquarters in Cairo advised Mansfield that additional team members were being sent in to deal with the difficult situation. "After several nights of waiting, the new members parachuted in . . . British Brig. Gen. Charles Armstrong with three British officers, three enlisted men, and my new commanding officer, U.S. Army Col. Albert B. Seitz. (It was reported upon landing that Seitz burst into a joyous 'Yee-haw,' cowboy style whoops to the delight of the Yugoslavia welcoming party.) At the same time several tons of badly needed military supplies were dropped." At the time, Seitz thought that the friction between Tito and Mihailovich "did not appear insurmountable," an opinion that would change as he spent time on the ground. He came to realize that, "I was there simply to give an Allied illusion to the Yugoslavs. The mission was British and the whole show would remain a British show. I would be permitted to see or talk to Mihailovich only at the discretion of the brigadier [Armstrong]. . . . I was even forbidden to address Mihailovich in French. Further, any message destined for my people would be subject to the brigadier's censorship." Even the British thought Armstrong was a little "stuffy." He was a regular officer, with no experience in guerrilla warfare, and given to strict military discipline. To top it off, he was "a non-smoking, teetotaler," according to Lees, "who was not at home in the Chetnik meetings at which 'raki' [a potent distilled spirit] was regularly passed around in a thick fog of cigarette smoke."

Despite the internal squabbles, the war continued. After several conferences with General Mihailovich a plan was developed to attack the fortified city of Visegrad, where over eight hundred German soldiers were garrisoned. "Orders were sent out to all Chetnik guerrilla leaders," Mansfield related. "Over 2,500 were gradually massed with their arms in the woods south of the city. There was no doubt that Mihailovich was out to put on a big show. . . ." The attack started at dawn on 4 October with a heavy mortar, artillery and small arms fire. "The fighting continued all morning, with our patrols gradually infiltrating until contact was made," Mansfield related. "By the afternoon we had the town and had killed or wounded over two hundred Germans. The balance withdrew. We quickly set to work to destroy the armored railroad car left behind by the Jerries. Then everyone pitched in to prepare charges for the huge steel bowsprit bridge, which we blew into the river that afternoon."

The guerrillas withdrew to Rogatica, a town in eastern Bosnia to rest and refit. While they were in the town, "Mihailovich heard a BBC broadcast announcing that the Partisans had taken Rogatica, never mentioning that Mihailovich's forces were there," Mansfield said. "At that time, around the town there was not a single German or a Tito Commie. For the first time, the BBC was glorifying Tito and his Partisans to the exclusion of Mihailovich despite the fact that the Chetniks, since the Italian surrender, were attacking the Germans everywhere. General Mihailovich was in a terrible temper." The BBC was repeating almost word for word what the Partisans were releasing in their communiqués. For example, after Mihailovich's forces conducted several attacks, Tito's Yugoslav People's Army of Liberation took credit, stating, "We captured Rogatica and a large quantity of war material. We carried out a big, successful attack against the Zagreb-Belgrade railway, and destroyed the line in 130 places along a forty-mile stretch. We also destroyed four bridges and killed about three hundred Germans guarding the line."

"From that point on," Mansfield recalled, "all reports over the BBC consisted only of statements by Tito as to what he said and did."

Because of the great buildup Tito was receiving in the British media, Mansfield and Seitz decided to undertake a tour of the various Chetnik forces throughout Serbia so he could report to the U.S. government on the effectiveness of Chetnik attacks on German troops. As Mansfield wrote:

> Traveling light, minus radio or any heavy gear, we moved northward from one guerrilla band to the next. Sticking always to guerrilla 'safe canals' for passage . . . our trip took us through scores of towns and villages under Chetnik control where hundreds of peasants, townsmen and guerrillas came out to greet us and shower us with flowers. At almost every stopping point, the people would hold a great feast in our honor . . . [W]e became regular gourmands, and on Thanksgiving Day, they even prepared a turkey dinner for us! With each guerrilla commander, we held long conferences to find out his past and proposed operations, the number of men in his group and how much they had in the way of arms and ammunition. We held mass inspections of guerrilla forces wherever we went and took many photos.

For a month the two men made their way across Serbia, "after walking and riding [horses] hundreds of miles, mostly over mountainous terrain," and staying one step ahead of the Gestapo. "Throughout this tour, we were amazed at the large amount of free territory in which we could roam at will. It was almost impossible to believe we were in German-occupied country with enemy troops only a few hours away. It was almost like a victory march . . . except for the Germans on our trail." At several points along their route, the Germans took hostages and burned down houses where the two had spent the night. It was common practice for the Nazi to exact a terrible price for opposing them. Hitler ordered that for every German killed, one hundred Serbs were to be killed; fifty for every German wounded. Major Hudson said it sickened him to hear the wailing lamentation for the dead . . . and see the villages burned. He noted, "This had a strong effect on Mihailovich. He felt his job was to defend the people, to be their shield. . . ." Michael Lees wrote, "Tito never worried about reprisals. In fact, he welcomed them because he got recruits from the devastated villages where the reprisals took place. Mihailovich, of course, was very concerned about the reprisals."

Homeward Bound

By December 1943, Mansfield and Seitz had amassed a great quantity of data and intelligence which they were anxious to deliver to their headquarters. In addition, "All supplies had been cut off [by the British] and we were unable to do anything further in coordinating guerrilla supply drops," Mansfield said. "[So] we decided instead to try to make it to the Adriatic Sea, over two hundred miles to the east and get to Bari, Italy, which had just been taken by the Allies. Colonel Seitz decided that we should not try to make the perilous journey together. The Gestapo were trailing us like hawks and we did not want to risk our eggs in one basket." Seitz left on Christmas Eve with a small escort, intending to walk to the coast, steal a boat, and work his way to southern Italy. Mansfield decided to stay and gather more information. By this time he was fairly conversant in Serbo-Croatian and felt comfortable communicating with the people.

Mansfield spent Christmas holed up in a little mountain village with a group of local guerrillas. "The guerrilla chieftain must have sensed that I was feeling rather low, [so] they secretly made preparation for a little feast, sending peasants down to nearby German-held towns to acquire food and wine," Mansfield recalled emotionally. "On Christmas Day, all the peasants and guerrillas dropped by to pay their respects, many bringing gifts. My pack boy chopped down a little pine tree and fashioned little tallow candles on the branches. A huge roast pig was served as a fitting climax. Such unsolicited care and generosity on the part of these people made me feel proud to be fighting alongside them." After the celebration, Mansfield continued. "During the following weeks I inspected more troops, took part in a road ambush in which we destroyed at least six trucks, killed or wounded twenty-five Jerries, and captured some loot, including more rifles and machine guns. German reprisals were heavy!" In mid-January 1944, he finally headed for the Dalmatian coast with a small guerrilla security force.

The group marched between forty to fifty kilometers a day up and down steep mountain trails until they reached the point of exhaustion. "Often we would find our route blocked by heavy German forces holding the towns and main roads," Mansfield recalled. "Then with the help of peasants and local guerrillas, we would find some back pass which we could slip through at night. More than once we were fired on, and on one occasion we were completely scattered until we rejoined each other the following day." At one point he ran head on into a German patrol and had to run for his life for over ten hours before evading the pursuers. Another time he was forced to dress up as a peasant in order to cross a German-held bridge. "I had a beard by this time so that I felt quite comfortable in crossing right under the eyes of the German guards." Mansfield passed town after town that had been burned down by Germans, Partisans, or Chetniks. "The country was poor and the people were starving," he said.

As Mansfield reached the coast, he began to see evidence of large Partisan forces. "When we came close to them, my small force would become panicky," he explained. "Most of the field commanders . . . were constantly complaining that they were being attacked by Partisans. . . ." The group finally reached the coast near Dubrovnik, Dalmatia. "The greatest hurdle lay ahead, we had to find a way across the Adriatic Sea . . . . [C]apturing a fishing boat would not be easy, the Germans kept close control over all craft. They operated plane and sea patrols up and down the coast. Furthermore, we were now in hostile territory, where the people were not as sympathetic as in Serbia. The Gestapo knew we were in the vicinity, so we had to watch ourselves carefully, find safe villages to stay the night, post an extensive guard, and change our location each night."

After failing to find a boat after several days, Mansfield's morale was at a low point until "[w]e received a report there was a British officer about three days to the north," he said. "I went to meet him . . . [and] who should I meet but Colonel Bill Bailey, my old friend, whom I had not seen in several months. It was a joyous meeting!" Bailey had been attempting to get out but had been stymied just as Mansfield had. The two conspired to contact their headquarters and request a pickup. "That night we waited feverishly for the 8 p.m. schedule . . . [W]ithin ten minutes after we had started pounding the key . . . Cairo came up! The operator was so excited that he put us off for a half hour while contacting headquarters [since both men had been out of contact with headquarters for several weeks]. On the following day, Cairo advised us to be at the rendezvous [an unguarded cove with the nearest German garrison three kilometers away] two nights later between the hours of 2000–0100 and flash two code letters out to sea five times every ten minutes. A surface craft would take us off."

On the appointed date, the two men "started out at dusk over the mountains for the point on the coast, which was six hours away by foot," Mansfield described.

> It was a bitter night, with rain and sleet sweeping at us. The terrain was almost impassable. We descended slowly, feeling our way in the darkness, to the two-mile plain extending out to the water. After cutting ourselves and stumbling down rocky ledges, we wallowed through fields of mud. Our hearts pounded as we waited in a ditch near the main road. When it cleared of traffic, two at a time we sauntered down the road for a hundred yards to a point where a trail led to our destination. Next we were pushing through brambles, scratching ourselves badly in the pitch darkness. Finally we reached our destination.

Rescue was not to be. "One look at the water and I knew we would never get out that night. It was a thundering sea, crashing up thirty-foot breakers against the rocks. For three freezing hours we sat on the rocks, flashing my little German torch out to sea—nothing happened."

At 0200 they had had enough. "Our native guide came to the rescue and walked us about a mile and hid us in the attic of his house, where we hid for two days, right in the middle of the Germans. We could see them from time to time in the distance through the shutters. The old man and his two daughters brought us food—everyone held their breath when someone came near the house. On the third night we made our way, with great difficulty, back up the mountain. Everyone was discouraged!" They made contact with headquarters and arranged another rendezvous at the same location—"We knew that if this time did not work out we would have to move somewhere else." On the following day the weather cleared and they made their way to the rendezvous. "Standing on the rocks, we took turns flashing out the [code] letters. We were there only twenty minutes when someone heard the low hum of a motor somewhere out in the water, but we could not see it. Worried as we were over the possibility that it was a German patrol boat, we kept flashing."

The boat approached the shoreline.

Finally we spotted it at once. Now we were too excited to contain ourselves. . . . [I]t was a large ML2 British-type PT boat. Before it pulled to a stop, a dingy was slung over, and we could see its muffled oars splashing as it made its way into shore. We all gave a soft cheer! . . . and quickly leaped down the rocks to a point where it could take us off and flashed our light. As it pulled alongside, we made out two British sailors and two passengers, a British naval officer and an American army captain. They leaped up on the rocks with pistols drawn. We quickly identified ourselves and were taken aboard for the trip to the PT boat. Within fifteen minutes all of us, Colonel Bailey, six Yugoslav guerrillas and I were aboard Allied territory at last!

The Mansfield-Seitz report reached Donovan, who was impressed with its thoroughness and pro-Chetnik stance and wanted to continue placing teams with Mihailovich. However, Prime Minister Winston Churchill convinced President Roosevelt that it would not be in the best interests of Allied solidarity if the United States did not follow Britain's lead in supporting Tito. As a result, Mihailovich was starved for supplies and was eventually overwhelmed by the Partisans. Mansfield angrily declared, "The British had sold him [Mihailovich] down the river!" After the war the leader of the Chetniks was tried by a military court and executed. Mansfield, after a short leave in the United States, was assigned to the Far East. From December 1944 to June 1945 he went behind Japanese lines with a small avenger group to organize Chinese guerrillas and to conduct ambushes and raids. From June 1945 until the end of the war, he led teams which parachuted into prison camps in China to evacuate American POWs. He capped his OSS career by assisting in the rescue of Gen. Jonathan Wainwright and three of the surviving Doolittle fliers. For his work in Yugoslavia, Mansfield was awarded the Bronze Star and the Yugoslavia White Eagle with Swords.

CHAPTER 4

Union II

Marine Platoon Sergeant Jack Risler pushed his equipment bag out of the small rear hatch of the B-17 Flying Fortress, and followed it into the turbulent slipstream. His body was pummeled by the blast of air and he knew instinctively that the bomber was going too fast—more than 150 knots—and he experienced a bad opening shock but the adrenaline rush of the jump lessened the pain. His metal static line stretched tight, yanked the canopy from his British-made parachute, and he felt the satisfying shock as it fully deployed. The chute slowed his descent, but at a jump altitude of only four hundred feet the ground rushed up at him with dizzying speed.

Risler estimated that he spent less than thirty seconds in the air before hitting the ground. He leaped to his feet, smacked the quick-release cylinder in the middle of his chest and rotated it a quarter of turn. As he struggled to shed the harness, a scruffily dressed Resistance fighter grabbed him in a viselike bear hug and, before the flabbergasted Marine could react, planted a sloppy kiss on both his cheeks. "Hell of a reception on a combat mission," Risler allowed, "but, all in all, better than a German bayonet."

"Malice in Wonderland"

Jack Risler had enlisted in the Marine Corps in July 1940. After graduating from the Recruit Depot at San Diego, he was assigned to the guard force at Bremerton Navy Yard, Washington. Shortly after Pearl Harbor, Risler volunteered for parachute training since "guard duty was boring" and was assigned immediately to the West Coast jump school at Santee (later Camp Gillespie), California. Following six weeks of training, Risler was assigned to the U.S. Naval Air Station Parachute Riggers School at Lakehurst, New Jersey, where the Marine Corps had leased the jump towers from the 1939 World's Fair. After graduating in early 1943, Risler was transferred to New River, North Carolina, as a parachute instructor, where he came under the watchful eye of the school's senior instructor. The instructor asked him, "Would you like to do something exciting?" and then he was given the opportunity to volunteer for "hazardous duty behind enemy lines."

Within days of volunteering for hazardous duty, Risler was on his way to Washington, D.C., to receive training from the OSS. He reported to "Area F," the Congressional Country Club located only thirteen miles northwest of Washington in Bethesda, Maryland. The club had been leased by the OSS for the duration of the war for $4,000 a month and the promise of repair for any damages. In *OSS Training in the National Parks and Service Abroad in World War II,* John Whiteclay Chambers II noted that, "The former watering hole for Washington's power elite, the club had fallen onto hard times as a result of the depression and the war, and its board of directors was happy to lease it to the OSS." The estate quickly turned into a school for unconventional training: fairways became obstacle courses and small-arms ranges, sand traps turned into demolition beds, the club house provided office and work spaces. The site was supposed to be top secret, but when one newly assigned agent paid for his cab ride, the driver said, "Oh, you're one of those guerrillas." Every cab driver in Washington knew what was going on.

The training was tough and dangerous. Machine guns on the fifteenth tee fired live ammunition over the heads of trainees. Two trainees were killed on the range and another died during a mock attack on a bridge. Risler started the day at sunrise with hours of physical conditioning and didn't end until mock missions were completed well after dark. The classroom instruction was honed by practical application. Night after night, hundreds of trainees stalked the fairways in an attempt to ambush their instructors, who acted as enemy soldiers. At times the training was a little too realistic—the caddie shack fell victim to an overzealous demolitionist. "Sometimes we'd ambush the milk truck," one trainee recalled. This happened so often, in fact, that a signal system was developed to let the milkman know when the coast was clear. On occasion, missions were conducted off the property. A French group became adept at raiding the local farms to steal pigs, rabbits, chickens, and eggs, which they would then feast on in the woods. When the well-known syndicated columnist Drew Pearson, a Congressional neighbor, penned a series of unflattering pieces about Colonel Donovan, the trainees ambushed his farm as well.

It was at Area "F" that Risler met William E. Fairbairn, the legendary close-combat expert, who had spent three decades in Shanghai mastering the martial arts. The OSS "borrowed" him from the British to train the men in hand-to-hand combat. During one training session, Fairbairn told him to, "Come at me."

"I didn't want to hurt the old man," Risler recalled, "and instead I ended up on my ass!" One trainee described the demanding training as "malice in wonderland."

Parachute Training School

After completion of OSS training in November 1943, Risler and eight other Marines—Maj. Bruce Cheever, Gunnery Sgt. Robert LaSalle, Platoon Sgt. Larry Elder, Sgts. Homer Mantooth, Fitz Brunner, Charles Perry, Don Roberts, and John P. Bodnar—were transferred to the No. 1 Parachute Training School (PTS) at Manchester's Ringway Airfield. They were billeted in an old brick-walled estate (Durham House), nicknamed "House on the Shore," several miles southwest of Manchester, England. The PTS was the training ground for the SOE. Major Cheever and Gunnery Sergeant Elder were the first to arrive; the rest followed several days later. When Risler arrived at the mansion, he was surprised to be met by the casually dressed Cheever—uniform pants, shirt, and a silk scarf—and offered a drink, not the normal Marine reporting in procedure. "Great place, this Durham House," Risler commented.

The parachute course at Ringway was condensed into one action-packed week during which the students completed five jumps, one of which was at night. The school was run by a British captain, who had been training agents to jump into Europe since 1940. Trainees included Americans, Belgians, Canadians, Czechs, Dutch, Norwegians, and Poles. For security purposes, no names were used. The men were all called "Joes," the women, "Josephines." Security was vital for their survival. A number of training aids were used: aircraft fuselages in the hangars to show the trainees how to exit the aircraft; trapezes for teaching correct flight drills; wooden chutes to practice falling and rolling; and the "Fan," a steel cable wound around a drum with the end attached to a parachute harness. When the trainee jumped from a platform twenty feet from the ground, his weight caused the drum to revolve; however, its speed was controlled by two vanes which acted as air brakes and thus allowed the trainee to land with the same impact as he would when using a parachute. A one-hundred-foot steel tower was used to separate the men from the boys. A parachute canopy was stretched across a large metal hoop and suspended from the tower by a cable. The student climbed to the top of the tower, attached the parachute harness, and stepped out into space. He was suspended in mid-air until the instructor felt he was in the correct position for landing and then released. This method provided the pupil with a real test of nerve before attempting his first free parachute descent.

The initial jump was conducted from a large modified hydrogen-filled barrage balloon named "Bessie" that was tethered to a winch vehicle. Four students and a "dispatcher" were crammed into a wicker basket. On a signal the balloon was released and, after reaching an altitude of eight hundred feet, the vehicle moved slowly forward, keeping the cable at an angle, out of the jumpers' way. Risler said that many of the commands were different from what he had learned in the United States. "The jump master was called the 'dispatcher,' " he said. "He called out 'running in' as the aircraft approached the landing zone. When the red light came on, he gave the command, 'Action station.' The number one man swung his legs into the hole. When the green light flashed he said, 'Number one man go.' Then the next man and so on."

At altitude, the jumpers dropped one by one through a thirty-six-inch hole in the bottom of the basket—"jumping through the hole," often without seeing the ground because of England's persistent fog.

Risler recalled, "If the jumper pushed off too hard or looked down when dropping through the hole, he would invariably hit his head or nose on the opposite side. This was known as 'ringing the bell,' which had painful consequences."

The night jump was made from a pre-war Whitley twin-engine bomber. Risler with all his training had to relearn the British method of parachuting. The reason for the different style of jumping was due to the difference of the American parachute verses the British parachute. The American chute comes out of the pack after the risers and suspension lines, where the British chute operates in the reverse order: the chute comes out first, then risers and suspension lines. There is less of an opening shock with the British chute than the American and once on the ground, the jumper can get out of the chute much faster.

Chance Encounter

After completing training, Risler and the others were able to wrangle a forty-eight-hour pass to the big city. Wartime London, with its blackouts and nightly air raids, was not exactly a tourist paradise—but then again, it offered liberty-bound Marines a little more fun than hand-to-hand combat in the country club garden. As luck would have it, they ran into Marine Maj. Peter J. Ortiz, who had just returned from a very successful clandestine mission to France. "Glad to see the Marine uniform in London," he greeted them. After introductions and explanation of what they were doing in London, Ortiz asked, "Want to do something exciting?" and went on to say that he was looking for volunteers to join him on a classified mission. Risler remembered thinking, "Where have I heard this before?" but agreed to the invitation along with the others.

"I'll see what I can do," Ortiz responded.

Major Peter Ortiz had a reputation for adventure. He joined the French Foreign Legion, rising to the rank of acting lieutenant before returning to the United States. During his six years' service, he fought in a number of engagements in Africa and was wounded once. He received several French decorations—Croix de Guerre with two palms (one gold star and one silver star), the Croix des Combattant, the Ouissam Alouite, and the Médaille Militaire. When war broke out, he returned to the Legion and received a battlefield commission. In June 1940, he was wounded and captured. He spent fifteen months as a prisoner of war before escaping to the United States and enlisting in the Marine Corps.

After graduation from boot camp, Ortiz was commissioned. Because of his experiences and language skills—French, German, Spanish and Arabic—he came to the attention of the major general commandant. "The rather unique experiences and qualifications of Lieutenant Ortiz indicate that he would be of exceptional value to American units operating in North Africa. It is suggested that [his] services be offered to the Army. . . ." He was also promoted to captain from second lieutenant and assigned to Tangier, Morocco, as the assistant naval attaché, under Col. William A. Eddy. During this assignment, Ortiz volunteered to lead a special operations group. In a memorandum for Gen. William J. Donovan, director of the Office of Strategic Services, he noted, "I was placed in command of a group of five Spaniards and a British radio operator to determine the enemy's [German] armored strength." Ortiz left his men in an observation post while he crept alone toward an enemy position. "It was an extremely dark night, still raining heavily, the visibility so poor that I could scarcely see bushes and trees a few yards away."

Ortiz scouted several wadis until, "Suddenly, at very close range automatic weapons to my front and right opened fire on me. Before I could fall to the ground, a bullet had gone through my right hand and another had grazed my right leg. Rolling a few yards to my left . . . I could make out the dim silhouette of a vehicle . . . I managed to throw a Mills grenade but it fell short and had little effect. I then got in a well-aimed Petard Grenade. It exploded with a terrific blast and stopped the automatic weapon fire from the front and I heard excited shouts and cries of men in pain." Ortiz managed to get away and make his way back to Algiers for medical attention. He was eventually returned to the United States. After recovery, he was assigned to the OSS Naval Command for duties in the Haute Savoie region in occupied France. The three-man Allied mission— Frenchman Pierre Fourcaud, British agent H. H. A. Thackthwaite, and Ortiz—code named Operation Union, was ordered to survey the strength and organization of the French Resistance, the maquis. In late May 1944, Ortiz was withdrawn to England for further assignment.

Union II

Ortiz proved as good at his word and within days the men reported to the London headquarters of the SOE. This was based at 64 Baker Street, and led to the SOE's occasional nickname of "the Baker Street Irregulars," after Sherlock Holmes's fictional group of young helpers. It was also known as "Churchill's Secret Army" or "The Ministry of Ungentlemanly Warfare" because of the Prime Minister's interest in its operations. Soon after arriving, the men learned they were going to be part of General Donovan's new strategy of using heavily armed contingents known as an Operational Groups (OG) to take direct action against the Germans. Their mission was to assist the resistance, sabotage, seize key installations, and to prevent retreating German units from destroying them. Ortiz, code name "Chambellan," was assigned to lead Marine Operational Group Union II, consisting of U.S. Army Air Corps intelligence officer Capt. Francis T. "Frank" Coolidge, codename "Aimant" (who served with Ortiz in the French Foreign Legion and would subsequently lead a team (Spaniel) in China), five Marines—LaSalle, Perry, Bodnar, Brunner, and Risler—and Joseph Arcelin, code named "Jo-Jo," a representative of Gen. Charles de Gaulle's French Forces of the Interior (FFI, *Forces Françaises de l'Interieur).* Arcelin, who did not speak a word of English, was given the false identity papers of a French-Canadian Marine named George Andrews.

Union II's objective area was the Glières Plateau in the Haute Savoie region of southeastern France. The remote plateau was a natural landing area, very open, soft terrain and covered with pastures. Few roads traversed plateau, making it easier to defend against a road-bound armor and mechanized infantry attack. Starting in 1942, the plateau had become a mecca for the French resistance. A year later, the OSS/SOE estimated that over three thousand ill-trained and poorly-armed maquisards (resistance fighters) had assembled in the plateau's vastness. In January 1944, Major Ortiz and two others were sent into the area to determine the maquisards' military capabilities and requirements. As a result of their reconnaissance, tons of weapons, ammunition, and clothing were delivered, in one of the largest parachute drops of the war. In July 1944 the German army mounted a brutal offensive against the Glières Battalion, killing almost 150 and dispersing the organization.

In late July, the team received word that the mission was set for 1 August 1944. Each team member drew a .45 caliber pistol, a Winchester folding stock carbine, Fairbairn stiletto, maps of the objective area, and 50,000 French francs ($1,000) to pay for incidentals. Major Ortiz carried a suitcase containing a million francs for the resistance. They packed their personal equipment in a wire-reinforced canvas bag that was attached to a cargo chute. Risler noted that, "the night before we left, Major Ortiz paid for a going-away party at an exclusive restaurant . . . I could not help but reflect that this might be our 'last supper.'" On Sunday, 30 July the team was taken to the RAF airfield at Knettishall and on Monday they made a practice jump from a B-17 from the 388th Bomb Group (Heavy), the same group they would use for the mission. OSS headquarters had decided that the team would be inserted as part of a massive supply drop by the 8th Air Force, code named Operation Buick.

Operation Buick

During the critical first weeks of the invasion of France, the Eighth Air Force's 3rd Air Division diverted almost two hundred B-17s from the air campaign to maquis supply missions. For Operation Buick, three combat wings (4th, 13th, and 45th) consisting of thirty-nine B-17s each were assigned to drop on four targets. One wing went to the Chalon-sur-Saône area; another wing dropped 451 containers west of Geneva; a third wing dropped 463 containers to the maquis in Savoie, and. finally, seventy-five B-17s, escorted by P-51s of the 359th Fighter Group (mission 179) delivered 899 containers to Haute Savoie. In all, 192 B-17s dropped 2,281 containers, at a cost of six planes slightly damaged.

Ortiz's Union II team was part of the Haute Savoie drop. After an early breakfast, the team attended the aircrew briefing and then each boarded a separate aircraft. Risler remembered that, "The bombers took off at sixty-second intervals, climbed to seventeen thousand feet and formed into three formations, low, middle [the team flew in the middle formation], high. It took the B-17s an hour to gain formation and altitude." As the formation neared the coast, the on-board Rebecca radar picked up the Eureka ground transponder, guiding them closer to the objective. Flying over Normandy, Risler said the weather was perfect:

he could see barrage balloons and some flak bursts. North American P-51 Mustang fighters took station to escort them to the drop zone. The bombers reduced altitude to three thousand feet as drop zone Ebonite appeared. The lead pilot talked to a maquis over the S-phone—a radio-telephone for ground-to-air communications—with specific directions while decreasing altitude to four hundred feet for the drop. "The zone is clear, and the signal fires are burning," the Frenchman reported. "The three signaling fires were built in equilateral triangles, prepared with old tires that were soaked with gasoline and tar."

Risler thought they were "flying too low because I could see cows with bells around their necks! I felt the plane slow down and the waist gunner slapped me on the shoulder." He pushed his jump bag through the rear exit hatch and then leaped out himself. "We were using the English parachute with a wire cable static line about 3/16 of an inch in diameter. I was worried that the cable would get wrapped around my arm or leg or form a kink and snap." This happened to one of the jumpers. Sergeant Bodnar jumped from another aircraft. "We normally would jump at about one thousand feet. Because of the [terrain] limitations, we had to make this jump at four hundred feet," he remembered. "As soon as we were out of the aircraft our chutes opened and the next thing I remember is I was on the ground. Boom! It happened that fast." Risler thought the air speed must have exceeded 150 mph. "The B-17 pilots tried to slow the plane down, however they were afraid of the mountains. For this reason they lowered the landing flaps, which did reduce the air speed, but still had plenty of propeller rpm. This caused a bad propeller blast, plus they went to full power as soon as we left the aircraft."

Risler hit the ground and was immediately embraced by a jubilant Frenchman. After freeing himself, he scrambled to find his equipment bag among the hundreds of containers that littered the ground. In all the 78 B-17s dropped 864 containers loaded with 1,096 Sten guns, 298 Bren automatic rifles, 1,350 Lee-Enfield rifles, 2,080 Mills anti-personnel grenades, 1,030 Gammon grenades, 260 automatic pistols, 51 P.I.S.T. antigun guns, 2 1/2 million rounds of ammunition, several tons of explosives, medical supplies, clothing, rations, bicycle tires, and chewing gum. A man ran up to Risler and frantically pointed to a group of men gathered around a still form lying on the ground. He had a sinking feeling in the pit of his stomach as he ran toward the group. He made his way through the men and discovered Sergeant Perry's crumpled form. His parachute failed to deploy after the steel static line snapped six inches from the drogue. Without a reserve, there was nothing he could do to save himself. Minutes later he found out that Gunnery Sergeant LaSalle was also a casualty and barely mobile after badly wrenching his back in the jump. The mission was off to a very rough start.

The team spent the rest of the day assisting the maquis in gathering the widely dispersed weapons and equipment. Risler said, "By nightfall the plateau was well defended. Captain Jean Bulle, the maquis commander established road blocks and ambush sites around the drop zone. Fortunately the Germans did not react quickly. We found out later that they were waiting for reinforcements." The next morning, Sergeant Perry was buried with full military honors. An altar of packing cylinders, decorated with red, white, and blue parachutes, was erected as a bier for the rough-hewn coffin. An honor guard of maquis stood in two ranks, while several dignitaries spoke of the "soldier who came from far away America to help us in the liberation of our country." Local women had painstakingly sewn a homemade American flag which was buried with the Marine.

For the next several days the team instructed the maquis on the functioning and maintenance of the weapons and planning attacks on the Germans. Ortiz took the opportunity to inspect several of the resistance companies in the area. He was accompanied by Capt. Jean Bulle, the local maquis commander and legendary hero (He was later killed by the Germans while attempting to negotiate a bloodless surrender. The SS shot and killed him and then dumped his body alongside the road.) "On the twelfth, we traveled in two cars as far south as we could," Risler said, "to link-up with other resistance groups around the town of Beaufort. Gunnery Sergeant LaSalle was in such extreme pain that we left him with a priest in a mountain safe house." The group set out by foot with their equipment and weapons. "We spent the night in a barn owned by a local resistance fighter. He gave us cheese, bread, and wine and refused payment. 'It's for France,' he explained fervently." The team did not realize at the time that a French spy had informed on them and the Germans were in hot pursuit.

Sergeant Brunner recalled that, "On 14 August we proceeded to Beaufort where we made contact with other F.F.I. [*Forces Françaises de l'Interieur*] companies and from there went on to Montgirod where we were told there were heavy concentrations of Germans. We were able to enter the town but had no sooner done so than we were heavily shelled by German batteries located in the hills around the city."

Risler said that, "We reached the center of town when the shooting started. Four maquis that were with us were wounded, two seriously. When the Germans swarmed into town, we were forced to hide them in the parish church. Several houses were on fire as we retreated." The team withdrew up a steep hill north of the village where they hid in the thick brush. After dark, they were able to make their way past the surrounding enemy positions. "It took us until almost mid-night to cross the Isere River and find a hiding place about a thousand yards from the small village of Longefoy."

The next morning, Ortiz left Captain Coolidge in charge and went alone into the village. "I contacted the mayor and requested food," Ortiz said. "He was very nervous"—the mayor had learned that the Germans had killed the two maquis that had been left in the church, then burned the building to the ground and killed several hostages for harboring "terrorists." "They burned the place down," Sergeant Bodnar bemoaned, " . . . and killed them all." The longer Ortiz talked to the mayor, the more "his confidence returned he and others became very hospitable." Risler said fondly, "The mayor's daughter—a very attractive young woman—brought us bread, cheese, sausage, and wine." Ortiz was excited to learn that the Allies had landed in Southern France (Operation Anvil). However, the mayor cautioned him that German forces were on the move. One convoy had passed through the village earlier that morning headed northeast. "I spent the rest of the afternoon observing enemy movement in the valley," Ortiz said. "After dark we went into the village and spent the night in the mayor's house."

The team decided to return to their headquarters on the plateau so they could better coordinate their activities with the invasion force. "At first light we crossed the Isere River at Centron," Risler said, "We were overconfident and got careless." Just as they reached the main highway, a heavily armed convoy—two hundred German soldiers in ten to twelve trucks with machine guns mounted on rings over the cabs and a half-track—from the German 157th Alpine Mountain Division came around a blind curve and put the Americans under fire. "Ortiz was in the lead, followed by Bodnar, myself, Arcelin, Brunner, and Coolidge," Risler said. "The Germans caught us flat footed. There was no place to go, except back to the village in an attempt to cross the river again and seek cover on the other side. The village was the only cover available. . . . [T] here was a steep drop on one side and a mountain on the other." Sergeant Brunner recalled, "Major Ortiz, Sergeant Bodnar, and Sergeant Risler withdrew into the southwest section of the town. Captain Coolidge, Jo-Jo, and I took the southeast. We retaliated as best we could while working our way under fire toward the east." Risler said that, "The three of us reached a stone wall, under covering fire from Brunner and Coolidge. We returned fire with our carbines and retreated through the village."

About this time, Captain Coolidge was hit in the right leg but he kept going. Brunner said, "I called out to Jo-Jo and told him to follow us but he stayed in the village. Captain Coolidge and I reached the river. I dove in, and swam across under fire. The current was very swift and I had some difficulty reaching the opposite shore. The captain and I got separated and did not meet up again until two days later." As the other three retreated from house to house, Risler came upon a young mother and two small children. "I told them to get down but they didn't understand English," he said emotionally. "The toddlers were crying. . . . I felt sorry for them. . . . I remembered what the Germans had done to the last village." Ortiz told the two men to get out while he held the enemy off. Both refused. Several terrified townspeople implored the Marines to give up to save the village. Finally the Germans had the village surrounded, cutting off any hope of escape. They were trapped, and it was only a matter of time until they brought up heavy weapons to destroy the town.

"Since our activities were well known to the Gestapo, there was no reason to hope that we would be treated as ordinary prisoners of war," Ortiz explained. "For me personally the decision to surrender was not too difficult. I had been involved in dangerous activities for many years and was mentally prepared for my number to turn up. Sergeant Bodnar was next to me and I explained the situation to him and what I intended to do." Bodnar recalled, "Major Ortiz said that he was going to talk with the Germans and that we should try and sneak out while he did. I told him, 'Major we're Marines. We work together, we stay together!' "

Surrender and Captivity

The decision was made. Ortiz would surrender to save the village and his men. During a lull in the firing, he shouted a surrender proposal in German . . . and stepped into the street. The Germans continued to fire but fortunately Ortiz was not hit and kept walking toward the enemy. Finally the firing stopped and he met with the German commander, who agreed to spare the village inhabitants. Ortiz motioned for his men to come out, and when more did not appear the German officer demanded to know "where the rest of the company was."

Risler said that, "The Germans got mad because only three Marines surrendered. They thought there was more." During a subsequent search of the village and the surrounding fields the Germans captured Arcelin, who was wearing Perry's uniform and was considered to be a Marine despite a very limited English vocabulary—the team taught him some English, mostly profanity, according to Risler. Arcelin was able to continue the ruse during the entire period of his captivity.

After being disarmed and searched, Ortiz called his men to attention. "We are Marines," he said, and ordered them to adhere to the Geneva Convention by giving their captors name, rank, and serial number. This show of discipline so impressed the Germans that they started treating them with marked respect. The men were placed under heavy guard and taken to the German headquarters at Bourg St. Maurice for interrogation. Upon arrival they were searched again. Ortiz lost his identification card and 35,000 francs but managed to conceal 65,000 francs. "We were taken before Major Kolb, the German officer responsible for our imprisonment," Risler explained. "He was a short, heavyset retread from World War I, who had fought against the Marines in 1918." Ortiz was surprised by the amount of information Kolb knew. "In great accurate detail he described our air operation, the burial ceremony of Sergeant Perry, various engagements, and the manner and position of our movements. He said the information was obtained by a shepherd who was one of his field agents."

Kolb ordered the prisoners to be taken to Albertville. "Ortiz rode in a staff car, while we rode in the back of a truck," Risler recalled. "I thought that we were going to be executed because there were three shovels in the bed of the vehicle." He was aware that Hitler had issued orders to execute all OSS agents who were caught and before leaving a junior officer had stalked by and pointed a pistol at them. "Kaput!" he exclaimed. Looking back, Risler thought that Kolb disliked the SS-Totenkopfverbände, the SS unit which ran the concentration camps, and that's why they weren't turned over to them. As a ploy, Ortiz told the team to claim they were paratroops from the Normandy landings but Kolb quickly saw through the ruse. The convoy stopped every few minutes. "The Germans were afraid of maquis ambushes," Risler said. "They sent out security patrols to investigate suspicious terrain and often traveled in circles, backtracking, and only traveled with larger convoys. They were so concerned about the maquis that they abandoned broken down vehicles rather than take time to repair them." During one of the frequent stops, the irrepressible Ortiz used his lighter to try to set fire to the car, hoping in the confusion that he could escape. "However," he said, "I succeeded only in making the rear seat smolder. The Germans ranted and threatened in the usual Teutonic manner, but did not use physical force."

On 21 August the small convoy reached Chambery, the headquarters of the 157th Alpine Division where Ortiz brazenly requested to see the commanding general. His request was granted and upon entering the general's office he boldly proposed that the division surrender to his team. The amazed general responded, "It's lucky I don't have you shot!" and threw Ortiz out of his office. For several weeks they were transported to various locations. "At one point we were taken through a tunnel to northern Italian town of Susa, where we were strip searched in the town square . . . much to the amusement of the town's women. Our captors found the money we had hidden in our boots." From Susa they were taken to Bardonecchia, a rest and recuperation center for German troops. "Bodnar tried to convince one of the older guards to let us go and desert but he didn't want to go because of his family. We then decided to overpower him but before we could carry out our plan, we were moved to another camp where the conditions were poor."

In late September or early October, the team was taken to Stalag VII A, a prison camp near Munich. "We were crammed into a heavily loaded railroad boxcar where it was almost impossible to sit down," Risler explained, "with only a small opening for air. Many prisoners passed out on the three-day trip." Within days they were transferred to *Dulag*, a transit camp and thrown into solitary confinement, where they were interrogated three or four times a day by an officer of the *Kriegsmarine*, the German navy. Risler thought he looked like Hermann Goering. At first the interrogator was friendly, but soon showed his true colors when the Marines refused to "cut a record for the folks back home," an obvious propaganda ploy. In November they were transferred to Marlag/Milag Nord, a permanent camp for naval POWs located about twenty miles from the German city of Bremen. There were only thirteen Americans in the camp; most of the other five to six thousand men were British, with some French, and quite a few Royal Marines that had been captured at Dieppe and other commando raids. Ortiz was kept in *Marlag* "O", the officers' section of the camp, and the others in *Marlag* "M," for NCOs.

Each camp contained a number of single-story wooden huts; twenty-nine in Marlag and thirty-six in Milag. Most of them were barracks, while the others contained kitchens, dining rooms, washrooms, guard barracks, storehouses, a post office, and other administrative buildings. The barracks were divided into rooms each accommodating fourteen to eighteen men who slept in two and three-tiered bunks. The POWs occupied themselves in various ways. There was a camp theater in Marlag and the POWs performed concerts and plays. Each camp had its own sports field, and there was also a library with around three thousand books. Prisoners ran courses in languages and mathematics, as well as commercial, vocational, economic, and scientific subjects. Sports equipment and textbooks were obtained from the Red Cross and YMCA. POWs were allowed to send two letters and four postcards each month. There were no restrictions on the number of letters a POW could receive. Naturally all incoming and outgoing mail was censored. A popular diversion was provided by the "Milag Jockey Club" which held race meetings every Saturday evening. The "horses" were wooden models that raced on a thirty-six-foot track, controlled by dice. The POWs bet on the races, and money was raised and donated to the Red Cross.

The prisoners' relationships were excellent—bound by their common dislike of the German guards. The prisoners outdid themselves in devising dirty tricks to play on their captors. Risler remembered one particularly nasty ruse that had the prisoners chuckling for months. "Several men bargained two hundred cigarettes from the Red Cross packages for a bottle of cognac that had already been opened. They told the guard they would have to make certain it had not been watered. The German fell for it and gave them the bottle, which they took into the barracks and emptied it into a container. Then [they] peed in the bottle, sealed it and gave it back, saying the price was too high. The guard got real upset but couldn't take any action." The camp had a homemade radio they kept hidden in a plywood Red Cross box. "The radio was hidden in a hole under the floor. Every day a man would record the 2100 BBC broadcast and send the news around the camp. The Germans scoured the camp but never found the radio."

In early February, the Marine prisoner detachment grew by another member. Marine 2nd Lieutenant Walter Taylor, the operations officer of an OSS intelligence team attached to the U.S. Army's 36th Infantry Division, was captured while on a mission behind German lines.

Taylor was a veteran of OSS operations in Corsica and was attached to the U.S. 7th Army, 36th Division, for Operation Anvil. The 36th was the right flank of Gen. Alexander Patch's northward attack. Taylor, Capt. Justine L. Greene, USA (a well-known New York psychiatrist), and Cpl. James S. Sweeney, USMC, were tasked with reconnoitering German defenses near Grasse in southern France.

The reconnaissance team drove behind enemy lines to Mons, an observation post about twenty miles from Grasse. The following day, Taylor drove a local macquis agent to Saint Cezaire, about nine miles from Grasse, in a Citroen. The plan was for Taylor to wait in Saint Cezaire, which was reported to be under Resistance control , while the macquis agent advanced into Grasse and then returned with information. As they neared the town, they had to stop for a roadblock of land mines. The agent got out of the car to approach the mines, thinking they were laid by the Resistance. He was shot through the head within ten feet of the car.

At first, Taylor thought it was maquis friendly fire, but then he glimpsed a German forage cap. He threw the Citroen into reverse and started backing up as the car was riddled with rifle fire. Taylor crashed into the curbstone and then tried to open his door, but a German soldier jumped up from a ditch and lobbed a grenade. The explosion threw Taylor into the road unconscious, his left leg and hand seriously wounded. He regained consciousness as a prisoner; a German army company had moved into the town overnight. The Germans took him to Grasse, surviving a strafing run from American planes along the way. Even under these conditions, Taylor was able to destroy an incriminating document he carried and hid it behind the car seat.

After arriving in Grasse, Taylor was interrogated harshly until he vomited on the interrogator's uniform. While Ortiz and other Union II troops were being shunted about, Taylor was shuffled through six hospitals, a medical prison near Munich. After a month, Taylor was sent to a stalag in Moosberg. Finally, in January 1945, his wounds were declared sufficiently healed, and he found himself at Marlag.

By late March 1945, the inmates could hear artillery fire from the Allied advance. Everyone knew it was only a matter of time until the camp was liberated. Lieutenant Don Naughton USAAF, recalled, " . . . [T]he Germans announced that our camp was to be evacuated. Peter [Ortiz] immediately called a meeting of his small group of officers . . . we had been discussing escape possibilities for some time and it was obvious that the time was now." On 10 April, before they could carry out their plan, the camp was suddenly evacuated. A company of SS-*Feldgendarmie* (military police) suddenly appeared and that afternoon forced the prisoners to leave the camp. During the confusion, many of them were left behind. "We—Bodnar, Arcelin, Risler, and Charles Mulchy, a Navy gunner's mate—tried to hide under the kitchen floor," Risler said. "There was only a foot of clearance . . . barely enough room to crawl and we had to remain in the same position for hours while the Germans searched the camp for holdouts. They even brought in dogs, but we had sprinkled pepper around to hide our scent."

The other prisoners prepared to leave. Lieutenant Naughton recalled, "The day was hectic. We were issued tinned food and a half loaf of black bread and ordered to take a bare minimum of personal items. In a last attempt to postpone the march, [Ortiz] went to the senior Allied officer, a British Naval captain, to request that he refuse to have his prisoners march. Ortiz was turned down. After stalling as long as possible we were finally on the road." About three hours after starting out, the column was attacked by American P-51 fighter aircraft. "We were in the open with nothing but open fields on either side so we all scattered off the road and into the fields. The P-51s roared down the road, machine guns yammering. They killed and wounded a number of prisoners and continued on their way. The dead and wounded were left behind and the march continued." The American aircraft did not realize that the Germans were emptying prisoner of war camps ahead of the Allied advance and thought the column was escaping enemy soldiers. "We were targets of opportunity," Naughton lamented.

Another alert swept the column. "We were passing through an area with woods on our left," Naughton said. Taylor and two British officers, Maj. Fred Meade and Capt. John Greenwood, joined him and Ortiz. "We ran until we fell down exhausted and then just waited to see if we were missed." It was a daring escape; the Germans would have shot them on sight. "We spent ten days hiding, roving at night, blundering into enemy positions hoping to find our way into British lines," Ortiz recalled. "Luck was with us. Once we were discovered but managed to get away, and several other times we narrowly escaped detection. . . ." Lieutenant Naughton described one of the close calls. "We were hidden in some heavy underbrush in a small and sparsely wooded area when we heard children playing. We kept quiet as possible but in the late afternoon we were concerned we may have been seen. Lieutenant Taylor could move like an Indian and he decided, with Peter's approval, to check our surroundings. He came back shortly and reported two Hitler youth were watching our hideout as though waiting for someone. We decided to make a run for it. We held each other's hands so as to stay together and broke out of the underbrush and ran as fast as we could into the darkening open field. We were about a hundred yards away when a couple of German soldiers opened fire with their machine pistols but the darkness saved us and we got away."

Ortiz recalled, "By the seventh night, we had returned near our camp. I made a reconnaissance of [the camp]. . . . There seemed to be only a token guard and prisoners of war appeared to have assumed virtual control of the compounds." Marine historian Major Robert Mattingly wrote, "The little band was now in bad physical shape. A combination of little food and drinking swamp water had made them all sick—Taylor was covered with boils, and Ortiz was very weak. . . . [T]he men decided it might be better to live in their old huts than starve to death outside." By this time, there were few German guards and the prisoners basically ran the camp. "We decided it was time to 'revisit' the compound," Naughton said. "We were walking down the road when two German officers passed us and said 'Good Morning.' " They merely walked through the gate and returned to their barracks to await the arrival of the British advance.

Several days later, the Allied prisoners heard the unforgettable skirling of bagpipes. A piper, sitting on the turret of a Sherman tank, grandly announced the arrival of the 1st Scots Armored Group. True to form, Ortiz volunteered the team to join them and "bag a few more Germans." His request was respectfully declined. Instead, they were flown to Brussels and then to Paris for V-E Day. Risler commented that their uniform would have "made a DI sob. Marine overseas caps, Navy black shirts, khaki tie, Army O.D. pants, and paratroop boots." The team was given thirty days leave upon returning to the United States and told to report to the West Coast afterward. When the war ended they were in training for a mission to jump into Indo China.

Risler, Bodnar, and LaSalle were awarded the Silver Star for their exploits, while Ortiz received a second Navy Cross. Risler and LaSalle were discharged in July 1946 when their enlistments were up. Bodnar remained in the Marine Corps, retiring as a sergeant major. Brunner was killed in action on a subsequent operation.

PART II

Pacific Theater

CHAPTER 5

Tulagi

arly in the morning of 1 May 1942, Japanese flying boats from the
Yokohama Air Corps bombed and strafed the Australian government's facilities on Tulagi, a small island just north of Guadalcanal in
the Solomon Islands. Later that day, Royal Australian Air Force (RAAF)
Sgt. C. W. "Bill" Miller, piloting RAAF Consolidated PBY Catalina A-24-17,
focused his binoculars on the Japanese five-ship task force steaming for
the southern tip of Guadalcanal. "Send out a sighting report," he ordered.
His radio operator tapped out the message in the clear—no sense in
sending it in code, the Japanese knew they had been spotted. The RAAF
radio station on Malaita Island picked up the signal and relayed it to the
twenty-four commandos of No. 1 Section, 1st Independent Company, at
the Advance Operating Base (AOB) on Tulagi, signaling that an invasion
force was on the way. The next day, two Australian coastwatchers, Jack
Read on Bougainville and D. G. Kennedy on New Georgia, reported that
a large force of Japanese ships, believed to be part of the Tulagi invasion
force, were heading toward the southern Solomons.

Commando Captain A. L. Goode and Flight Officer R. B. Peagam,
11 Squadron RAAF, decided it was time to evacuate Tulagi and the
seaplane base on the nearby island of Gavutu-Tanambogo. All other
nonessential civilians had been evacuated in early February by the

Morinda, an old inter-island steamer chartered specifically by the Australian government for the evacuation. On 3 May, after destroying everything they couldn't carry, the Australians sailed away on the *Balus*, an old copra schooner that had been hidden in the mangroves swamp on the south coast of Florida Island. Every day the mast had been covered with fresh palm branches to conceal it from air observation. The *Balus* sneaked out of the harbor for Vila in the New Hebrides. Two hours later, the Japanese invasion task force sailed in. Coastwatcher Martin Clemens wrote in *Alone on Guadalcanal: A Coastwatcher's Story*, "At 0530 on 3 May . . . a squat black craft was reported from the direction of Tulagi. It was the *Balus* with the RAAF, lock, stock, and barrel. They had escaped the notice of the Jap aircraft because of low cloud and slight rain."

The Japanese landing force, code named RXB Landing Force, consisted of approximately four hundred men of the Kure 3rd Special Naval Landing Force (*Kaigun Kure Daisan Tokubetsu Rikusentai*), under the command of Special Lieutenant (j.g.)* Junta Maruyama, commanding the 2nd Company. Special Lieutenant (j.g.) Kakichi Yoshimoto led the 3rd Company and Special Lieutenant (j.g.) Sakazo Takamura led elements of the 1st Company. The SNLF was reinforced by a 54 man antiaircraft unit (*Mitsuwa Butai*) under Lieutenant Toshichi Mitsuwa and a 132-man civilian Hashimoto Construction Force (*Hashimoto Butai*) led by Shim'ya Hashimoto. Major General Oscar F. Peatross wrote in *Bless 'em All: The Raider Marines of World War II* that the landing force was " . . . accompanied by interpreter and guide T. Ishimoto. . . . Before the war, Ishimoto had worked on Tulagi as a carpenter, while moonlighting as a spy for his Imperial Majesty's government."

Late in the evening on 2 May, the transport *Tosan Maru* dropped anchor in Tulagi harbor. "In practice the transports stood offshore about three miles," Warrant Officer Takeo Iwata, commander of the 1st Platoon, 2nd Company explained, "But in the RXB operation they came right into the harbor." The heavily armed 2nd Company clambered into three of the ship's landing craft (*Kokosuka*). Lieutenant Maruyama's *Kokosuka* carried his headquarters

---

*Special Lieutenant (junior grade) were officers who had completed a special course, as opposed to graduating from the Naval Academy; they had joined the Imperial Japanese Navy when young and needed a long year of service to qualify for a commission.

TULAGI

Tulagi, the seat of the British Solomon Islands Government, is a long, narrow island surrounded by coral beds. The island is approximately 4,000 yards long and just 1,000 yards across at its widest. A 350-foot-high heavily wooded ridge , runs along the northwestern two-thirds of the island. On the other side of a saddle corridor running across the island, a smaller southeastern ridge continues down the island.

The developed portion of the island was centered in the southeastern section around the coastline in the corridor between the two ridges. The resident commissioner's home and office (the "Residency"), complete with a cricket field, tennis court, and golf links was located in the saddle on the southern end of the island, at the foot of Hill 281, called Tori-dai (bird hill) by the Japanese. The promontory would figure prominently in the ensuring battle. The buildup area contained numerous government buildings, a radio station, a prison, and a small hospital. Numerous concrete wharves fronted the northeastern coast.

platoon, 1st Platoon (Iwata), one section of the 3rd Platoon (W.O. Kikuo Tanaka) and the company signalers. The other landing craft carried 2nd Platoon, the remainder of the 3rd Platoon and the medical section. Seaman Engineer (SME) Tameichi Shimmamoto, 4th Squad, 2nd Platoon, 1st Company, described his thoughts waiting for the run to the beach. "We are going to carry out an opposed landing on Tulagi at 0100. It is before a fight, and there in not a tremble in our hearts. I believe the most beautiful part of a Japanese is this present mental state, transcending life and death."

Just after midnight the landing craft sped toward the north side of Tulagi. Third Platoon's SME Yodoyama Mori crouched down in the crowded landing craft. "Our 120-130 men started to head for the coast. . . . We placed bullets in our "I" type [bolt action rifle produced by Italy] rifles. Approaching the coast, 500 meters, 400 meters, 300 meters, 200 meters, and 100 meters and then 50 meters and carefully landed on the pier. No resistance! It seems the enemy has escaped and burned their barracks." With no opposition, the landing force focused on unloading supplies and

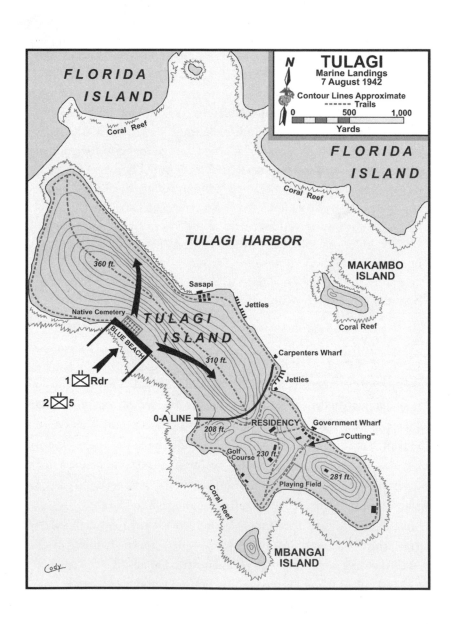

N

TULAGI
Marine Landings
7 August 1942

Contour Lines Approximate
------- Trails

0   500   1,000
Yards

FLORIDA
ISLAND

Coral Reef

FLORIDA

ISLAND

Coral Reef

TULAGI HARBOR

MAKAMBO
ISLAND

360 ft.

Sasapi

Native Cemetery

Jetties

TULAGI
ISLAND

Coral Reef

BLUE BEACH

Carpenters Wharf

310 ft.

1 ⊠ Rdr

Jetties

2 ⊠ 5

0-A LINE

208 ft.

RESIDENCY

Government Wharf

"Cutting"

Golf
Course

230 ft.

281 ft.

Playing Field

Coral Reef

MBANGAI
ISLAND

Cody

equipment. "We completely occupied Gavutu and Tulagi by 0415," Mori said. "The 7th Construction Unit, RXB Detachment, began unloading their equipment immediately." One of their first priorities was to construct defensive positions. Lieutenant Maruyama concentrated the main defenses on Hill 281 and a nearby ravine on the southeastern end of the island. The defenses consisted of dozens of tunneled caves dug into the hill's limestone cliffs and machine-gun pits protected by sandbags. Base construction and improvement of existing facilities—a ship refueling point, a communications facility, and repair of the seaplane base on Gavutu-Tanambogo—were also started. They worked hard. Author Stanley Coleman Jersey, in his comprehensive book *Hell's Islands: The Untold Story of Guadalcanal*, noted, "Reveille on Tulagi was at 0400. Breakfast was ready twenty minutes later. Work normally began at 0630."

Retribution

The United States was quick to respond. In early April, the U.S. Navy's highly classified Fleet Radio Unit Pacific (FRUPAC) located at Pearl Harbor had picked up indications of a large force of Japanese warships and a dozen troop transports moving toward the Solomons. Admiral Chester W. Nimitz, Commander-in-Chief Pacific Fleet (CinCPac) directed Allied forces toward the Coral Sea area to interdict the Japanese. On 27 April, the U.S. aircraft carrier USS *Yorktown*'s Task Force 17 (TF 17), sortied from Tonga to join a second carrier, the USS *Lexington*'s Task Force 11 (TF 11) northwest of New Caledonia. On 3 May, the two task forces were notified of the Japanese Tulagi invasion and began preparations to retaliate. At 0701 on 4 May, *Yorktown* launched three air strikes against Japanese ships anchored near Tulagi. Brigadier General Samuel B. Griffith wrote in *The Battle for Guadalcanal*, "The strike caught the Japanese by surprise. A destroyer, two minesweepers, and a destroyer escort went to the bottom." Jersey noted, "Sailors from Yoshimoto's 3rd Company had been unloading cargo from the transport at the time of the attack; seven were wounded and three killed. No member of the Kure 3rd on land had died, but twenty-nine were wounded."

Despite the damaging air attacks the Japanese proceeded with the construction of the naval seaplane base at Tulagi and Gavutu,

KURE 3RD SPECIAL NAVAL LANDING FORCE

The Japanese Special Landing Force was the marine troops of the Imperial Japanese Navy (IJN). The IJN did not have a separate marine force until well after World War I. Prior to that, the IJN formed naval landing forces from individual ship's crews as needed for special mission. The sailors' basic training included infantry training to prepare them for such temporary missions. It was in the late 1920s that the IJN first started forming Special Naval Landing Forces (SNLF) as separate standing units. Japan's four largest naval bases—Kure, Maizuru, Sasebo, and Yokosuka—all raised multiple SNLF units, which took their names from the bases.

The SNLF first saw action in the 1932 Shanghai Incident when 2,500 of its troops participated in the fight for the city. At the start of World War II, there were sixteen SNLF units, which were increased to twenty-one units during the war. The units ranged from 750 to 1,500 men organized into two rifle companies and one or two heavy weapons companies, which were much larger than their Army counterparts. The rifle company was commanded by a naval officer and consisted of a headquarters, four rifle platoons, and a machinegun platoon. The rifle platoons had a platoon headquarters, three rifle squads (thirteen men each, with one bipod-mounted machinegun), and a weapons support squad (thirteen men with three 50mm "knee

receiving more shipments of troops and construction workers over the next several months. The bulk of the 3rd Kure SNLF was sent back to Rabaul, leaving just Yoshimoto's 3rd Company, two platoons of the 1st Company (WO Yoshiharu Muranaka and WO Katsuzo Fukimoto) and the Tanaka platoon. The reconfigured unit was designated the Yoshimoto Detachment. After completing construction of the base, the Japanese turned their attention to Guadalcanal. In early July, they started construction of an airfield. As Edward J. Drea wrote in *Japan's Imperial Army: Its Rise and Fall, 1853-1945*, " . . . the navy unilaterally dispatched an airfield construction unit to Guadalcanal in the Solomons to build a forward airstrip to support future operations." U.S. Army Air Corps B-17s and B-24s reported its progress on a daily basis. General mortars"). The machinegun platoon had four squads, each having at least ten men and two tripod-mounted machineguns. In a defensive role, the typical SNLF was augmented by antiaircraft, coast defense, anti-boat, and field artillery batteries, plus service and labor troops.

The War Department Handbook on Japanese Military Forces noted that, "During the early part of the war, the SNLF was used to occupy a chain of Pacific island bases. Wake Island was taken by one such force, while another seized the Gilbert Islands. Later they were used to spearhead landing operations against Java, Ambon, and Rabaul. . . . During this period [they] were used as mobile striking units."

Stanley Coleman Jersey wrote in Hell's Islands: The Untold Story of Guadalcanal that, "The Kure 3rd SNLF was formed on 2 February 1942 at the Naval Training Center, Kure Barracks. Ninety-five percent of its personnel were reservists; the balance consisted of recent inductees and apprentice seamen. The unit was led by Cmdr. Minoru Yano of Sasebo, a career officer; at thirty-nine he was younger than most of the men in his charge. When Executive Officer Lieutenant Nagata read the muster roll that first day, 1,122 enlisted men and 44 officers answered. Their average age was forty-three."

Douglas MacArthur's Joint Intelligence Center-Pacific Ocean Area (JICPOA) noted, "An enemy airdrome appears to be nearing completion on Guadalcanal and another is under construction."

The steady and rapid southward extension of Japanese power through the Solomons threatened the U.S. line of communication with Australia. The Joint chiefs of Staff were alarmed. Admiral Ernest J. King, commander-in-chief, United States Fleet, and chief of Naval Operations (COMINCH-CNO) directed an offensive in the Lower Solomons to seize Tulagi and adjacent areas. On Tulagi, rumors were rife of an American attack. "One sea infantryman, while on pier duty at Tulagi, said that a boat came from Gavutu and warned that an American task force was approaching the Solomons and may land at Tulagi and Gavutu on

1ST MARINE RAIDER BATTALION

The 1st Marine Raider Battalion was an outgrowth of President Franklin D. Roosevelt's interest in establishing a commando force similar to the British organization. In a letter to Lt. Gen. Thomas Holcomb, the Commandant of the Marine Corps, Admiral E. J. King wrote, "The President proposed the use of 'commandos' as essential parts of raiding expeditions which attack (destroy) enemy advanced (seaplane) bases in the Pacific Fleet area." At the same time, Marine Capt. James Roosevelt, the president's son, wrote the commandant a letter proposing "a unit for purposes similar to the British Commandos and the Chinese Guerrillas." Finally, Col. William J. Donovan proposed being appointed a brigadier general in the Marine Corps Reserve for the purpose of taking charge of the "Commando Project." Under this pressure, the commandant "staffed" the proposals through the Corps' senior leadership. While not generally supportive—his successor, Maj. Gen. Alexander Vandefrift, would note "Neither General Holcomb nor I favored forming elite units from units already elite."—the commandant nevertheless decided to activate the special unit. Lt. Col. Merritt Austin "Red Mike" Edson was picked to lead the new unit and given carte blanch to comb Marine units for those men "deemed to be suitable."

The next issue became what to call the organization. Names ranged from, "Commando," to "First Destroyer Battalion," to "1st Shock Battalion," before General Holcomb personally selected "Raiders." The first special unit was activated on 16 February 1942 and designated the 1st Marine Raider Battalion. Manning this new organization caused considerable heartburn among the other personnel-starved Marine units, which were also trying to gear up for deployment. The battalion consisted of four rifle companies (A, B,C, and D) and a weapons company (E) of two .30-caliber light machine gun platoons, a 60mm mortar platoon, and eventually a demolitions platoon. A small headquarters company provided essential administrative, logistical, and command and control services. Each rifle company was composed of 137 officers, enlisted Marines and Sailors organized into three platoons. Three 8-man squads made up a rifle platoon. They were armed with .30-caliber Springfield rifles and two .30-caliber Browning Automatic Rifles (BAR).

30 May," SME Mori noted. Nothing happened but the rumors persisted. On 1 July, the Yoshimoto Detachment was incorporated into the newly formed 84th Guard Unit and the fifty-three-year-old Yoshimoto was relieved by Cmdr. Masaaki Suzuki. A month later, Tulagi's radio station received an alert from the 8th Fleet Signals Unit. " . . . [E]nemy is gathering power along the east coast of Australia . . . you should keep close watch."

On 5 August, Amphibious Task Force Tare steamed through the dark waters of the Pacific. For the men of the 1st Raider Battalion who were slated to take Tulagi, it was a time of reflection. Major Justice Chambers, commanding officer of "Dog Company" recalled, "I don't think that any of us will forget that last night before we landed. Officers and men realized that all their training the last few months was finally going to be put to the test. I personally was worried to death and kept going over my notes for fear that I had forgotten some detail in the orders. As we headed up for Tulagi in the darkness of the night the men wrote their last letters home and I collected them, knowing that for some of them it would probably be the last letters they would write."

At 0300 7 August, Transport Group Yoke, with USS *Neville* in the lead, turned onto course 058 degrees to pass to the north side of Sealark Channel and then to 115 degrees to head directly for Tulagi. *Neville* reported, "No shots fired, no patrol boats encountered, no signs of life were evident. . . ." As the ship approached the transport area, fifteen fighters and fifteen dive bombers from USS *Wasp* (CV-7) (sunk on 15 September 1942 by Japanese submarine I-19) strafed and bombed Tulagi, destroying several seaplanes in the harbor.

Seize, Occupy and Defend

"On August seven, this force will recapture Tulagi and Guadalcanal Island, which are now in the hands of the enemy."
—Rear Admiral Richmond Kelly Turner,
Commander Amphibious Force

Lieutenant Yoshimoto's observer on Savo Island was the first to spot the gray silhouettes approaching the roadstead in the early morning light. At first he thought they were another convoy bringing men and material;

however, as the ship's profile became clear, a jolt of adrenalin surged through his bloodstream—American warships! "Petty Officer Third Class Osmu Yamaoka of the Tulagi radio communications section had been on duty when at 0600 a runner alerted him that a group of strange ships had been seen near Savo Island, . . . " Jersey wrote. At 0613, the cruiser USS *Quincy* (CA-39) opened fire with her eight-inch guns, followed immediately by the rest of the bombardment ships. Twelve minutes later, at 0625, Radio Tulagi sent an emergency report to the 25th Air Flotilla headquarters on Rabaul, "Enemy surface force of twenty ships has entered Tulagi. While making landing preparations, the enemy is bombarding the shore, help requested."

On Guadalcanal, coastwatcher Martin Clemens was startled by explosions. "Starting about 0610, very heavy detonations, at very short intervals, were heard from Lunga and Tulagi," he later wrote. "There was no doubt what they meant . . . I could hardly comprehend that help had finally come." Journalist Richard Tregaskis noted in *Guadalcanal Diary*, "It was fascinating to watch the apparent slowness with which the shells, their paths marked out against the sky in red fire, curved through the air." The Americans weren't the only shooters. At 0700, as the Navy's minesweepers came within range, the Japanese antiaircraft unit on Gavutu took them under fire with their three-inch guns. Jersey noted that, "The Mitsuwa unit found the range of the [USS] *Hopkins* and fired several times without scoring any hits. There were close calls, but the Japanese shells were of a small caliber and their light charges inflicted no damage."

At 0715, Radio Tulagi reported, "Enemy has commenced landing," and at 0800, "Enemy forces overwhelming. We will defend our posts to the death, praying for eternal victory." Peatross wrote, "This was the last transmission from Radio Tulagi, as a few seconds later, a shell from one of the naval gunfire support ships put the station off the air permanently!"

"Land the Landing Force"

In the early morning darkness, the sky was punctuated by flashes of light as the light cruiser USS *San Juan* (CL-54) and destroyers USS *Monssen* (DD-436) and USS *Buchanan* (DD-484) bombarded Tulagi with hundreds of five-inch and eight-inch shells. Aboard the transports,

OPERATION RINGBOLT LANDING FORCES

Operation Ringbolt, the code name given for the seizure of Tulagi Island, was part of Operation Watchtower, a division-sized operation to seize Tulagi and Guadalcanal commencing on 7 August 1942. The 1st Marine Division, under the command of Maj. Gen. Alexander A. Vandegrift was organized into two landing forces: Guadalcanal (Group X-Ray) and Tulagi (Group Yoke), under Brig. Gen. William H. Rupertus, the assistant division commander.

The Tulagi assault force called for the 1st Marine Raider Battalion (Lt. Col. Merritt A. Edson) and the 2nd Battalion, 5th Marines (Lt. Col. Harold E. Rosecrans) to land on the south shore, in column, then wheel right (east) and attack down the long axis of the island. This landing would be followed by further landings by the 1st Parachute Battalion on Gavutu and Tanambogo, plus a mop-up sweep by a battalion (less one company) along the Florida Island's coastline fronting Tulagi Bay.

At 0800 (H-Hour) the 1st Raider Battalion was to land on Beach Blue, a narrow shelf on the island's west coast, two thousand yards from the northwestern tip of the island on the western shore. Dog Company commander, Maj. Justice Chambers explained the battalion's scheme of maneuver. "Dog and Baker Companies were the two assault companies followed by Able and C Charlie. Dog Company, which I commanded, and Baker Company, which Nickerson [Lloyd] commanded, landed abreast . . . Nickerson on the right and I was landing on the left. We were landing through a Chinese cemetery."

the raiders began climbing down the cargo nets into the Higgins boats (first model ramp-less wooden thirty-six-foot landing craft) that would take them ashore. "As we passed across the deck," Pfc. Thomas D. "T. D." Smith said, "the sailors clapped us on the back and said, 'Give 'em hell—see you tonight.' " Private First Class Ashley Ray was scared. His platoon commander had told the men, "By this time tomorrow, some of you will be dead!" The battalion was embarked aboard six transports—a hundred men each on the USS *Neville* (APA-9) and USS *Heywood* (APA-6), while the main body was embarked on four flush-deck, high-speed destroyer transports—USS *Little* (APD-4), USS *Colhoun* (APD-2), USS *Gregory* (APD-4), and USS *McKean* (APD-5). The first waves crossed the line of departure right on schedule and headed for the beach.

Major Chambers was in the first wave. "On the way in I had my head up a little bit so I could see over to where the cruiser *San Juan* was firing support fires. This was an antiaircraft cruiser, and had many five-inch guns. She laid down a terrific barrage. She fired almost like an automatic rifle, they were coming so fast." The heavy bombardment forced most of the Japanese defenders to remain under cover in the network of caves and tunnels they had carved deep in the limestone cliffs. "During the air raids our commander would be the first one in the shelter," Seaman Tomisaburo Hirai noted angrily. "He would often tell us to always be brave. But he is the one who is not brave." Only scattered, ineffective rifle fire met the first waves of Higgins boats but it was enough to remind the men in the open boats that at least some Japanese had survived the shelling. Peatross noted that, "The bullets splattering into the water near Major Nickerson's boat were effective enough to cause the sailors manning the bow machine gun to duck. The coxswain, however, stayed on course and soon his boat grounded on the reef . . . with a sudden and terrific jolt, staggering those men who had nothing to hold onto."

The first wave landed exactly on schedule at 0800 (H-hour). Until now, the landing had taken the *Rikusentai* by surprise and the Marines landed unscathed. The only casualty had been a Marine who had died from an accidental discharge aboard ship. "It was the last place that the Japs thought we would land," Chambers said. "The best beach on Tulagi was at the other end of the island and the Japanese had clearly expected that any hostile landing would be made there. So they had very lightly fortified the beach where we landed." The heavily laden men climbed clumsily over the sides of the Higgins boats into chest deep water—chin-deep for the shorter men. " . . . Everybody had to plunge into the water and wade to shore [fifty or more yards to the beach]," Chambers recalled. "This was no fun, as we found out during our training at Samoa, because coral reefs are dotted with holes and at any moment you are likely to step into water that is over your head. I once went down completely over my head but I bounced right back up. . . ."

Peatross credited rifleman-scout Pfc. Clifford J. Fitzpatrick, 1st Squad, 1st Platoon, Baker Company, with being the first Marine to begin the "U.S. Pacific-island-hopping offensive." "Once ashore, Lt. [Eugene M.] Key quickly sorted out his platoon, and the 1st Squad Leader, Corp. Benjamin C. Howland Jr., sent Fitzpatrick on ahead up the steep slope and followed after him. . . . [T]he rest of the squad followed him." Chambers explained that, "The minute we got across the beach—there was not much to speak of and immediately we were in very heavy vegetation going up very steep hills. The boys knew what our job was . . . get up on the ridge and take off into the jungle. It was, I would estimate, twenty to thirty minutes at the most when we reached our initial objective, the ridge line. So far we had hit no resistance." By 0815, Lieutenant Colonel Edson received a message from the beach, "Landing successful, no opposition." Baker Company crossed the island's spine and continued down the slope to a small village called Sasapi on the opposite side of the island.

When Chambers's Dog Company reached the top of the ridgeline, he radioed the battalion to give a situation report. "There was a faint trail that ran along the ridge but we couldn't see a thing," he said. "Our maps were laid out with target squares and we were supposed to use code designations . . . we were moving in assault situation in an area where you couldn't tell where you were." Major Samuel B. Griffith II asked, "What is your present location?" Chambers replied, "I can't tell you very well. All I know is I'm standing under one hell of a big tree on the trail right on the ridge line." The response didn't satisfy Griffith, who fired back with, "Use the code designations and grid." At this point a frustrated Chambers responded heatedly, "If you can figure this out you're crazy. I haven't got time to fool with this anyway, out!" The exchange was more than just a little report; naval gunfire ships were on station and needed the information to start pounding the Japanese positions ahead of the assault.

The second wave, consisting of Maj. Lewis W. "Silent Lew" Walt's Able Company and Maj. Kenneth Bailey's Charlie Company landed shortly after the first waves cleared the landing beach. Charlie Company turned right and moved rapidly along the shoreline to its initial objective, the OA line. Walt's Able Company had a much more difficult time. The southwest slope of the ridge was extremely steep. Peatross mentioned that, "it required a major effort to keep from falling off, much less move ahead." It took Walt and his exhausted men more than two hours to reach their objective and report to Edson's command post on the ridge. Finally Echo Company, the last unit to come ashore, reached the ridge and prepared to support the advance with 81mm mortar fire. At 0900, two M2A4 Stuart light tanks from Charlie Company, 2nd Tank Battalion landed behind Bailey's company but did not get into action. "One got bogged down in a ravine, and I never did see that damn tank again," Griffith said. "Then the other one had a mechanical breakdown, so they were actually of no use to us at all."

Echo Battery, 11th Marines, with its 75mm "Pack" howitzers went ashore in wooden Higgins "Eureka" landing craft. "A 75mm Pack Howitzer was a difficult piece of weaponry that was manhandled ashore piece by piece, then put together and pulled by a jeep," Pfc. Howard Schnauber said. "We had to move through the 'Tulagi Pass,' the short-cut through the steep hill separating one side of the island from the other. The slot was level, but it had two caves dug into the limestone, large caves that house quite a number of Japs. The only way past them was for the foot Marines to shoot into the entrance as the jeep pulled the howitzer past. This system worked well and we managed to get the gun to the opposite side."

Shortly after the second wave landed, Lieutenant Colonel Edson and the battalion headquarters group debarked from the *Little* and boarded a "free boat" (a boat free to move wherever the commander desires to permit him to issue orders and make necessary changes). As the boat headed shoreward, the engine stalled and the craft began to flounder. The embarked staff tried to flag down an empty craft but the coxswains had explicit orders to return directly to their ship and ignored the frantic signals from Edson and his staff. Peatross wrote that, "Finally, after much frantic waving and not a few strongly worded threats from Edson, an empty boat came alongside . . . and landed them, much later than scheduled." Edson initially established his command post a few yards northeast of the cemetery but then moved it to the Residency at the crest of the ridge. Platoon Sergeant Francis C. Pettus was a member of Edson's command group. "Our observation group climbed the central ridge and established its first OP in a tree overlooking Sasapi, where we were able to observe a squad from Baker Company in a flat south of the village. This squad seemed to be puzzled because it had encountered no enemy."

At 0830, Lt. Col. Rosecran's 2nd Battalion, 5th Marines (2/5) landed over Beach Blue, crossed Tulagi, and attacked northwest to the end of the island without encountering the enemy. Rosecrans then reorganized and moved into position to support the Raiders. "To protect the left flank of the Raiders as they landed on Beach Blue . . . Baker Company, 1st Battalion, 2nd Marines, seized the Haleta promontory on neighboring Florida Island," Brigadier General Griffith wrote in *The Battle for Guadalcanal*. Baker's landing was unopposed.

Raider Attack

By 1100, all four Raider companies were on a line stretching from Carpenter's Wharf to the shoreline northwest of Hill 208 in the following order from left to right: Baker, Dog, Able, and Charlie. Edson called the company commanders to his command post to brief them on his plan of attack. "One company in assault on the south side of the ridge, one company in assault on the north side, each backed up by a company," Griffith explained. Platoon Sergeant Pettus noted that "[t]he operations plan called for naval shelling on the southern part of the island when we reached the OA line, and the battalion's advance was halted. Machine guns and mortars were set up, the machine guns west of the central ridge and the mortars east of it. They opened fire on the houses in the low, small plane south of us. A number of Japs were killed in the houses, but some ran out and escaped temporarily. Several houses were set ablaze by mortar fire." *San Juan* shelled Hill 281 ahead of the Raider attack. In a five minute barrage, she fired 289 rounds but failed to dislodge the *Rikusentai*, who were well dug in. An hour and a half later while providing support for the Gavutu landing, a loaded five-inch shell cooked off in a gun mount, killing seven and wounding eleven sailors. Meanwhile the *Buchanan* was shelling the Tulagi radio station, while the *Monssen* poured a hundred shells into Japanese antiaircraft positions south of the hospital. Later the *San Juan* shifted its fire to the prison.

At 1130, Edson gave the signal—a green flare—to start the assault. "We came under fire almost immediately as we began to move along the ridge,"

Chambers said. Two of his men—Pvts. Leonard A. Butts and Lewis A. Lovin—were hit by machine gun fire as they moved down the face of the ridge. The 3rd Kure's *Rikusentai* had shaken off the effects of the air and naval gunfire bombardment and were manning fighting positions dug in the hill. "We thought that coconut trees would not have enough branches to conceal snipers," Chambers said, "But we found that the Japs were small enough to hide in them easily and so we had to examine every tree before we went by."

Bailey's Charlie Company ran into a buzz saw of enemy fire from the seaward side of Hill 208 despite the fact that the height had been pounded with over 1,500 five-inch shells. Chambers recalled, "Bailey had gotten into a cricket field [golf course]. It was quite open country and the Nips by now were beginning to get organized and were fighting back." It took the company an hour and several men killed and wounded to clear the hill with small arms fire and hand grenades. One of those wounded was its popular commander. As "Ken Dill," Bailey's code name, leapt on a troublesome bunker and attempted to kick through the roof to grenade it, he was shot in the leg. As he was being evacuated, he said, "That Jap Arisaka isn't a bad rifle after all." The Raiders learned that Japanese machine-gun dugouts contained ten to twelve men. When one man was killed, another stepped up and manned the gun, requiring every man to be killed, a dangerous and time-consuming process.

Charlie Company lost its forward momentum and Edson didn't know why. "Eddie [Lt. Col. Edson] was pretty upset about it and sent me down to find out," Major Griffith said. "When the company broke out onto the golf course it got bogged down." Griffith assumed command and got it moving again. "That afternoon—I'd say about 1400—we had taken the golf club house, which had been occupied by the Japs. We found a lot of uniforms hanging, binoculars, rice left in bowls, raw fish, and stuff like that."

Dog Company, under fire, crossed the north-south road cut below the Residency. "As we cleared the bridge," T. D. Smith recalled, "we started taking fire from the right and right front." Chambers appeared and "ordered us to move out, 'right now and to hell with the fire!'" At one point Chambers had taken cover when he heard someone ask, "What's going on here?" "I look up," Chambers recalled, "and there's

CODE NAMES

Lieutenant Colonel Edson used code names for some of his key officers, which provided immediate proof of identity under hectic conditions. He was "Red Mike," because of his red beard; Maj. Sam Griffith, his executive officer, was "Easy"; Capt. Ken Bailey, Charley Company, became "Ken Dill"; Maj. Lew Walt, Alpha Company, became "Silent Lew"; Maj. Justice Chambers became "Joe Pots" (for chamber pot); and Capt. John B. Sweeney, in charge of the command post security, became "John Wolf." The simple system would twice prove invaluable on Tulagi, and again during the second night at Edson's Ridge.

Edson standing there big as life smoking a cigarette! I said, 'Colonel, what are you trying to do, get me killed?' " Edson was drawing fire. "All Edson said was, 'Keep them moving,' and then moved on," Chambers exclaimed . . . "I think that episode was probably responsible for me getting wounded later on so many times . . . because I thought this was the way a battalion commander should act." After reaching the base of the ridge, the company worked its way toward the Residency on the high ground on the left. "I was pretty well satisfied with the progress that the company had made at this point."

Nickerson's Baker Company was working its way along the boat docks on the northeastern side of the island when Japanese sniper fire hit the lead platoon. One man went down in the open. The platoon commander, Lieutenant Key, was shot to death as he leaped over a stone wall to rescue the man. Then Pvt. Thomas F. Nickel was killed as he attempted the rescue. A third man, Navy Lt (j.g.) Samuel S. Miles, the battalion junior surgeon, leaped over the wall and met the same fate. The remaining members of the squad finally spotted two snipers, assaulted their positions, and killed them. The snipers may have been from WO Sadayuki Kato's 2nd Platoon. Jersey noted that, "PO1c Nakasuke Miyagi and his squad of nine—with sharpshooter PO3c Ryosuke Kuwabara, supported by PO3c Harubumi Ishida and his seven men with sniper SM Yoshimi Hamaota—were able to block the Marine advance [for a short time]." Baker Company continued to advance until it reached a point adjacent to the government wharf, where it dug in for the night. "I was now pinching Nickerson out," Chambers explained. "The island had narrowed down, so I had the left flank all the way down to the ocean at this point."

Dog Company had to cross a ravine and up a hill on the other side. "Several things happened once we got in the ravine," Chambers explained. "There were some snipers in back of us [possibly from WO Tsuneto Sakado's platoon which had several snipers]. I know I was leaning my head around a big coconut tree and a Jap laid a round right alongside my head. That's when I thought they were using explosive bullets, because this thing really banged when it hit the tree." Chambers's luck ran out a short time later. "After we got across the ravine and were going up the other side working against the area where the antiaircraft was located, I spotted some Japs firing down on Bailey's people. I got my 60mm mortars set up and was calling in the fire. All of a sudden there was this great flash of fire right in front of me, maybe ten or fifteen feet in the air. [Shrapnel] smashed my left wrist, broke my right wrist, and took a hunk out of my left leg."

Chambers refused to be evacuated and continued to lead his company, "walking and hobbling," until they reached the final objective, a gun emplacement near the beach. About 1500, the company was held up by two enemy positions. "We were having some trouble because there were some Nips dug in underneath a house," Chambers said. "The boys cleared it out, but a trench line gave us some problems. One of the men threw a grenade in and the Nips threw it right back at us. We did this a couple of times before the Marine let the fuse run before he threw it. I saw this pair of hands come up to catch the grenade again. . . . [I]t went off . . . and we didn't have any more trouble." A short time later, they reached the gun emplacement and found it empty, the Japanese had pulled out. "At this point," Chambers explained, "I decided to get back to the aid station. I had a piece of shrapnel in the back of my kneecap and I was bleeding pretty good in my wrists . . . and I was sore as hell, but I was ambulatory." And then he added, "If they shot at me hard enough, I could still move pretty fast!"

Walt's Able Company advanced against light resistance, trying to stay abreast of Charlie Company on the right. At one point the company became concerned with the amount of firing in Charlie Company's area. Walt sent a fire team to see if help was needed. Along the way the team knocked out a machine gun nest and, together with several Charlie Company men, helped clear the way to advance. Later that afternoon, Able was pinned down by heavy automatic weapons fire from the forward slope of Hill 281 where there were numerous enemy concealed positions. The company suffered quite a number of casualties from the galling fire. About 1600, the fire slackened off, which allowed the company to pull back to a better defensive position and prepare for the expected Japanese counterattack. Raider Henry Popell recalled, "We moved over the ridge and men are being dragged back wounded. It is now five in the afternoon . . . [O]ur 1st Platoon is in a bad way in an attempt to take out a number of machine guns. . . . [T]hey have to withdraw. . . . [D]arkness is now falling."

Bonzai

Edson decided to call it a day and dig in for the night. "By this time Edson had moved forward to the Residency and established his command post there," Griffith said. "We fully expected a counterattack." Pettus described the Residency as "a large, white, wooden building located on the crest of the hill, which formally had been occupied by the highest British official in the Solomons." By this time, the battalion had come up against Hill 281, which captured maps and documents indicated was the main Japanese stronghold. Lieutenant John "Tiger" Erskine*, the Japanese-language officer, translated them and found that Suzuki's command was located in the ravine west of the hill, which paralleled the south end of the Raider lines. The map showed two machine guns at the foot of the hill behind the hospital, one on top, and two 8mm antiaircraft guns on top of the southeast promontory. "Bird Hill" was Suzuki's key defensive position.

It was just too late in the day to mount a coordinated attack; besides, the battalion occupied the high ground, making it difficult for the enemy to attack. At this point the battalion extended in a somewhat

*Lt. Erskine was a 1941 graduate of the Japanese Language School at the University of Hawaii. "Tiger" Erskine earned his nickname because of his stature—65.5 inches tall and 104 pounds.

continuous line, depending on the nature of the terrain, stretching from Government Wharf across the crest of Hill 230 down the ridge to the beach—Baker Company, with elements of Headquarters Company attached, Easy Company, Able Company, and Charlie Company (less one platoon) were in position in that order from left to right, with Charlie Company right flank resting on the beach. Dog Company's lines ran from the beach on its left flank and up the ridge line. Easy and Fox companies, 2/5, had moved up to reinforce the left flank.

The Raiders quickly turned to and tried to dig in—under the watchful eyes of their officers and SNCOs—in an attempt to get below ground before dark. Edson had trained them well, capitalizing on his observations of Japanese tactics during his assignment with the 4th Marine Regiment in Shanghai, China (1937-1939). He studied how the Japanese conducted night attacks by first sending in scouts to locate the perimeter lines and crew-served weapon positions. They sought weaknesses, particularly seams between units or gaps in the defense. The scouts would generally follow terrain features through dense cover in an attempt to get close to the enemy positions. The main body might make considerable noise in order to drown out the movement of the scouts. During the attack, the main body generally followed clearly defined terrain features—a crest, draw, ridge line—for ease of control and orientation. The effort of the attack was to close with the enemy and destroy him in close combat—with the bayonet.

All along the line, Edson's men laid out grenades and stacked ammunition close at hand so it would be easy to reach in the dark. Machine gunners carefully sited their guns in an attempt to get overlapping bands of fire. Communicators strung wire linking the command posts. The password for the night contained words with the letter "L"—"Lily's thistle," "Philippines," and "Lola's thigh." Chambers noted, "Any one of them was supposed to keep you from getting shot by your own men because the Japs couldn't pronounce the letter 'L.'" Night fell. The exhausted Raiders peered anxiously into darkness, straining to hear the man-sound of a Japanese infiltrator. Warrant Officer Albert E. "Bud" Fisher, Easy Company's 2nd Machine-Gun Platoon, said, "We were all pretty nervous as darkness fell. The Nips came out of the caves making all sorts of weird noises." Chambers explained, "The Japs tried every trick on us that we had been told they would, yet we really never imagined they would. They shouted, whistled, and sniped at us all night long. . . . [A]t first there was considerable promiscuous night firing, the Japs trying to locate our units by [shooting] at us at random. But our men learned to hold their fire and not give away their position unless attacked in hand-to-hand assault."

Sometime around 2300 a large force of *Rikusentai* boiled out of the ravine and struck the seam between Able and Charlie Companies, splitting them and leaving their flanks dangling in the air. Able Company quickly refused its right flank and prepared to repel boarders. It was not long in coming. Private Pete Sparacino recalled that, " . . . There was movement to the front . . . the enemy found a gap and began running through the opening. Some Japanese crawled within twenty yards of [Frank] Guidone's squad. Frank began throwing grenades from a prone position. His grenades were going off fifteen yards from our position and we had to duck as they exploded. The enemy was all around. It was brutal and deadly"—but the new line held, killing twenty-six Japanese within twenty yards of the front line foxholes. However, a few infiltrators got through. Platoon Sergeant Pettus recalled that, "Some thirteen Japs charged through Company A's line and ran over our small bivouac area on the lawn [in front of the Residency], going into the house behind us. Two of our observers were wounded at this time."

Griffith remembered "a series of attacks but the real force of the counterattack hit the center of the position; this gave us the first indication of how dumb the Japs were, because the center of the position was by any evaluation of the terrain just naturally the strongest." That said, Griffith explained that "we knew the Japanese were good fighters [but] I think we were taken by surprise by the viciousness and tenacity of these night attacks. Normally if you make a couple of attacks and get your ass kicked and burned badly, as they did, you'd think they'd stop." In all the *Rikusentai* launched two major attacks and at least five separate small scale assaults against Edson's command post near the Residency. Platoon Sergeant Pettus said that, "When the Japs got into the house . . . Captain John B. Sweeny gave the word for the machine guns to fire. Some of the

Japs were killed in the house and some were killed as they tried to run out. There were thirteen dead in and around the building. All of the Japanese outside were dragged in, and the house was set afire. This saved burial, but it destroyed a perfectly good building!"

A temporary casualty collection point had been established about two or three hundred yards on the south side of the Residency, where a large number of wounded had been gathered, including the indomitable Justice Chambers. "When I got there it was dark but I could see all these white figures lying around. The Navy had sent in white blankets to wrap the wounded." A number of Japanese had been bypassed and they were starting to cause trouble. "There were a lot of people down below us . . . hollering and shouting . . . and jabbering in Japanese." Chambers was afraid the wounded were directly in the path of a Japanese assault. "They shifted us back to the west and up the slope and laid us along a path that ran along underneath the ridge line. We were all jammed in there together . . . then all hell broke loose!" The Japanese were attacking. "Both . . . sides were firing mortars and there was a lot of rifle fire . . . and we're lying there with this stuff bursting around. We had no protection whatsoever except a blanket. I heard them coming!"

Chambers started moving the wounded. "Those who could walk I told to get moving and help each other out. There were a few Corpsmen and they started taking men out on stretchers . . . it was a mess!" Chambers found a trench along the trail. It was full of Marines, one of whom he recognized. "Get some men out here and get these wounded to where they can be safe," he ordered. "From then on out I had no more concern about the wounded." For this action, Chambers was awarded the Silver Star. The next morning he was evacuated to the beach. "They were carrying me down on a stretcher and the Japs shot at me all the way, which was another little black mark I had in my book against the Japanese." Chambers was taken aboard the hospital ship USS *Solace* and ended up in Wellington, New Zealand, where he recovered in time to lead the 3rd Battalion, 25th Marines, in the Iwo Jima campaign where he received the Medal of Honor.

By first light, the surviving Japanese had melted back into their caves and bunkers that honeycombed Hill 281. Edson sent 2/5's Echo and Fox companies, along with his own Charlie Company to clear them out. The troublesome terrain was flanked on three sides and pounded with 60mm and 81mm mortar fire. Platoon Sergeant Pettus recalled one incident. "Soon we saw Japs running up the south slope of Hill 281, one of them with a white cloth tied around his head ran to one of the antiaircraft positions and tried to take off the gun. This was about six hundred yards from our OP. The Jap was pointed out to Captain Adams, who killed him with his .03 rifle. In a few minutes Marines were seen coming up the hill and we ceased firing. Hill 281 was ours shortly after this."

By late afternoon the battalion had made such good progress that Edson radioed General Vandegrift and told him that organized resistance on the island had ended—Tulagi was "secure." The fact remained that well-armed *Rikusentai* were still holed up and had to be hunted down before the island was truly secure. The Raiders stayed on the island for three more weeks before being transferred to Guadalcanal. During that time, they were subjected to naval bombardment. "Many mornings," Pettus said, "our reveille on Tulagi was announced by Japanese destroyers or submarines. This bombardment was frequent, but casualties were surprisingly light. At dawn one morning a single destroyer lay at the mouth of Tulagi Harbor. White and blue clad Japs were scurrying across its deck and soon the ship's guns were pointed in the direction of our CP. Its first shells went over and landed in the harbor. One salvo straddled the government wharf and another landed among dispersed Higgins boats, causing no damage. However, one salvo landed in China Town killing a Marine and a sailor."

A few days later, the battalion was transferred to Guadalcanal. During the conquest of Tulagi, the 1st Marine Raider Battalion suffered thirty-eight men killed in action and an additional fifty-five men wounded in action. All but three of the estimated 350 Japanese defenders were killed. Griffith "estimated that another fifty to sixty Japs escaped from Tulagi by swimming to Florida [Island]."

CHAPTER 6

Gavutu-Tanambogo

Flight quarters sounded well before dawn for the pilots of the USS *Wasp* (CV-7)'s air group and by 0530, the first planes barreled down the flight deck. Tulagi and Gavutu were among the early targets assigned to Lt. Cmdr. Courtney Shands's Scouting Squadron 71 (VF-71) comprising four division Grumman F4F Wildcat fighters. As they approached Guadalcanal, Shands took the flight down to the deck to avoid the possibility of anti-aircraft fire from Savo Island. At 0600, they flew over the Navy transports preparing to disembark the landing force. After passing the ships without challenge—there was a real danger of friendly fire from anxious gunners—the 4th Division of Shands's flight climbed to five thousand feet above Tulagi to serve as the combat air patrol (CAP) for the strafers. Shands took the 1st Division around the northwest tip of Tulagi, where he split it. He and his wingman, Ensign Sam W. Forrer, swung down the north coast toward Gavutu Seaplane Base. The other two F4Fs in the division piloted by Ensigns Don G. Reeves and Raymond F. Conklin headed for Tanambogo, to work over the seaplane facilities there. The 2nd Division, Lt. S. Downs Wright and Ensign Roland H. Kenton headed south toward Gavutu and Tanambogo and the 3rd Division, Lt. Charles S. Moffett and Ensigns William M. Hall, and Thomas M. Purcell Jr. went to strafe an enemy bivouac area just north of the small village of Haleta on Florida Island.

Shands could not believe his good fortunate. Spread out below him at anchor were over a dozen Japanese flying boats and float planes of the Yokohama Air Group. According to author John Lundstrom in *The First Team and the Guadalcanal Campaign: Naval Fighter Combat from August to November 1942*, "Four Kawanishi H6K4 Type 97 flying boats [Allied designation, 'Mavis'] swung at moorings along Tanambogo's north shore, while in the quiet waters off Tulagi's east coast, gasoline barges serviced the other three for a dawn takeoff . . . six [Nakajima A6M2 Type 2 sea fighters, 'Rufe'] Type 2s drifted in line just off Halavo, a small village on a peninsula of Florida [Island] a mile east of Tanambogo. Two others under repair reposed ashore on Tanambogo." The Type 2 was the amphibious version of the standard A6M2 Zero carrier fighter and was used to provide fighter coverage for advanced seaplane bases. A green flare arched over the harbor as Shands's 1st Division started its gun run.

"*Ku-shu-keihoh*! (Air Raid)"

Captain Shignetoshi Miyazaki, Imperial Japanese Naval Air Service (*Dai-Nippon Teikoku Kaigun Koku Tai*), was in command of Gavutu's flying-boat unit and had ordered three aircraft on an extended patrol in response to a dramatic increase in American naval radio traffic. Master Chief Petty Officer Masaichiro Miyagawa, as the duty noncommissioned officer, had the responsibility for ensuring that the three flying boats were serviced and ready for the 0700 launch. Thus far everything was going well. The aircrews had been ferried to their planes moored off the eastern shore of the island. They were in the process of, "warming up their engines by taxiing about in Gavutu Harbor, their blue and white guidance lights flickering," according to author Jersey. "Petty Officer Kyosho Mutou was at the controls of his flying boat, waiting patiently for the signal to take off. Lieutenant Commander Soichi Tashiro, third in command of the air unit, was making his final instrument adjustments. When the green takeoff signal flare was fired, the Kawanishi jockeyed into position."

Suddenly the telephone rang in headquarters. Master Chief Petty Officer Miyagawa picked it up and was startled to hear, "*Ku-shu-keihoh* (air raid)!" It was too late for him to do anything because Shands and his

GAVUTU-TANAMBOGO

Gavutu and Tanambogo are coral islets—little more than steep hills rising sharply from shallow reef-bound beaches—off the southern coast of Florida Island, eighteen miles north of Guadalcanal in the Solomon Islands. Gavutu is only 250 yards by 500 yards in size, while Tanambogo is about half that in area. The two are connected by a stone causeway five hundred yards long and just eight feet wide. They are dominated by high ground, Hill 148 on Gavutu and Hill 121 on Tanambogo, both honeycombed with caves and mutually supportive machine gun bunkers. Intelligence reports indicated that they were garrisoned by only two hundred naval troops and construction workers. The assault on Gavutu, code named Acidity, was scheduled for 1200 on 7 August 1942 by the 1st Marine Parachute Battalion.

wingman were already streaking across the harbor, barely fifty feet off the surface, spewing .50-caliber tracers into two of the moored four-engine flying boats. The aircraft instantly burst into flame, illuminating the taxiing aircraft. Like moths attracted to flame, Reeves and Conklin spotted the flames and bore in on the lumbering Kawanishis. Their .50-caliber bullets shredded the metal fuselages, exploding the fuel tanks and incinerating the crews at their stations. In a matter of minutes, Shands's 1st Division had destroyed five Type 97s and the four boats that serviced them.

Shands's two-plane 2nd Division spotted four other flying boats moored in a semicircle around Tanambogo's north coast. The Wildcats made several firing passes, destroying the aircraft and leaving them burning in the water. On one of his passes, Lieutenant Wright spotted a silver rubber boat filled with flight personnel near one of the burning aircraft. He came around in a tight turn and opened fire. The thumb-sized bullets walked across the boat, tearing it to pieces and throwing the passengers into the flaming water. As the 2nd Division worked over the flying boats, Shands and his wingman found another lucrative target: a line of six Nakajima sea fighters moored close together just off Halavo's shoreline. The two made several firing passes and destroyed them all.

In the roughly thirty-minute "turkey shoot," VP-71 virtually destroyed the Gavutu/Tanambogo branch of the Yokohama Air Group Flying-Boat Unit. The squadron's attack was so violent that a pilot from another squadron blurted out, "[We] cleared out to keep from getting shot down by our own fighters who were going wild and shooting at everything in sight!" For this early morning action, Lieutenant Commander Shands and several of his flight were awarded the Navy Cross for "destroying seven enemy fighters and fifteen patrol planes. This victory eliminated all local air opposition in the area . . ."

As VP-71 cleared the area, three flights from VSB-6 (Scout Bombing Squadron) off the USS *Enterprise* bombed and strafed the two islands. The first strike, eighteen Douglas SBD-3 Dauntless dive bombers with 1000-pound bombs, took off just after dawn. Seven aircraft hit Gavutu and three bombed Tanambogo. Two hours later, nine dive bombers loaded with 500-pound bombs strafed targets on both islands and at 1000, twelve VSBs dropped 1,000-pound bombs on the islands. As a result of the air attacks, most of the above-ground structures were destroyed or severely damaged, including the concrete seaplane ramp, which was to have serious consequences on the parachute battalion's landing plan.

Defend to the Last Man

Captain Miyazaki stared in horror at the flaming pyres marking the wreckage of his command—"It was a horrifying sight," he said—and vowed to take vengeance on the Americans. "We will defend to the last man. Pray for our success," he radioed the 25th Air Flotilla headquarters on Rabaul. As the last of the American planes flew off, Miyazaki ordered his men to come out of the shelters they had taken cover in during the attack and take up arms. He knew it was only a matter of time until the Americans landed on the island. Despite the violence of the attack most of his men had survived the air assault. To defend the twin islets, Miyazaki had a total of 536 men—over twice the number of the American intelligence report—the 54-man Mitsuwa antiaircraft unit (two 13mm antiaircraft guns) under Sp. Lt. (j.g.) Toshichi Mitsuwa, a unit of the Kure 3rd Special Naval Landing Force (*Kaigun Tokubetsu Rikusentai*), 342 men of Miyazaki's Yokohama Air Group, and 144 civilian technicians and laborers from the 14th Construction Unit, commanded by Lt. Cmdr. Kiyoshi Iida. The *Rikusentai* platoon was the only trained infantry but the others could certainly handle light infantry weapons.

The Japanese defenders were armed with a variety of weapons, including rifles, light and heavy machine guns, two 13mm antiaircraft guns, and the ubiquitous 50mm grenade discharger (knee mortar). They occupied dozens of caves, bunkers, and tunnels positioned throughout the islets but their primary defensive positions were organized around two heights: Hill 148 on Gavutu and Tanambogo's Hill 121. The Japanese had honeycombed the hills with tunnels and rock-hewn chambers, some as big as twenty feet by twenty feet. The two heights were within machine gun range of each other, giving the Japanese excellent defensive ground to stop an attack against either hill. The Japanese were past masters at camouflage. Their rifle pits and machine gun positions were dug into the sides of the hills and carefully camouflaged with rocks and soil. Barrels were often filled with debris and placed around the openings to provide extra protection from direct fire. Finally, the positions were constructed with narrow embrasures, making them extremely difficult to spot. Often a Marine was right on the position before he saw it. Snipers were often positioned in trees and other expected locations to kill unit leaders and to limit movement. One particularly effective sniper managed to swim to one of the partially destroyed seaplanes on the coral reef and use it as his firing position. The garrison was well prepared to defend the islands and to defeat the invaders on the beach or die in the attempt—surrender was absolutely unacceptable.

The Landing Force

The 1st Marine Parachute Battalion, under the command of Maj. Robert H. Williams, embarked on the attack transport USS *Heywood* (APA-6), was scheduled to land on Gavutu's northeast coast at four hours after the landing on Tulagi (H+4 hours, 1200 7 August, 1942). The four-hour delay was the result of a shortage of landing craft. There were not sufficient craft for simultaneous landings on Tulagi and Gavutu-Tanambogo. Parachutist Private First Class Leonard Kiesel recalled, "The Raiders [1st Raider Battalion] had got use of the landing barges first, and we had to stay on board 'til they made their landing on Tulagi Island. And then the barges come back to us. And by that time the Japanese on Gavutu were alerted." Major Williams's landing plan called for a two company assault—Company "A" and Company "B" in that order—across the seaplane ramp, with Company "C" in reserve, prepared to support either of the assault companies. The initial assault was directed against the north and southeast faces of Hill 148, while the third company passed around the right flank to take a position on the Gavutu end of the causeway to interdict any flanking fire from Tanambogo. After Gavutu was captured, Company "C" was to seize Tanambogo. The Parachute Battalion numbered 397 men, including 30 naval personnel (24 Corpsmen, 5 doctors, and a U.S. Navy chaplain).

At 0800 three minesweepers, USS *Hovey* (DMS-11), USS *Hopkins* (DMS-13), and USS *Trever* (DMS-16) moved in to support the Raider landing on Tulagi. As they passed Gavutu, Lieutenant Mitsuwa's 13mm gun on Hill 148 opened fire, straddling the American formation but without causing damage or casualties. *Hopkins* and *Trever* responded with their three-inch main battery and 20mm cannon. *Trever* gunners scored a close hit and temporarily put the gun out of action. A short time later, a flight of SBD Douglas dive-bombers dropped several 500-pound bombs but failed to knock it out. The antiaircraft cruiser USS *San Juan* (CL-54) and destroyers USS *Monssen* (DD-436) and *Buchanan* (DD-484) bombarded Gavutu, causing heavy damage to all the above ground structures but causing very few casualties among the garrison. The battalion's after-action report noted, "Although these prepared fires gave all the appearance of really 'softening up' the objectives and giving all the members of this battalion a feeling that the objectives would be easily taken, this did not prove to be the case. . . . [T]he dugouts and gun positions were exceedingly well and build and disposed. . . . [T]he enemy suffered few casualties as a result of the preliminary bombardment."

Leonard Kiesel stood on deck waiting for the order to go over the side. "We were all lined up on the railing of the *Heywood* watching the Navy planes strafe the two target islands. I remember seeing a Japanese gas and oil storage unit go up in smoke. . . . [W]e were all anxious and excited, but had to wait our turn to board the Higgins boats." At 1000 the men started climbing down the cargo nets into the pitching boats. Ground swells were

1ST MARINE PARACHUTE BATTALION

The 1st Marine Parachute Battalion came into existence on 28 May 1941, with the formation of Company "A," at Quantico, Virginia, with Capt. Marcellus J. Howard as its first commanding officer. In the summer of 1941, the 2nd Parachute Company was transferred from the West Coast to Quantico and merged into the 1st Battalion. Captain Robert H. Williams assumed command of the two-company organization. At the end of March 1942, a third company was formed, giving the battalion an overall strength of 332 officers and men, less than 60 percent of its table of organization strength. The concentration of the companies at Quantico gave them an opportunity for tactical training but a shortage of transport aircraft kept the battalion from executing large-scale parachute jumps. Captain Williams felt that "paratroopers are simply a new form of infantry."and took advantage of his battalion's ground time to train accordingly: hand-to-hand fighting, hikes, and callisthenics filled their days. A reporter from *Time* magazine noted that the parachutists were a "tough-looking outfit among Marines, who all look tough." With the Japanese attack on Pearl Harbor, the battalion prepared for deployment, and in May and June 1942, it sailed to New Zealand as part of the 1st Marine Division. Upon arrival, Captain Williams learned that it had been assigned to seize the islands of Gavutu-Tanambogo in the Solomon Islands.

causing the landing craft to rise and fall as much as several feet making a jump from the cargo net into the boat a risky proposition for the heavily loaded Parachutists. Kiesel recalled, "When we finally climbed down the [cargo] net into the barges, the water had turned a bit rough. The barges were bouncing up and down and when I attempted to drop off the net into a waiting Higgins boat, my knees were almost driven up to my shoulder blades!" The loaded boats (twelve *Heywood* boats and one ramp boat from the *Neville*) formed three waves, corresponding to the landing plan:

- First wave—Navy Lt. R. E. Bennink, Company "A," 130 Marines, 4 Higgins boats

- Second wave—Navy Ensign G. C. Brown, Company "B," 130 Marines, 4 Higgins boats
- Third wave—Navy Lt. D. W. Ellis Jr., Company "C" and Headquarters, 140 Marines, 4 Higgins boats and 1 ramp boat.

The boats proceeded to an assembly area where they formed a circle and waited for the signal to proceed to the line of departure (LOD). Private First Class Lawrence Moran recalled, "We left *Heywood* around 1000 and circled her for about two hours . . . I got seasick from all the bouncing around." Lieutenant Bennink received word at 1141 to start the seven-mile run to the line of departure. The second and third waves (Ensign Brown and Lieutenant Ellis) followed at five minute intervals. The Higgins boats rolled heavily in the choppy water, allowing sea water to come over the sides, drenching men and equipment. The boats gathered at the line of departure for their difficult run to the beach. Because the island was almost surrounded by coral shoals, the landing had to be made on the northeastern side of Gavutu, not far from the causeway connecting it with Tanambogo. "Consequently our boats had to pass along the eastern shore of the island, between it and the promontory of Florida on which Halavo lay, then turn sharply in toward the beach," Moran explained. "During this turn we were exposed to fire from Tanambogo."

As the wave made its way to the beach, the *San Juan* opened fire, bombarding Gavutu with 280 rounds of five-inch high-capacity shells in four minutes. The destroyer *Monssen* closed to within five hundred yards of the island and unleashed 92 rounds of five-inch against suspected Japanese positions. Private First Class Robert W. Moore was in the second wave. "As we approached the cement dock [Lever's pier] Marine Gunner Robert Manning looked over the bow of the landing craft and said, 'There couldn't possibly be anyone alive there.' It had been blasted and shelled from one end to the other and the island was absolutely bare except for a few coconut trees that seemed to have survived."

As the last shells of the naval bombardment exploded, the first wave approached their designated landing spot. "These boats intended to land at the concrete seaplane ramp," General Vandegrift noted, "but the heavy naval gunfire and bombing preparations had tumbled huge blocks of cement in the path of the leading waves. . . ." A coral reef surrounded the two islands except for a narrow channel leading to the seaplane ramp. The landing plan called for the three waves to land over or in the vicinity of the ramp but the bombing and naval gunfire had reduced it to a mass of rubble, forcing the boats to land slightly north in a more exposed location on a nearby small beach and concrete pier standing some six feet out of the water. As the boats approached the channel they presented a lucrative target for the Japanese machine gunners. Colonel Joseph H. Alexander wrote in *Storm Landings: Epic Amphibious Battles in the Central Pacific*, "The intermittent reef surrounding Gavutu-Tanambogo had served to channelize the American assault landing into one open sector, which proved to be well covered by Japanese Nambu machine guns." Their heavy caliber slugs punched holes completely through the boats' one-inch thick plywood hull, killing and wounding several Marines. "They [landing craft] were painted gray to look like steel [but] you could shoot a .22 bullet right through them," Kiesel said.

The first wave beached about twenty-five yards apart and the men went over the sides—the early Higgins boats did not have ramps—and started pushing inland. The battalion's after-action report noted, "The leading wave (Company "A") was permitted to land without being fired upon. As soon as this wave hit the beach, it was taken under rifle and machine gun fire. Stanley Jersey wrote, " . . . [W]hen the Americans were within range, the order came: *Hassha o hajime!*—commence firing!" The battalion after-action noted: " . . .[T]he second and third waves were subjected to rifle and machine gun fire while still embarked in the boats." The *History of U.S. Marine Corps Operations in World War II, Pearl Harbor to Guadalcanal* stated that, "The second wave, at the request of the senior Marine officer, came in closely behind the first and touched the beach only a minute and a half later. Three Marines were hit before they could leave the boat and others were shot down in the water as they splashed ashore. While the boats were backing off one was hit and sunk, apparently by a hand grenade thrown from shore, and two of its crew were killed. The third wave followed in closely and landed at 1206, eight minutes ahead of the scheduled time. Again several Marines were hit in the boats and the rest rushed ashore in the face of heavy fire."

Private First Class Kiesel recalled, "One of our coxswains was hit and killed instantly. His assistant took over and hunched down in the bottom of the boat, steering by reaching his hand up to the wheel. About fifty yards out he uttered, 'This is as far as I go boys.' We had to bail over the sides . . . [into] chest deep water, bullets singing by . . . I considered ducking under the water and going in that way . . . Another 'Chute' just in front of me stumbled and went down. I thought he had slipped; after catching him by the shoulders, I dropped him instantly, half his face was gone!" Because of the heavy sniper fire, the boats had to withdraw some thousand yards before making a rendezvous to treat the wounded. Lieutenant Ellis, third wave commander, brought his boat in and transferred the wounded to a damaged boat and sent them to the *Neville*. While his boat was withdrawing, two of his crew were wounded. During this time enemy fire from both Florida and Gavutu had become so heavy that the boats at the rendezvous had been forced to withdraw farther down the channel.

Private First Class Moran was in the second wave. "We landed . . . on a concrete ramp at about a 45-degree angle. I had a hell of a time getting out . . . the Japs were not zeroing in on our boat or I would have been a goner. . . ." Private First Class Moore's boat didn't even make it to the beach. "As we approached the sea wall and dock [about seventy-five yards out] we hit a coral reef and the bow of the boat swung to the left . . . [W]e all plunged into the water, not realizing it was up to our necks . . . [B]ullets were whizzing around us and heavy fire hitting the water— you could hear the sound of shells flying by." Private First Class Kiesel was hit in the water. "I was finally able to move better, when 'Wham,' I was knocked off my feet. I knew I was hit. I managed to crawl up to the beach and . . . got behind a piece of concrete . . . and applied a tourniquet to my leg to stop the bleeding." Private First Class Moore reached the seawall. "We commenced firing, that is, everyone but me. My piece [Reising sub-machine gun] would not fire . . . I tried everything I knew to get it to operate. No luck. I was weaponless with the enemy firing at the Marines, including yours truly!"

The battalion after-action report noted, "This fire came from Hill 148, Hill 121, the small island, Gaomi, and it is strongly suspected, from the wrecked four-motor seaplane. . . . In addition to these fires the enemy is believed to have had time to send snipers up predetermined trees on all these islands." Lt. Ronald F. Adams, a platoon commander in Company "C" recalled, "As we headed for the point where we were to land, all thirty men in my platoon were lying down, but I was standing in the middle of them with my binoculars. Standing in the stem was my captain, Capt. Richard Huerth. About three hundred yards off-shore, we were hit by a round of bullets. I looked forward and the coxswain was slumped over dead. I looked behind me and there was Captain Huerth sitting on gear of some kind and blood was gushing out his nose and mouth, and of course he, too, never reached the shore. As we approached the shore, the boat ran into some underwater concrete piling. We had to bail out over the side, and we waded in to shore through water up to our chests." Captain Huerth was evacuated to a ship with a doctor but he could not be saved.

The battalion after-action noted, "When the leading wave landed it pushed inland about seventy-five yards where it was pinned down by fire from Hill 148 and Hill 121. The 2nd and 3rd waves upon landing found themselves subjected to an intense fire. It was evident that the enemy had every intention of fighting to the last man." Heywood's commanding officer, Capt. Herbert B. Knowles said, "From daylight to noon this little island was subjected to repeated bombing attacks and bombardment from cruisers and destroyers. The results have been most disappointing . . ." Jeter A. Isely and Philip A. Crowl wrote in *The U.S. Marines and Amphibious War, Its Theory, and Its Practice in the Pacific* that, " . . . the defenders opened up . . . Those on Tanambogo joined, taking the Marines under a raking enfilade fire . . . [T]he pier was swept by a stream of lead . . . [T]en percent of those set ashore by the first boats were casualties."

Japanese snipers caused a number of casualties and disrupted the advance. Private Robert M. Howard, a member of the division intelligence section, was pinned down near the wharf.

The enemy kept us confined to a small area for some time, due to many well placed snipers, and machine guns on top of the two hills.

The snipers were well camouflaged, with clothes made of palm tree leaves and bark. They were so well camouflaged in many cases that they could not be seen unless you were directly under the tree. These snipers were usually tied in the trees, and sometimes had light machine guns, but usually a .25-caliber rifle. They covered the sound of their weapons with the sound of our machine guns, and they sometimes got off two shots during one machine gun burst. Due to the fact that they fired when there was noise to cover their own rifle fire, and to their being well camouflaged, they were very effective. Their choices were sergeants and officers whose insignia were exposed.

Private First Class Moore recalled, "We faced a murderous fire from Hill 148. We attempted to make ourselves the smallest target you could imagine and finally managed to reach the base of the hill. There was some sort of a small wash running from its base. . . . [I]t was there that I saw my first dead Marine, Cpl. Harold E. Johns, who was a [parachute] rigger in Headquarters Company. I have never forgotten it." Private First Class Kiesel could not move because of his leg wound. "Every time I moved to change the tourniquet, the Japs would pepper the area. . . . [T]here were Japanese all around . . . underground, in caves . . . [T]hey were right close." He finally spotted the troublesome enemy position about seventy yards away. "They were busy manning the one gun that was still working. I quickly took aim and fired three shots. I know I killed one and wounded another. . . . [N]o more firing from that pesthole, thank God!"

With minutes of the landing, Major Williams was severely wounded by a bullet in the chest as he led a group of men up Hill 148. Lieutenant Norman R. Nickerson, Company "A" was close by. "I saw Williams fall and rushed to his aid with my platoon, where we formed a protective shield around the major until a corpsman arrived." Pharmacist's Mate Second Class Les Ferrell dumped sulfonamide powder on the wound and applied a battle dressing. "Major, you're damn lucky it was a machine gun that hit you," Ferrell told him. "It had so much velocity it went right through you." Major Charles A. Miller assumed command of the battalion but by this time, "The battalion C.P. was in considerable turmoil," according to the battalion's after-action report. "The battalion commander was wounded, the communication officer and the intelligence officer were killed. Gavutu was secured, not by any direct action on the part of the battalion headquarters, but by the persistent and courageous action of individuals and small groups of men." Major Miller

NAVY CROSS CITATION

The President of the United States of America takes pleasure in presenting the Navy Cross to Lieutenant Colonel Robert H. Williams, United States Marine Corps, for extraordinary heroism and devotion to duty while serving with the FIRST Parachute Battalion, FIRST Marine Division, during the assault on enemy Japanese forces at Gavutu, Solomon Islands, on 7 August 1942. Fighting against very great odds, Lieutenant Colonel Williams and his command daringly stormed strongly entrenched enemy forces and succeeded in securing a beachhead for further operations. Although he was wounded during this forward thrust, his outstanding spirit of aggressiveness and leadership was an inspiration to his entire Battalion, reflecting great credit upon Lieutenant Colonel Williams, his command, and the United States Naval Service.

The President of the United States of America takes pride in presenting the Navy Cross (Posthumously) to First Lieutenant Walter Xavier Young, United States Marine Corps (Reserve), for extraordinary heroism and devotion to duty while serving as Communications Officer, FIRST Parachute Battalion, FIRST Marine Division, during the assault on enemy Japanese forces at Gavutu, Solomon Islands, on 7 August 1942. During the extremely dangerous initial landings on Gavutu, First Lieutenant Young, on his own courageous initiative, fearlessly attacked several of the enemy in a single-handed attempt to neutralize a dugout which commanded a portion of the dock and constituted a grave menace to his comrades. Although fully aware of his imminent peril, he determinedly continued his voluntary action until, while effecting a daring entrance, he was fatally wounded by rifle or pistol fire from within the dugout. First Lieutenant Young's heroic spirit of self-sacrifice was in keeping with the highest traditions of the United States Naval Service. He gallantly gave his life for his country.

established the command post and aid station in a partially demolished building near the dock area.

Despite the heavy enemy fire, the Parachutists crept forward knocking out bunker and caves. Platoon Sergeant Merritt C. Walton was one of those courageous men. "Although fully of his extreme personal danger," the Posthumous Navy Cross citation stated, "Platoon Sergeant Walton voluntarily proceeded to reconnoiter the position of a hostile machine gun which threatened his platoon's right flank. After skillfully spotting the weapon's location, he courageously participated in a daring attack and realized success in silencing this deadly menace before he died of fatal wounds. Platoon Sergeant Walton's unflinching determination and unconquerable fighting spirit were in keeping with the highest traditions of the United States Naval Service. He gallantly gave his life for his country." Platoon Sergeant Roland F. Kachinski was another heroic individual who lost his life. "When the right flank of Company A was subjected to withering fire from a hostile machine gun, Platoon Sergeant Kachinski, on his own courageous initiative, launched a lone attack against the enemy. Effectively throwing grenades and engaging in perilous hand-to-hand combat, he fought with such tenacious determination and fearless aggressiveness that he was able to destroy the gun position before receiving fatal wounds. Platoon Sergeant Kachinski's relentless fighting spirit and unswerving devotion to duty were in keeping with the highest traditions of the United States Naval Service."

Company "A" made slow progress against the Japanese on Hill 148 because of the heavy fire from Tanambogo. "I saw a sandbag fortification at the other end of the causeway [Tanambogo side] with a machine gun," Private First Class Moran explained. "This weapon was shooting at our guys trying to take the hill. Some Marines from Company 'A' managed to toss a grenade at a cave adjacent to the hill and killed two or three Japs, but there were some still alive. The entrance was plugged with sand bags and I could not see too well because of the dust that had been blown through the embrasure." A machine gun team came up and set up their gun about twenty yards from the entrance. "I told the guys that I saw some Japs still alive," Moore said. About this time, Lt. Walter X. Young, the battalion communications officer arrived. "The lieutenant set his Reising-gun on full automatic and started blasting the emplacement," Moore recalled. "From the emplacement I heard a loud single shot and the lieutenant fell, shot through the neck." The company continued to push ahead but it was stymied by the heavy fire. Unless something developed quickly, Company "A" risked being shot to pieces.

Company "B" inched its way to the left through heavy enemy fire toward the southern end of the island. The company was fortunate to be defilade and partially protected from the Japanese positions on the high ground. "We got to the end of the island and started up the east side of the hill under extreme fire," Private First Class Moore recalled. "It was slow going with casualties all along the route." Company "C" was pinned down by Japanese machine gun and sniper fire from Tanambogo. At 1430, Major Miller requested reinforcements and air and naval gunfire to knock out the enemy positions. Commander Harry D. Felt's air group off the USS *Saratoga* launched five SBDs armed with 1,000-pound bombs. Their raid set fire to fuel and ammunition dumps, which exploded and burned for over two hours. A plume of black smoke from the fire rose several hundred feet in the air over Tanambogo. Commander Felt requested another strike after observing dugouts and trenches on Hill 121. Within a few minutes fifteen dive bombers arrived on station and began bombing the enemy positions. In addition, destroyers *Buchanan* and *Monssen* unleashed an intense concentration of five-inch shell fire. The combination air and naval bombardment greatly reduced the Japanese fire from the island and allowed Company "B" to begin their assault of Hill 148.

Private First Class Moore made it to the base of the height. "The hill was approximately 140 foot high and there were caves and dugouts all the way up. The first Japs I saw in one of the dugouts were big men in gray uniforms [probably the Mitsuwa unit]. . . . Vesey [Pfc. William K.] was in a Jap dugout swearing and stabbing any enemy . . . over and over with his bayonet. . . . I [learned that] Platoon Sgt. Howard D. Pumroy and 2nd Lt. Walter W. Kiser had been killed." Kiser had been shot in the lung while leading his platoon and lay bleeding to death while a corpsman vainly attempted to save his life. Pumroy had been shot in the head while trying to find a way around a Japanese position and died instantly. "There was a constant machine gun fire coming from a tin roof building," Moore recalled. "We were pinned down for some time, I don't recall just how long, and we had not reached our goal."

By 1400, Company "B" had reached the crest of the hill. At that moment, an SBD dropped a bomb on the summit. "As I started up the incline, two dive-bombers started to drop bombs near the top of the hill," Private First Class Moran said. The mistake cost the company two men killed and several wounded but did not stop the assault. They began clearing the Japanese fighting positions with grenades, hand-to-hand combat and explosive charges. Captain Harry L. Torgerson developed a novel method for destroying the Japanese emplacements. He bundled several sticks of TNT together, lashed it to a long board and stuffed it into the caves with a short fuse so the Japanese could not push it out. He personally destroyed more than fifty of the emplacements and came out with only a broken wrist watch and his pants blown off! Company "B" and a few men from Company "A" continued to attack Hill 148 from its eastern flank. Individuals and small groups cleared out dugout after dugout under rifle and machine gun but by late afternoon, Gavutu was essentially secured. However, Private Howard recalled, "The enemy was still to be found in many places. They had the island tunneled from one side to the other. At night the Japs were very active. They sometimes used firecrackers to draw machine gun fire, and then threw hand grenades in our emplacements. They used darkness to cover their movements. Some reinforcements swam across from Florida Island, using a log to keep their rifles out of the water."

Night Attack

At 1800, Company "B," 1st Battalion, 2nd Marines, under the command of Capt. Edgar Crane arrived pursuant to Major Miller's early afternoon request for reinforcement. Miller ordered the reinforced company to seize Tanambogo in a night landing. Crane was told there were just a few snipers on the island. It is difficult to understand how Miller could misconstrue the heavy machine gun fire his battalion was receiving from Tanambogo's Hill 121 for "scattered sniper fire." At the time there were almost 250 Japanese defenders on the island. Captain Crane planned to land on a small pier on the northeastern tip of the island about 1845 in an

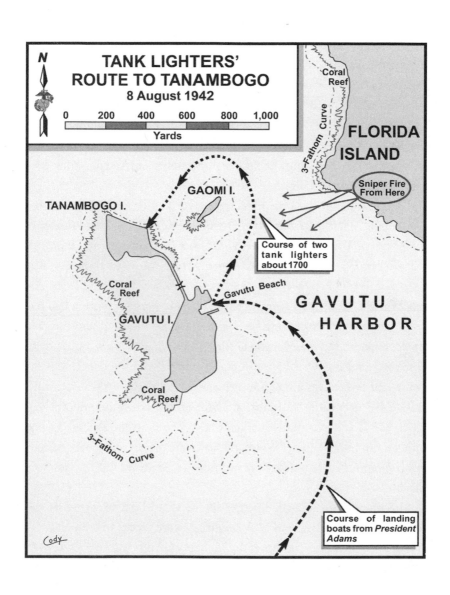

TANK LIGHTERS'
ROUTE TO TANAMBOGO
8 August 1942

0   200   400   600   800   1,000
Yards

N

Coral
Reef

FLORIDA
ISLAND

3-Fathom Curve

Sniper Fire
From Here

GAOMI I.

TANAMBOGO I.

Course of two
tank lighters
about 1700

Coral
Reef

Gavutu Beach

GAVUTU
HARBOR

GAVUTU I.

Coral
Reef

3-Fathom Curve

Course of landing
boats from President
Adams

Cody

attempt to take the Japanese positions from the rear in darkness. Flight Officer Cecil E. Spencer, an Australian guide, was attached to Company "B." He recalled, "We had about five minutes of naval gunfire support prior to landing. As we were coming in, the last shell hit a fuel dump on the beach lighting it up just like day, and the Japs opened fire from their dugouts on Tanambogo Hill." Captain Crane's boat with about thirty men made it to shore without incident and the men deployed along the beach but the other boats were silhouetted and taken under heavy fire. "Only two boat loads of our men got ashore," Spencer explained. "The coxswain of the third boat was shot in the head and killed and the other members of the crew wounded." One of the embarked Marines took over and piloted it out of danger.

Lieutenant John Smith, the company executive officer was in the second boat. Author Richard W. Johnson wrote in *Follow Me, The Story of the Second Marine Division in World War II*, "As the ramp of Smith's boat descended, the lieutenant charged across the sand shouting over his shoulder; 'Follow me!' As the men stumbled from the boat, the Japs brought all of their fire to bear and there was no place to go but down. The lieutenant already had vaulted across the sand and into the thicket beyond. His platoon edged slowly sideways to join Crane's men, which were taking what shelter it could find behind the concrete pier." Lieutenant Smith was alone and behind the Japanese lines. "Painfully, cautiously," according to Johnson, "he began circling behind the Jap positions . . . and eventually worked his way back to the beach." At one point he ran into a Japanese soldier who "whirled, bayonet flashing, and Smith shot his first Japanese." Sometime later, Smith was able to join the men at the pier.

The Marines of the 4th Platoon in the third boat managed to get two machine guns in action. However, they were forced to withdraw "as soon as we opened fire [because] the Japs spotted our tracers." Coxswain John Stanley Evans Jr. kept his boat on the beach according to his Navy Cross citation, "although two other landing boats turned back due to intense hostile fire." The intense enemy fire forced Crane to withdraw. He managed to get all but twelve of his men and all the wounded aboard Evans's boat, which was able to successfully withdraw and take them to the USS *Neville* for treatment. Chief Pharmacist Mate William F. Graham was one of the dozen men that were left behind. "It was Captain Crane who gathered us together and led us back, wading chin deep in water along the causeway," he said. "In the darkness, both Japs and the Marines were firing at us." The Marines were unaware that they were friendlies. "Crane . . . shouted, 'I'm Captain Edgar Crane, Company "B," 2nd Marines.' A 'chute' yelled, 'No he is not, he is a Jap, I can tell by the accent. Shoot the Jap son-of-a-bitch!'" Graham related that Crane hailed from Galveston, Texas, and had a well-developed southwestern drawl. Fortunately, Captain Torgerson was on hand and yelled, "Hold your fire, I know this guy!"

Pharmacist Mate Second Class Walter C. Wann received the Silver Star for crossing the causeway several times under heavy machine gun fire to assist Crane's wounded. His citation read in part, "Ignoring the enemy fire and with complete disregard of his own life, he sprinted back and forth, carrying and rendering aid to wounded Marines." Unfortunately, Wann was killed in action on 4 November 1942. The abortive landing cost Company "B" eight dead and fourteen wounded. In addition, one sailor was killed and several wounded.

The Parachutists' action can be explained by the fact that Japanese reinforcements were swimming to Gavutu from Tulagi and Florida under concealment of a heavy rain. Platoon Sergeant Harry M. Tully, an expert rifleman was located in a position where he could watch the water for the tell-tale sign of a swimmer using a floating log for cover. Second Lieutenant Herbert L. Merillat wrote in the September 1942 issue of the *Navy Information Bulletin*, "Sergeant Tully spotted a suspicious log float to the beach only six feet from where he lay in wait. He patiently waited for over a quarter of an hour until a Jap lifted his head. Tully shot him, ending the enemy's reinforcement attempt." Other swimmers reached the island and caused several casualties but were soon hunted down and killed. In another action that night, a group of holdouts was wiped out when they launched a bonsai attack from a cave on the southern slope of Hill 148. Scattered rifle and machine gun fire went on all night long, as anxious Marines defended their hard-won positions.

NAVY CROSS

The President of the United States of America takes pleasure in presenting the Navy Cross to Captain Edgar J. Crane (MCSN: 0-7017), United States Marine Corps (Reserve), for extraordinary heroism as Commanding Officer of Company B, First Battalion, Second Marines (Reinforced), SECOND Marine Division, during initial landings on enemy Japanese-controlled territory in the Solomon Islands Area, 7 to 9 August 1942. After leading his men to the successful completion of a dangerous and important mission on Florida Island, Captain Crane withdrew his company and proceeded by water to reinforce the attack on Gavutu and Tanambogo Islands. Although menaced by the withering blasts of hostile weapons, he brought two of six boats in to attempt a landing but was forced by extremely heavy machine-gun fire to remain in the water for four hours before he was able to get ashore, completely unarmed. With the small number of men still under his command, Captain Crane obtained arms from friendly troops and continued action against the enemy. His aggressive fighting spirit and courageous devotion to duty, maintained despite great personal risk, were in keeping with the highest traditions of the United States Naval Service.

Reinforcing Gavutu

The decision was reached late in the evening that Lt. Col. R. G. Hunt's 3rd Battalion, 2nd Marines would reinforce the Parachutists and to seize Tanambogo. Companies "L," "K," and "M" were to land on Gavutu and mop up the remaining Japanese. Company "I" was given the task of taking Tanambogo. Sergeant Warren Fitch recalled, "Company L was alerted at 0400 on the eighth to get ready to go ashore and to take what we needed for seventy two hours. At daybreak we loaded into landing boats." Private First Class Richard N. Vorwaller of Company "M" was a member of a .30-caliber machine gun team. "Our heavy .30-caliber machine guns along with spare parts and boxes of ammunition were lowered into the waiting boats. Our packs held three days' 'C' rations, a poncho, an extra pair of socks, and a belt of machine gun ammunition. We also carried a

The President of the United States takes pleasure in presenting the Navy Cross to John J. Smith (0-8521), Second Lieutenant, U.S. Marine Corps (Reserve), for extraordinary heroism while serving with the First Battalion, SECOND Marines (Reinforced), SECOND Marine Division, during initial landings on enemy Japanese-controlled territory in the Solomon Islands Area, 7 to 9 August 1942. When reinforcements were urgently needed elsewhere, Second Lieutenant Smith and his company withdrew from positions on Florida Island where a dangerous mission had just been completed, and proceeded by water to assist in the attack on Gavutu and Tanambogo Islands. Although menaced by the withering blasts of hostile weapons, he attempted a landing but was forced by extremely heavy machine-gun fire to remain in the water for four hours before he was able to get ashore. With the small number of men still with him, Second Lieutenant Smith immediately obtained arms from friendly troops and, although suffering a painful wound, participated in a vigorous action which forced the enemy to retire. His aggressive fighting spirit and courageous devotion to duty, maintained despite great personal risk, were in keeping with the highest traditions of the United States Naval Service.

hundred rounds of .30-caliber ammo for our 30.06 bolt action Springfield rifles. We had one canteen of water, a bayonet, a fighting knife and a gas mask."

As the landing craft were filled, they formed up and headed for Gavutu. "None of us really knew what war was like," Private First Class Vorwaller said. "We were not afraid, a little apprehensive maybe, but not really scared. . . . [An] older man opened the bolt of his rifle and fed a clip of shells into it. A man asked, 'Are you loading your rifle?' to which the other man answered, 'Hell yes man! This is war!' At his reply, everyone in our boat loaded his weapon." Unlike the previous day, the 3rd Battalion's approach to the island was not subjected to heavy fire. "When the boat hit the beach I was first out," Sergeant Fitch said. "There were several Marines lying there and I landed in the middle of them, thinking to get news from them as to what the situation was. I looked to the right where there were four dead; I looked to the left there were also four dead." Private First Class Robert C. Libby recalled, "Right after landing . . . I saw my first dead Japanese defender lying face down, with a rather large hole in the back of his head. Naturally, momentarily stunned, I stared and then moved on. . . . "

The unblooded men of the 3rd Battalion quickly became veterans. First Lieutenant Frederick W. Riggs recalled, "Pushing ahead and climbing on shore we were immediately subjected to intermittent fire from Tanambogo, off our right flank." A Marine from Company "I" said, "Our sergeant had drilled into our minds over and over on the ship, 'When you hit the beach, stay low. Don't make a target.' Amazingly, he lit out straight ahead and was killed immediately. After landing, I found myself next to a Navy corpsman who had a softball sized hole in his shoulder. Under his directions, I packed his wound with sulfa and bandaged it." Sergeant Fitch and his squad ran into an enemy occupied position. "There was a log and sandbagged bunker just ahead . . . we tied five sticks of dynamite to the end of a twelve-foot board. This was lit and shoved into the bunker. When it exploded the whole top seemed to raise about two feet and then settle to ground level. The bunker was then quiet." A platoon of engineers was attached to the battalion from the 2nd Pioneer Battalion, under 1st Lt. Harold A. Hayes. "We proceeded to dispose of bomb duds and blow caves after the Japanese refused to come out. . . . [A]t one cave, as I was placing a charge, a shot went off and I wasn't sure if someone was shooting at me. . . . [I]t turned out an officer had shot himself with a rifle, using his toe to pull the trigger."

Sergeant Fitch's squad cautiously advanced along the shoreline to the southern end of the island when it ran into several Japanese.

We encountered some caves in a rock ledge. . . . [A] couple of nude Japs ran out of them onto the shallow reef, but with about twenty-five Marines firing at them, they didn't make it far. Now we started receiving fire, some at ground level and some at a height of fifteen feet. In order to return fire, we had to get out on the reef . . . to the Japs we must have looked like ducks in a shooting gallery. Our platoon sergeant took a bad groin hit; and a corpsman was killed going to his aid. A Marine behind me told me to step aside as I was in his line of fire. The split second I moved over he was hit in the left shoulder. As he was about three inches shorter than I was, it would have been a heart hit for me. Several more men were wounded around me. The firing from the caves let up and we retraced our route to the island.

Lieutenant Riggs's platoon moved to the top of Hill 148 where they had a bird's-eye view of the surrounding island, including an air attack on Tanambogo. "We watched the attack by our SBDs, which flew from the south, dropped their bombs and continued northwards towards Tulagi." Private Leonard Skinner's machine gun team set up near an open corrugated iron building on top of the hill. "I took a prone position a few feet from the machine gun where I could also bring my rifle to bear on Tanambogo. The noise of machine gun, and mortar fire was very loud and continuous. Suddenly there was even a louder roar and an instantaneous explosion, then all went black and quiet." One of the SBDs thought the hill was still controlled by the Japanese and dropped a 500-pound bomb. "The gun crew was killed and several other Marines were wounded and I was blown halfway down the hill," Skinner said. "I don't know how long I was unconscious. . . . [G]radually things started to get light and focused . . . and I found I was lying flat on my back." Skinner was lucky. He had been hit by small pieces of shrapnel that did not inflict any serious injury. "The doctor told me to just rest where I was for awhile. . . . [A]s I was anxious to get back to my squad, I took my rifle and joined what was left of my squad."

Taking Tanambogo

Shortly after noon, Company "I," under the command of Capt. William G. Tinsley was ordered to capture Tanambogo. The assault was to be supported by the parachute battalion's machine guns, as well as Tinsley's own guns from Gavutu. Two Stuart light tanks from the 2nd Tank Battalion were to land just ahead of the infantrymen to cover the southern and eastern side of Hill 121. At 1600, the *Buchanan* stood into Gavutu, slowed to steerageway, and opened fire with her five-inch battery on Tanambogo's heights at a range of 1,100 yards. After a ten-minute bombardment, she shifted fire to the flat area on the southeast side of the island. At 1620, the first of two Landing Tank Lighters ran up on the beach, dropped its ramp and the tank rolled off. A Marine sergeant standing forward of the lighter's engine room was killed instantly by the heavy enemy fire. The second lighter ran aground on the coral a few yards from shore. "When we couldn't get any nearer the beach," Boatswain Mate 2nd Class B.W. Henson reported, "I signaled the tank to run off, rather than stop to lower the ramp. I had told Lt. Sweeney [Robert J., the tank commander] to run right into the ramp and knock it down when I gave the signal that the stops were off."

The minute the tanks rolled off the lighters, they became the focus for much of the Japanese fire. Johnson wrote that, "as Lt. Robert J. Sweeney, the tank commander drove his two egg-shell monsters inland, screaming Japs ran at the tanks with pipes and crowbars to jam the treads. Sweeney's guns were all going, and so were the guns of his companion tank, but there was painful lack of room to maneuver. Rising from the turret to reconnoiter, Sweeney took a bullet through the head. The tank stalled and the crewmen fought their way out of it against Japs who were swinging knives and even a pitchfork." The second tank was also immobilized when it got stuck between two palm trees, unable to move either forward or backward. The Japanese threw "Molotov cocktails" and other inflammables onto it, setting the tank afire. Marine riflemen tried to support the tankers but there were simply too many Japanese. The tank commander and the driver were killed and two other crewmen severely wounded before most of the Japanese were killed by rifle fire. The next day forty-two Japanese were counted around the knocked out tank. Among the corpses was the executive officer of the Yokohama Air Group and several of the seaplane pilots. One of the Japanese survivors of the attack reported, "I recall seeing my officer Lt. Cmdr. Saburo Katsuta on top of the tank. This was the last time I saw him."

The Marines of Company "I" followed the tanks ashore. The company split into two groups, one group worked its way up the southern slope of the hill, while the other deployed to the right, then inland to assault the eastern slope. Immediately after establishing a beachhead, the 1st Platoon, Company "K" launched a bayonet attack. "At 1620 we fixed bayonets and charged, single file across the causeway," Private Skinner said. "Enemy machine gun fire started sweeping back and forth, frequently finding its mark. . . . [A]bout halfway across I dived to the ground and rolled over the side to break up my long exposure to the Japanese gunners. It was then I discovered another machine gun was located on Gaomi Island [to the right of the causeway], and this gun was sweeping the causeway . . . I immediately was back up and continuing the charge." The platoon suffered several casualties in the wild assault but reached the other end of the causeway and dug in. Richard Johnson wrote, "As the first few Marines reached the Tanambogo end of the causeway, the Japs rose from their holes to meet them. For a moment the Marines were engaged with bayonets, and the battle was hand to hand, man against man and steel against steel."

Throughout the remainder of the evening, Company "I" rooted out the last of the Japanese defenders. Most of them did not surrender, so their caves were blown up and the entrances sealed. The few remaining Japanese conducted isolated attacks, which caused some casualties, but for the most part resistance on Tanambogo had been crushed. In the battle for Gavutu and Tanambogo, 476 Japanese defenders and 70 Marines or naval personnel (28 Parachutists) were killed in action. Of the 20 Japanese prisoners taken during the battle, most were not actually Japanese combatants but Korean laborers belonging to the Japanese construction unit. MCPO Miyagawa was one of the lucky ones. He was taken prisoner on Florida Island after escaping from Gavutu. He believed that Captain Miyazaki had either killed himself or had been sealed in one of Gavutu's caves.

Colonel William A. Eddy, World War I hero and head of all OSS operations in North Africa in 1942–43. He developed an agent network that greatly assisted the Allied landing during Operation Torch. *Author's collection*

Sergeant Jack Risler, who received the Silver Star for heroic action as a member of Operational Group Union II, which parachuted into southern France in 1944 to help the French Resistance. *National Archives*

Colonel William A. Eddy, in Marine uniform, was the official translator for Saudi Arabian King Ibn Saud and President Roosevelt aboard the USS *Quincy* in February 1945. *National Archives*

General Drazha Mihailovich, leader of the Serbian Chetnik guerrilla group.
U.S. Government Photo

OSS Captain Walter Mansfield (extreme right), British Lt. Col. D.T. Hudson
(center) and OSS Col. Albert B. Seitz (left) liaison officers to the Yugoslavia
Chetniks. *U.S. Government Photo*

OSS Operational Group Union II at the funeral of Sgt. Charles L. Perry, a team member killed in the parachute drop into France. Left to right: Maj. Peter Ortiz, Capt. Francis Coolidge (U.S. Army), Sgt. Robert E. Lasalle, Sgt. John P. Bodnar, Sgt. Frederick I. Brunner, and Sgt. Jack Risler. *USMC Photo*

Marine Raiders disembarking from a fast transport (APD) in ten-man rubber boats (LCP-R). *USMC Photo*

Before and after photographs of Tulagi after the naval bombardment.
USN Photo

Gavutu-Tanambogo as seen by a carrier plane off the USS *Wasp* after early morning air strikes. The islets were captured by the 1st Marine Parachute Battalion after heavy fighting. *USMC Photo*

Tanambogo after the naval bombardment on 7 August 1942. *USN Photo*

Lieutenant Colonel Carlson (left) and Major James Roosevelt (commanding officer and executive officer, respectively, of the 2nd Raider Battalion) holding a Japanese battle flag after returning from the 17 August 1942 raid on Makin Island. *National Archives*

Marine Raiders retuning to Pearl Harbor after their raid on Makin Island. Many of them have on dyed shirts to help camouflage them during the night landing. *USMC Photo*

A .30-caliber machine gun position on Edson's Ridge just before the bloody Japanese assault on 12–13 September 1942. *USMC Photo*

The morning after the bloody Japanese attacks on Edson's Ridge. A line of Marines can barely be seen in the smoke- and fog-shrouded air behind the killing ground. *USMC Photo*

Lieutenant Colonel Victor H. Krulak, commanding officer 2nd Parachute Battalion after successfully pulling off a diversionary raid on Choiseul. *USMC Photo*

Captain Frank Farrell, the OSS agent who investigated the Nazi spy ring in China at the end of the war. *USMC Photo*

Captain Frank Farrell, 1st Marines intelligence officer, and two unknown Marines in the Guadalcanal jungle in 1942. *USMC Photo*

CHAPTER 7

Gung Ho!

At 0300 16 August 1942, the USS *Nautilus* (SS-168) made landfall off the coast of Makin Atoll on a mission to land Marines of the 2nd Raider Battalion, under Lt. Col. Evans F. Carlson, on the Atoll's largest island, Butaritari. "Arrived off Makin at 0300. Scouted the eastern corner of the island down to Butaritari until 0540," Carlson noted in his diary. Lieutenant Commander William E. Brockman ordered the boat to periscope depth and within minutes he was peering through the night scope. The island was totally blacked out and even at high power he could not make out any distinguishing features. "The view was not particularly noteworthy: palm trees, a sandy beach, and lots of water," then-Lt. Oscar F. Peatross noted, "identical to thousands of other islands in the Pacific. The church steeple, the sole prominent cultural feature and a key reference point in all our briefings and rehearsals, was not to be seen. . . . [W]e now wondered if we were in the wrong place."

Brockman ordered the helmsman to maintain course, careful to keep the sub two miles from the outer fringe of the barrier reef so as not to run aground. Throughout the next day, the *Nautilus* continued to creep slowly along the coastline, carefully observing the island for signs of the enemy. "All of the officers and key noncommissioned officer of the raiding force had an opportunity to observe the objective area through the periscope,"

LIEUTENANT COLONEL EVANS F. CARLSON

Lieutenant Colonel Evans F. Carlson was a controversial figure because of his ideas on guerrilla warfare and unorthodox methods of troop indoctrination and training that he based on his experiences with the Chinese Communist 8th Route Army before World War II. He personally interviewed each man in the battalion—"Carlson's eyes were stern," Pvt. Al Flores said. "They made me feel like a preacher was looking at me." Carlson believed there should be no caste differences between officers and enlisted men. Officers would not have special mess facilities or clubs—saluting would be minimized. He emphasized teamwork and hard physical training, emphasizing how a Chinese battalion had marched fifty grueling miles over rough terrain and not one had dropped out. Carlson proposed a slogan for the battalion—"Gung Ho," which he translated as "work together."

Many of his contemporaries thought he was a communist because of his book *Twin Stars over China,* in which he praised the Red Army. One of his officers said, "There was a feeling on the part of the old timers that he had communist leanings and was called a 'pinko' behind his back." He was told, "Don't touch him with a ten-foot pole." After being officially censored for publishing *Twin Stars over China,* Carlson resigned his commission in April 1939 to speak publically about the ongoing Sino-Japanese War.

In 1941, he applied for recommissioning but thought it would be turned down. "I know what will happen," he told a friend, "someone will say, 'What'll we do with the SOB?'" Despite his misgivings, he was brought back on active duty, given a commission as a major in the Marine Corps Reserve, and assigned as commanding officer of the 2nd Raider Battalion.

Peatross said. During the daylong reconnaissance, Brockman determined that the "set and drift of the current along the landing beach shifted direction rapidly as the day wore on." He discussed the discovery with Carlson because of the difficulty his men would have in controlling the direction of their small rubber boats during the next night's landing.

Just after dark, Brockman ordered a course correction so he could check on the alternate landing beach. However, "Rip tides and strong currents off Ukiangong Point rendered this impracticable in the time remaining," Brockman wrote in the after-action report. *Nautilus* had a schedule to keep, she had to meet the USS *Argonaut* (SS-166), her sister boat carrying 134 men from Company "B." *Nautilus* carried 87 Raiders from Company "A." At 2116, the two submarines rendezvoused within fifteen minutes of the scheduled time, "during a heavy rain squall, a fact which evidenced most excellent navigation on the part of that vessel [*Argonaut*] . . . ," Brockman noted. "After passing the operation order for the attack to *Argonaut*, the two vessels proceeded in company to the debarkation point." At 0300 17 August, the raider force commenced embarking in boats.

Diversion Objective

The 221 men of the 2nd Raider Battalion who were crammed aboard the two submarines had been selected to conduct a quick hit and run raid on Makin Island to "destroy enemy forces and vital installations and to capture important documents and prisoners." Admiral Chester W. Nimitz personally selected the target, according to John Wukovits in *American Commando: Evans Carlson, His World War II Raiders, and America's First Special Forces Mission*. "Nimitz considered hitting Wake, Tinian, Attu . . . but concluded those would be too difficult. Instead he selected Makin." Commodore John M. Haines said, "After considering all factors, an objective in the Gilbert Islands seemed most realistic. This was an area of deepest Japanese penetration . . . [I]ts exposed position might have left it sufficiently sensitive to a raid as to bring out the reaction we desired, which was to deter the immediate reinforcement of Guadalcanal. That is how Makin Atoll was selected as the target and August 17, 1942, as D-Day." A successful raid would offer a welcome boost to home front morale after a succession of defeats. Nimitz looked at the raid as the Navy's answer to the Doolittle Raid on the Japanese home islands in April 1942.

Carlson had requested three submarines for the raid. "I can let you have two," Nimitz shot back. "We're short of men, short of ships, and short of planes." The *Nautilus*, commanded by Lieutenant Commander Brockman, and the *Argonaut*, commanded by Lt. Cmdr. John R. "Happy

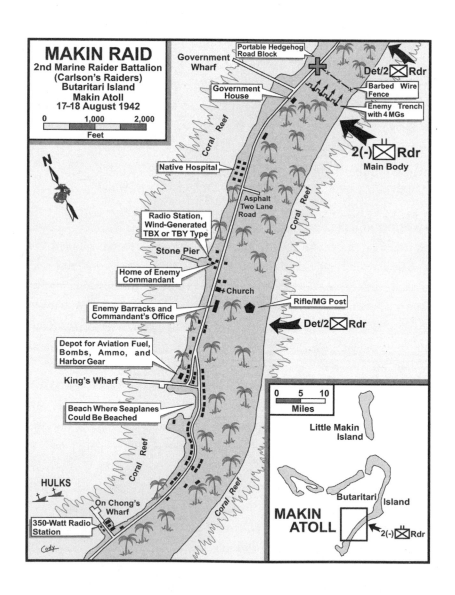

MAKIN RAID
2nd Marine Raider Battalion
(Carlson's Raiders)
Butaritari Island
Makin Atoll
17–18 August 1942

0   1,000   2,000
Feet

N

Government
Wharf

Portable Hedgehog
Road Block

Det/2 ☒ Rdr

Government
House

Barbed Wire
Fence

Enemy Trench
with 4 MGs

2(-) ☒ Rdr
Main Body

Coral Reef

Native Hospital

Coral Reef

Asphalt
Two Lane
Road

Radio Station,
Wind-Generated
TBX or TBY Type

Stone Pier

Home of Enemy
Commandant

+ Church

Rifle/MG Post

Enemy Barracks and
Commandant's Office

Det/2 ☒ Rdr

Depot for Aviation Fuel,
Bombs, Ammo, and
Harbor Gear

King's Wharf

Beach Where Seaplanes
Could Be Beached

Coral Reef

Coral Reef

HULKS

On Chong's
Wharf

350-Watt Radio
Station

Cody

0   5   10
Miles

Little Makin
Island

Butaritari Island

**MAKIN
ATOLL**

2(-) ☒ Rdr

MAKIN ATOLL

The atoll is the northernmost coral isle in the Gilberts group. It is located 3 degrees north of the equator, about two thousand miles southwest of Hawaii. Peatross described the atoll as consisting of "several small, reef-girt islands arranged in a rough isosceles triangle. The deep lagoon enclosed by this triangle is approximately ten miles across at its widest point. Butaritari Island, the largest island in the atoll (about eight miles long by a half mile wide), forms the southeastern base of the triangle." The island's western portion was covered by coconut palms, thicker on the south side, and salt brush. The lagoon side is lined with mangrove swamps. Much of the central portion was covered with salt brush and swamp, except near the short line. A packed-coral road ran along the lagoon side of the island's entire length. Just west of the island's center portion lies the old British administrative center, which included the Government House and native hospital. The island's native population numbered about 1,700 just before the war. There were several villages, but the main one was Butaritari east of the government area. There were four concrete or stone piers that jutted out into the lagoon from this area (from east to west): Government Wharf, Stone Pier, King's Wharf, and On Chong's Wharf. The island was bordered by reefs on both sides, 100-200 yards across on the southern ocean side and 500-1,500 yards wide on the northern lagoon side.

Jack" Pierce, the two largest submarines in the American fleet, were assigned for the raid. Peatross said that, "Although our submarines were classified as 'large,' they had never been intended to serve as troop transports: consequently they were very crowded." Carlson was forced to leave fifty-five men (twenty-five from "A" Company and thirty from "B" Company) behind. "Our gear was stacked, poked, tucked, and stowed in every nook and cranny," Peatross said. "Our rubber boats were rolled up and stowed in the torpedo loading scuttles along with the cans of fuel for their motors. Medical supplies and other fragile valuables were secured inside wherever space could be found. Extra rations for the embarked troops, mostly cases of canned fruits and vegetables were also stashed about the ship and were soon the targets of foraging Raiders."

Training

Initial Raider training was completed in San Diego, and then the men shipped off to Hawaii in May. Carlson moved the two companies in mid-July to Barber's Point, at the southwest corner of Oahu. He picked the location because of its high surf, which was thought to be as rough as Makin. "The landing craft selected for our raid was our old standby, the ten-man rubber boat [LCR-L] which, of course, could and did handle more than ten men," Peatross said. "Each boat was equipped with an outboard motor whose exposed ignition system could be drowned out by heavy dew, [and] an 'auxiliary power system' consisting of one paddle per man." Private William McCall remembered jokingly, "The training at Barber's Point was fun. We trained in our skivvies and some were dressed in their 'where-withals.' The sun baked our skin brown and there wasn't a woman in sight!"

Because submarines were not available for training, Carlson anchored two buoys set distances offshore to simulate the missing boats and get the men hardened to paddling in case the motors failed. "Sometimes the motors would run," Pvt. Ben Carson recalled, "but many times they wouldn't. The buoys were quite a ways beyond the surf line. We practiced, practiced, practiced—during the day and at night, when there was a pretty good wind blowing." Private First Class Ray Bauml echoed Carson's memory of the troublesome outboards. "They would never start and out came the paddles. The boat crew had to paddle like hell to get anywhere, especially against the ocean drift." Negotiating the surf line required seamanship skills and quite a bit of luck. The boat captain had to judge the wave action just right and then have the paddlers "give way together" to keep the boat heading toward the beach. If he judged the waves wrong, the boat might broach or "bend right in the middle," Carson said. " . . . The boat would unbend itself so fast that those seated in the back half . . . would go airborne and, most often as not, end up in the water."

Following the boat team training, Carlson concentrated on platoon, company, and then two-company tactical operations. "At this stage we practiced with all our equipment," Peatross explained, "And as our training progressed, we began to concentrate on the seizure of specific tactical objectives ashore." Even though they did not know the name of the objective, they used unidentified photomaps ("terra incognita") of the target to lay out an outline using strips of target cloth to mark specific objectives. On 4 August, the Raiders conducted a successful rehearsal for Admiral Nimitz and several of his staff members. The event marked the end of their training; all that remained was the word to go. "We had no doubts as to our readiness to handle anything that might await us as the objective," Peatross said. "And it was with feelings of great self-confidence and no little satisfaction that we broke camp and boarded trucks for the move back to Camp Catlin." Lieutenant Wilfred S. "Frenchy" LeFrancois proudly proclaimed, "Behind us were days, weeks and months of the most strenuous, back-breaking, soul-trying preparations. . . . The unit had perfected itself in landing on beaches regarded as inaccessible, and traversing terrain considered as impassable. We had been taught bayonet fighting, how to handle grenades and Molotov cocktails, judo, knife work, unerring marksmanship, how to use rubber boats, how to camouflage our bodies, demolition techniques, and how to live off the country."

Terra Incognita Plan

Initial intelligence reports indicated that three days after the Pearl Harbor attack, three hundred Japanese of the 51st Special Naval Landing Force (SNLF), sometimes called Japanese Marines (*Rikusentai*), and base personnel of the Yokohama Naval Flying Corps occupied the Makin Atoll and started construction of a seaplane base to extend Japanese air coverage over Allied territory. Just prior to the battalion leaving for the raid, the battalion intelligence officer, Capt. Gerald "Jerry" Holtom, learned from a native fisherman on Christmas Island that "the Japanese garrison comprised about forty-five to fifty Marines of the SNLF under the command of Warrant Officer Kanemitsu." According to the fisherman, the Japanese garrison had started constructing defensive positions on the lagoon side of the island and, following American air raids preparations had been intensified. The native was able to point out the Japanese headquarters and communications center, barracks, and a small rifle range on a map and provide hydrographic informa-tion on the surf, tides, and coral reefs. He also told Holtom about a "half-breed" who he claimed was a Japanese spy. Altogether, the infor-mant's information gave the battalion a fairly comprehensive picture of the objective.

On 3 August 1942, Carlson issued Operations Order 2-42. In it he stated, "An enemy force, estimated to consist of not more than 250 officers and men, and possibly supported by seaplanes and one or two surface craft, occupies Butaritari." He included the higher estimate despite Holtom's information. The inflated Japanese strength estimate came close to disaster for the force during the operation. The Navy's order (71-42) further expanded the enemy threat. "It is reasonable to believe that occa-sional destroyers and submarines put it there [Makin Atoll] . . . [and] that seaplanes are based there. The lagoon entrance . . . is reported (without confirmation) to be guarded by land-based guns . . . as the bulk of the commercial installations are at the town on the main southern island [Butaritari], it is believed that the enemy regards this as the vital area and that he has disposed his defenses accordingly."

As set forth in the order, Carlson envisioned the battalion's scheme of maneuver to be:

Company "A" (less one rifle section), under 1st Lt. Plumley [Merwyn "Plum"] will land at 0430 and will move rapidly north by east and secure the road junction. It will be responsible for the destruction of all enemy forces southward, inclusive of the entire Ukiangong Point area. Vital installations will be destroyed, documents and prisoners captured. Upon completion of this task this company will rendezvous in the vicinity of the road junction.

Company "B" (less one rifle section), under Capt. Coyte [Ralph] will land at 0430 and will move rapidly inland and secure the road. It will be responsible for the destruction of the enemy in the area west of this road. It will land one squad for the purpose of securing its left flank. The company will be prepared to move north-east through the area north of the main highway on order. Vital installations will be destroyed, documents and prisoners captured.

The order stated that, "the mission was to be completed and the troops withdrawn on the same day." During the planning and workup for the raid, Carlson was trying to determine how to deal with a critical personnel issue: his executive officer, Maj. James Roosevelt, the president's son. Both Carlson and Nimitz thought that it was unwise to expose Roosevelt to the possibility of death or injury . . . or even being captured . . . and discussed it with him. Roosevelt was unable to convince either man that he should be allowed to go on the operation . . . so he telephoned the Commander-in-Chief. President Roosevelt was said to have called the chief of Naval Operations, Adm. Ernest J. King, and told him politely, "Look, my son's an officer in that battalion; if he doesn't go, no one goes!" The issue was settled. Private Carson recalled, "We all knew that taking Roosevelt was a hell of a risk. The story among us privates was if he gets caught by the Japanese, he'd be pretty badly beat up. Once it was settled, though, nothing was said anymore."

Underway

In the early morning hours of 7 August, working parties loaded the battalion's supplies and equipment on board the two submarines. "Shortly after midnight on 8 August, the Raiders began loading onto trucks that would take them on a short ride to the submarine base," George W. Smith wrote in *Carlson's Raid: The Daring Marine Assault on Makin*. "They left camp under blackout conditions and as quietly as possible. There was no need to alert anyone else of their departure." At 0900, 8 August 1942, the submarines pulled away from the pier at Pearl Harbor on the outward leg of their four thousand mile cruise. They steamed past Battleship Row where the blackened, twisted remains of the USS *Arizona* jutted above the water, Hospital Point where the *Nevada*, the only battleship to get underway during the Japanese attack, was beached, and out the channel to the open sea. A patrol plane swooped low over the pair and waggled its wings in a gesture of "Good hunting!" The escorting destroyer stayed with them until nightfall, after which the two submarines proceeded independently to the objective area. The Pacific Fleet after-action report noted, "No contact with enemy forces was had en route and almost the entire trip was made on the surface, thereby making the boats habitable despite the large number of men carried."

The officer who wrote the Pacific Fleet's report was not on board either of the submarines. "Sleeping space was at a premium," Peatross explained. "Raiders and sailors slept all over the place, with many hot-bunking. The forward and after torpedo rooms on each of the submarines had been converted into troop billets by the simple expedient of removing the torpedoes, except those carried in the tubes [the submarines had been ordered, "do not attack enemy vessels unless a favorable opportunity is presented for attack on a carrier or other capital ship"], and replacing them with sleeping 'racks' built of 2-inch by 4-inch stock and canvas, stacked in five or six tiers with only 12 inches of vertical space between tiers. Each tier was about four racks long and three wide, but there was no horizontal space between individual bunks. The men who slept in back had to slide in before those in front; to turn over it was necessary to get out of the bunk, which required the cooperation of all."

Sanitary conditions were primitive to say the least. There were no showers and the slightest bit of activity brought out instant sweat. Temperatures in the subs hovered over 90 degrees, with 85 percent humidity. "Crapper cops" made sure the men used the correct procedure in flushing the head. Turning the wrong valve would cause "old face-full" to erupt, splattering the noxious contents over the unfortunate victim and the telephone booth–sized space. "One of the unwritten laws on the trip was that Raiders in their bunks were not allowed to break wind, no matter what," Private McCall said in all seriousness. "Anyone that farted was threatened to be stuffed in the number four torpedo tube and shot out into the briny!" Many of the men had to fight off bouts of claustrophobia in the combined space. To help offset these anxiety attacks, the men were allowed topside twice a day—dawn and dusk—by boat teams for a ten minute period of physical training. "We were always glad to get on deck and not smell those body odors and other stuff that festered our sense of smell," Private McCall said. "Sometimes it would smell so bad down below, it would gag a maggot."

At one point just before surfacing, Lieutenant Commander Brockman authorized the smoking lamp to be lit. "Immediately all of the smokers dashed for their cigarettes," Peatross recalled, "but it must have been at least five minutes before anyone could get enough fire from lighters or matches to light a cigarette because of the lack of oxygen." The battalion surgeon, Lt. William B. MacCraken assured everyone that there was enough oxygen to maintain life but, Peatross said, tongue in cheek, "There sure wasn't enough to burn a match." The men were fed two full meals a day—morning and evening—as well as soup and crackers at noon; coffee was available at any time. "There were so many people to feed that when the cook made coffee it was so weak you could stand in a barrelful and still see your toes," McCall joked. Each meal took three and a half hours to serve out of the tiny galley. There was no place to sit, so the men ate standing up wherever they could find a space. However, no one complained because they thought the food was excellent.

Two days from the objective, the Raiders practiced the debarkation procedure. "The rather complicated procedure required the boat teams to move from their billeting areas, scattered from stem to stern of the 381-foot-long submarine, fore or aft along the passageway to the middle of the submarine, climb a ladder, even-numbered teams to starboard, odd-numbered teams to port, move through a hatch onto the weather deck; get their boat out of storage and inflate it and carry it to the debarkation station corresponding to their boat team number," Peatross explained. In addition, the men had to pick up various odds and ends of equipment, crew-served weapons and ammunition that was stored somewhere in the submarine and make their way to the ladder—not an easy proposition in the cramped passageway. Once on deck, the men had to retrieve their boat from the torpedo loading tubes, unlash it, and move it to the air hose for inflation. The plan called for the boats to remain on the weather deck and, when all was ready, the sub would submerge, leaving them afloat and ready to motor to the assembly area alongside the *Nautilus*.

Landing (L-Day)
"It was organized grabass."
Private Dean Voight

The piercing blare of the klaxon, followed by "Prepare to Surface" added impetus to the Raiders' preparations for debarkation. Peatross recalled, "At last the *Nautilus* surfaced, the hatches were opened, and cool fresh air poured in. . . . [A]s we moved out onto the deck, we were met by weather conditions for which the adjective 'atrocious' seems wholly inadequate." The Navy's after action report noted that the wind was "raising moderate swells." The "moderate swells" were causing the submarine to roll and pitch. The heavily laden Raiders experienced a great deal of trouble trying to negotiate the slippery deck. "Rain was coming down in torrents," Peatross said, "[and] a strong onshore wind was whipping up whitecaps all around. . . ." The *Nautilus* log noted, "The ship at the time was experiencing great difficulty in maintaining position due to a current of about one and one-half knots which set us continuously to the westward and in towards the reef. The surf line could be faintly seen in the darkness [and] existing landmarks indicated the ship was within five hundred yards of the reef and the commanding officer was forced to continually kick ahead to keep clear of it. As the boats were being put over [the side] at this time, it was impracticable to run out from the reef for any great distance."

The men on deck struggled to retrieve the boats from storage and inflate them. One of the men failed to attach the air hose properly and it emitted a horrible screech from escaping compressed air, scaring hell out of the men who thought that it must have alerted the Japanese. The screech joined the loud rumble of the diesel engines, which Carlson hoped would be blocked out by the roar of the surf. The waves crashed into the submarine, throwing spray across the deck and making it nearly impossible for the men to fuel the outboard motors. Salt water mixed with gasoline, choking the engines. Many of the motors simply gave up the ghost and refused to start, while others sputtered for a few minutes and then died, forcing the men to paddle to the beach.

Because the submarines had to maneuver to keep from being carried onto the reef, the launch plans had to be abandoned. "The submarine was supposed to submerge and leave us in the water, but now we had to go over the side because of the swells," Sgt. Kenneth L. McCullough recalled. "They'd raise four to five feet and then drop about ten feet." The boat teams were experiencing a great deal of trouble, particularly the ones on the weather side of the submarine. They had to manhandle the four hundred-pound rubber boats over the side and hold onto lines to keep them from being swept away by the surging water. Two boats loaded with medical supplies

LANDING CRAFT RUBBER, LARGE

The World War II Landing Craft Rubber, Large [LCR(L)], was a sixteen-foot by eight-foot, four-hundred-pound manually inflatable rubber boat which could carry ten men. It was also known as the IBS (inflatable boat, small). Each boat came equipped with a two-cycle outboard motor, a five-gallon gas can, and a portable tank of carbon dioxide for inflating the boat when pressurized air was not available. The craft had a pointed bow and blunt stern for the attachment of a small outboard motor. A four-inch diameter "spray" tube ran around the outside of the craft, while three internal "spreader" tubes kept the sides from collapsing. Some boats were equipped with various devices for lashing down equipment. Crewman were assigned specific tasks: the senior man was the boat captain; others were assigned as the outboard motor mechanic, the coxswain, the fuel man, the inflator, and another in charge of the paddles. Each crewmember was cross-trained to handle the other's assignment. Taller men were generally positioned in the bow, while the shorter men were placed in the middle or stern positions. This assignment was used because the boat was usually walked out to deep water, and the taller men at the bow could keep their heads above water longer, controlling the boat while the shorter men climbed aboard and started the motor or paddled. The "paddlers" sat astride the side tube with their outboard leg propped up on the spray tube to keep their foot out of the water. This position was hard to maintain for long periods of time.

and ammunition broke free and sailed off into the darkness. Wave action quickly filled the remaining boats up to the gunwales with water, forcing the men to jump into the pitching, water-logged craft that blended so well with the ocean some men wondered if there was anything there at all. "You had to jump into the boat when it was at its zenith," Private First Class Brian Quirk recalled. "I remember when it came my turn to jump, and I thought, 'If I miss the son of a bitch, I'm going down like a rock.'"

Fortunately no one was lost and by 0410, all the boats were assembled at the rendezvous point near the *Nautilus*, except Carlson, who was still waiting for his boat from the *Argonaut* to pick him up. "As time crawled on and the debarkation seemed to be taking forever, tension on deck [of the *Nautilus*] increased noticeably," Peatross said. " . . . [F]inally when the boat was twenty minutes late . . . [I] was motioned to take Carlson off in my boat." Peatross took the battalion commander to the rendezvous point and transferred him to another boat. At this point the two companies were intermingled and had lost all tactical integrity. The boat captains were on their own, trying to keep some sort of formation as they struggled against the strong tide that was pulling them toward the reef. The darkness, foul weather, and failure of most of the engines made it impossible to organize the boats into company formations as had been planned.

Carlson soon realized that the initial landing plan had been overcome by events. The two companies would not be able to land on separate beaches so he decided to have them land on the same beach. "I signaled, as best I could, for all boats to follow me," he said. Corporal John W. Potter's boat had a working motor, so Carlson used him to pass the word. "Circle around and up and down to find as many boats as possible and send them straight to the beach." *Nautilus* recorded that, "All boats were clear at the scheduled time and had been given the correct course allowing for the current to take them to their landing beach." With the Raiders gone, the submarines moved four miles offshore, keeping contact with the landing force by voice radio.

The boats followed Carlson singly or in small groups depending on whether they had a functioning motor or whether they were being paddled. Those boats that had to depend on manpower had to be bailed out before they could proceed, as they were simply too full of water to paddle . . . and bailing with helmets took time. The men and equipment were soaked, which knocked out several radios and left much of the unit without communications. As the boats neared the breaker line marking the seaward edge of the submerged reef shelf, the men could see turbulent whitewater spilling down the face of the waves as the water raced for shore. The boat captains tried to time the wave sets but it was nearly impossible in the darkness and instead, they trusted to luck and their training. Several boats came a cropper as they struggled in vain to keep the bows headed toward the beach. "We were not prepared for the action those first rollers gave us," Pvt. Ben Carson recalled.

"The surf was running high and as our boat rode up the first wave we were turned sideways and ended up making a full circle before we headed down the leeward side of the wave." A huge wave threw Carson and three others out of their boat. "I grabbed a mouthful of air and rapidly sank to the coral reef as I was quickly dragged toward shore . . . I finally struggled to shore [without his weapon and ammunition]."

The battalion official report noted, "Fifteen of eighteen boats landed on the intended beach. Two boats landed about a mile to the northwest, but the occupants joined our main force during the fire fight. The other boat [Peatross and eleven men] landed over a mile to the southwest, which placed this group in the rear of the enemy when the battle started." Peatross soon found the two boats with the medical supplies and weapons that had earlier broken away but, "the only sounds we heard were our own voices, the roar of the surf, and the squawking of the sea birds . . . it was becoming more and more apparent that we had landed in the wrong place." Meanwhile the two companies landed right where they were supposed to but were badly intermingled. Private Brian Quirk summed it up. "The landing was all mixed up. Everything was in total disarray. It took us a while to get some sense of organization. Guys were running around in the dark making things even more confused. We decided to wait until dawn to get organized, so we just stayed where we were."

If the chaotic organization on the beach was not enough, an automatic weapon fired about 0530, just before dawn. Smith wrote, "Suddenly a burst of fire from a Browning Automatic Rifle (BAR) split the air. Carlson ran toward the sound, trying to find out if the gunfire was coming from the Japanese. He was soon told that it had come from a Raider (Pfc. Vern Mitchell) who apparently had allowed the bolt to slam shut when he loaded a magazine." Wukovits wrote that, "For the only time in his career, Carlson swore at one of his men." Everyone was exasperated. "They might as well just blow a bugle that says we're here, come find us," Private Quirk exclaimed, "We haven't even left the beach and we told them where we are." There was nothing Carlson could do except get his command off the beach. He ordered Lieutenant Plumly's Company "A" to move across the island, seize the road on the lagoon side and report his location with relation to the wharves, while he placed Captain Coyte's Company "B" in reserve and directed it to provide security for the left flank. In frustration, Carlson radioed the Nautilus, "Everything lousy!"

Lieutenant Plumly picked LeFrancois's 1st Platoon to take the point. "He told me the colonel wanted to know where we were, and that he wished us to contact the enemy . . . ," LeFrancois recalled. "Sergeant Clyde Thomason led the reconnoitering groups across the island, following the course of a shallow ditch for cover." Dawn was breaking as the Raiders worked their way toward the road. Within minutes the platoon spotted the dilapidated government pier jutting out into the lagoon, the island's flagpole and the Government House. LeFrancois and Thomason crept forward. "We were doing fine," LeFrancois said, "when two blasts roared from the left and double-O buckshot sprayed the wooden shack near us. Thomason shouted the password 'Gung' to keep our men from shooting at us in a cross fire. Then to our amazement, the countersign 'Ho' was shouted to us . . . and out came Charley Lamb [Lt. Charles] with two men. He had taken our shadowy forms for those of Japs." Small groups of Raiders were bent on carrying out their original instructions and were unaware that Carlson had changed them—Company "B" was originally assigned to be the lead element, not Company "A."

A boat team from Company "A" landed some distance from the main body and proceeded up the middle of the island. "We came to the road . . . headed north, with half the squad on each side," Sgt. James Faulkner explained. "Just as it was breaking daylight we sighted a bicycle coming up the road. When he got even with us we stepped out into the road and stopped him." Captain Holtom, who spoke and read Japanese fluently, happened to be with the squad and pointed out that a sign on the bike read, "Japanese Chief of Police." As they continued toward the Government House, their attention was diverted by shots. The prisoner took this opportunity to run . . . but he didn't get far before the Raiders opened fire and killed "the only prisoner taken in the operation."

As the platoon continued up the road, "A group of tall, well-built native men, women, and children was coming down it," LeFrancois recalled. "Apparently they had taken our firing for Japanese practice maneuvers. When they saw us they were startled but quickly became friendly." The natives told the Raiders that the Japanese were located near

On Chong's Wharf and that they had been on alert for the past couple of weeks expecting some kind of attack. Their estimates of Japanese strength varied from 80 to more than 150, which matched the intelligence report. The information was sent back to Carlson, who radioed the *Nautilus* to fire on the suspected enemy location. The *Nautilus* report stated, "At 0656 request was received from commanding officer Raider unit to open fire with deck guns on lake area off Ukiangoag Point . . . at 0703 starting [firing] at the extreme end of the point and working down it about a mile. A total twelve salvoes or twenty-four rounds were fired."

Shortly after the first request for fire, *Nautilus* received another. "Colonel Carlson requested [us] to take two merchant ships under fire. This presented a difficult gunnery problem, as no point of aim in deflection was presented due to lack of distinguishable landmarks, and the Nautilus' own position was only apparently known. . . . [A]t this time communication with the shore failed. . . . [F]ire was opened at 0716 and a total of twenty-three salvoes or forty-six rounds were fired . . ." Admiral Nimitz reported, "Both ships were hit and set on fire, and later sunk. One was a 3,500-ton ship, which the natives stated quartered sixty Marines. The other was a 1,500-ton patrol vessel." Immediately after ceasing fire, both submarines submerged because of an air threat and, "remained submerged for the remainder of the [day] as continued presence of enemy aircraft was anticipated to within two hours of darkness."

LeFrancois was uneasy after talking with the natives. "I wanted to be on our way," he said, "alert for a possible Jap ambush." The platoon continued to comb the area for Japanese. "We had just passed a group of fifteen shacks near a long house . . . when suddenly the point hit the ground and the rest of us followed suit." A truckload of Japanese appeared some distance away and stopped in the middle of the road. "The Japs jumped out of it and were joined by others, a total of more than thirty in all. They planted a large rising sun flag and ducked into the bushes beside the road." LeFrancois immediately deployed his platoon to take advantage of the terrain. "I could see the Japs creeping toward us in bunches along the narrow hundred-yard strip of trees and light brush between the road and the lagoon. They were perfect targets and were walking into a trap." He moved his left flank closer to the point so that his lines formed "sort of a pocket with frontal and a flanking fire to welcome the Nips. It was a perfect setup!"

Sergeant Thomason was in position to spring the ambush. "Let 'em have it!" he shouted. LeFrancois exclaimed, "There was about four minutes of inferno in which everybody in the area was blasting away at somebody or something. Anything out in the open was riddled. Then we realized we were the only ones making any noise, and let up. Later, I found our fire had been so deadly that this Jap combat group in its entirely had seen its last battle." That didn't end the threat however.

"A shot rang out . . . and all hell broke loose," Cpl. Howard Young recalled. "We had Japs in front of us, above us, alongside of us to our left and behind us also to our left. Two machine guns were sweeping the area above our heads; slugs were chunking into the bases of the palm trees. Snipers were coming very close . . ."

LeFrancois recalled, " . . . [E]nemy snipers were taking a grim toll. One slug kicked up dirt in my mouth. Then came a 'thunk,' [and] they

SERGEANT CLYDE A. THOMASON

For conspicuous gallantry and intrepidity at the risk of his life above and beyond the call of duty while a member of the Second Marine Raider Battalion in action against the Japanese-held island of Makin on August 17–18, 1942. Landing the advance element of the assault echelon, Sergeant Thomason disposed his men with keen judgment and discrimination and by his exemplary leadership and great personal valor, exhorted them to like fearless efforts. On one occasion, he dauntlessly walked up to a house which concealed an enemy Japanese sniper, forced in the door and shot the man before he could resist. Later in the action, while leading an assault on enemy position, he gallantly gave up his life in the service of his country. His courage and loyal devotion to duty in the face of grave peril were in keeping with the finest traditions of the United States Naval Service.

got Thomason. I inched my way over to him and felt his pulse. There was no heartbeat."

Snipers posed a major threat, particularly to radiomen, officers, and noncommissioned officers like Thomason, who was killed while leading his men. Many of the snipers were hidden in the tops of palm trees, concealed by the heavy foliage, their mustard-green uniforms blended right in with the tree growth. "I can say that the Japanese were near perfect at conceal-ment and camouflage," Platoon Sgt. Melvin Spotts said. "I only got one shot at a visible target; the rest of my firing was at things that could have been Japs but probably weren't." A sniper targeted Sgt. Victor Maghakian. "One picked me out and his shot caught me in the right arm. My arm went dead almost immediately but I still had the full use of my left as I dropped to the 'deck' and played dead for fifteen minutes until another shot by him revealed his position. When he showed himself I silenced him with my automatic rifle." The battalion intelligence officer was the victim of a sniper. LeFrancois recalled hearing a shout. "[Captain] Holtom has been shot and is dying! He needs medical attention!" Then came slowly the words, "Never mind!" Carlson noted, "[T]he bullet passed through his left chest and emerged behind the right shoulder. He lived only ten seconds."

Raising Cain

Lieutenant Peatross and his boat team had unknowingly landed behind the Japanese and were approaching the enemy barracks when LeFrancois's group started shooting. " . . . [A] very startled Japanese soldier burst from the barracks, his rifle firmly gripped at the ready, prepared to fire at anything coming his way. Without command and almost as one, three of our thirteen-man group fired, and the luckless Japanese fell to the ground dead . . . the first shots that any of us had fired in the war." The group continued scouting the road after searching the barracks. "We suddenly noticed some movement about four hundred yards down the road. . . . [A] Japanese with his rifle slung across his back came out of the bushes, picked up a bicycle, mounted it, and swiftly pedaled down the road in our direction." A Raider fired and missed. " . . . [T]he man [Japanese] ever so carefully laid down his bicycle, as if fearful of damaging the Emperor's property, unslung his rifle, calmly and almost deliberately walked to the side of the road, as if to select a position before he could get off a shot, however, four Raiders on the right fired at him, and in the dust raised by their fire, we saw him crumple." Two other cyclists were also killed, each oblivious to their dead comrades lying in the road.

The squad crossed the road and entered what had been described as the headquarters of the island commander. "We advanced upon it very cautiously," Peatross explained, "prepared to charge if necessary. But not a shot was fired, so we entered and conducted a thorough search." They discovered a radio set, which one of the Raiders got working, and a steel safe. "We spent several precious minutes listening on several channels, hoping to pick up some of our own radio traffic, but all we heard was Japanese. . . . [We] turned our attention to the safe, broke it open and found a bundle of Japanese bank notes and a quart-size bag of coins. Sam Brown [Cpl.], the safe-cracker and, hence, custodian of the cash, passed out the bank notes and a few coins, as if it were payday. . . ." As they approached another house just a few yards away, "a man dressed in a white shirt, khaki shorts, and a sun helmet . . . walked out of the house onto the porch and waved toward the area from which the bicyclists had come, as if signaling. Sam Brown immediately fired on the man killing him." Years later Peatross found out Brown had killed the island commander, WO Kanemitsu. Sometime earlier, a message was intercepted from Kanemitsu to the 6th Base Force stating prophetically, "All men are dying serenely in battle."

No sooner had Brown killed the Japanese commander than the squad received a "heavy volume of machine gun fire," which cost the lives of three Raiders and several wounded before the gun was knocked out. "With the rest of us providing such supporting fire as we could, Castle [Cpl. Vernon] crawled and dragged himself on toward the enemy position, firing his Thompson submachine gun as he advanced," Peatross said. "With complete disregard for his own personal safety, ignoring wounds that proved to be mortal, and by almost superhuman effort, he struggled close enough to the enemy position to throw a hand grenade, killing the gunner and two of the crewmen. The rest of us shot two riflemen positioned near the gun." About an hour later, Peatross was amazed to see a small Japanese car tearing down the road. "As it roared past us at full throttle, we all fired . . . it ran off the road and turned over . . . riddled with bullet holes, both the driver and his passenger were dead." About 1500, the squad discovered an abandoned Chevrolet truck bearing USMC markings. Peatross thought it may have been one captured on Wake Island.

After trying unsuccessfully to link up with the main body, Peatross's group made their way back to the beach and prepared their rubber boat for the withdrawal in accordance with the battalion order. "We watched the surf for about fifteen minutes to get a feel for the timing of the waves," Peatross said, "looking for the fifth wave which is usually smaller than the rest . . . [and] dragged the boat across the beach and into the water. Wading and pushing until we reached the surf, we piled in one at a time, grabbed our paddles, and dug in for all we were worth. We motored through the last breaker and into the open sea without mishap." Shortly thereafter, they spotted the *Nautilus*' green signal light and pulled alongside to unload. "I enquired about the rest of our force and felt a pang of vague uneasiness when the commodore told me that my boat was the only one to have made it back so far."

Trouble in River City

Starting around 1030 and lasting off and on until 1700, three groups of Japanese aircraft bombed and strafed the island. The first group, two Type 94 Nakajima three-seat reconnaissance floatplanes, dropped two bombs and after about fifteen minutes flew away. A second flight of twelve aircraft—two Type 2 Kawanishi four-motor flying boats, four zero fighters, four Type 94 Nakajima biplanes, and two Navy Type 95 Nakajima reconnaissance seaplanes—bombed and strafed for over an hour, without causing any Raider casualties. "I was really glad when that plane got past me without hitting anything with his bullets when all of a sudden the lead was flying again," Carson said. "There was a machine gunner in the rear of the plane and he was getting his jollies blasting the hell out of the road as the plane pulled up." LeFrancois recalled, "They strafed and bombed us, dropping sticks of antipersonnel bombs, but they missed us entirely."

Suddenly, to the amazement of the Raiders, two of the aircraft landed in the lagoon off Stone Pier. "It was a sight for sore eyes," LeFrancois exclaimed. "A four-motored transport had started to land on the water, and some of our machine guns and anti-tank guns, as well as a few rifles, opened up on it. The tracers streamed across the water and hit squarely on the plane. It nosed up, caught fire, tipped to the left, and sank swiftly out of sight." One of the aircraft tried to take off. Sergeant Buck Stidham fired at it with his .55-caliber Boyes anti-tank gun. "I kept firing . . . and got off thirty to forty aimed shots before the plane approached takeoff speed." Several men reported seeing it crash. "I am quite sure I hit it several times and like to think I had a small part in crashing it," he said. Nimitz reported that the large seaplane was bringing reinforcements. The final air attack occurred about 1630 and lasted for thirty minutes.

Spiritual Low Point

Shortly after the last air raid, Carlson began shifting the Raiders back to the beach and was ready to embark in the boats at 1930. Carlson thought it was the best time because "darkness had set in and the tide was high, enabling the boats to get over the reef. However, the speed of the waves and the rapid succession in which they followed each other had not been taken into account." Platoon Sergeant Spotts recalled, "Huge waves broke about a hundred yards from the beach and kept coming in rapidly with a very short interval between them. We would paddle until we struck the point where the surf broke. From there it was just a matter of time before we ended up back at the beach again. In my boat, we tried to get off for about five hours . . . finally around midnight we gave up and decided to wait until morning when the tide changed."

Carlson noted his boat's experience, which seemed to reflect the average struggle. "We walked the boat out to deep water and commenced paddling. The motor refused to work. The first three or four rollers were easy to pass. Then came the battle. Paddling rhythmically and furiously for all we were worth we would get over one roller only to get hit and thrown back by the next before we could gain momentum. The boat filled to the gunwales. We bailed. We got out and swam while pulling the boat—to no avail. We jettisoned the motor. Subsequently the boat turned over. We righted it, less equipment, and continued the battle. All this time I thought ours was the only boat having this difficulty, for all the others had left ahead of us. However, after nearly an hour of struggle men swam up to our stern and reported that their boat had gone back because the men were exhausted . . . I directed our boat be turned around and returned to the beach for our men were equally exhausted."

Only four boats made it to the *Nautilus* and three to the *Argonaut*. Peatross met them on deck. "I could see the worn faces and exhausted bodies of the men with whom the trials of the day had played havoc . . . [L]ater arrivals looked like zombies. . . . [T]hey had lost everything: weapons, equipment, shoes, and clothing, and above all their sense of unity." About 120 men remained on the beach, disorganized and dispirited. Carlson noted, "Rain and the fact that most of the men had stripped themselves of their clothes in the surf added to the general misery. This was the spiritual low point of the expedition." More importantly, many of the men had lost their weapons and were now helpless if the Japanese attacked. Late that night, "One man [Pvt. Jess Hawkins] who was posted as security above the beach line was challenged by a Japanese patrol of eight men," Carlson reported. "He was seriously wounded but managed to kill three of [the] enemy." Spotts recalled, "We must have scored several hits for they squealed like stuck hogs and didn't bother us in this position again." The action caused Carlson to write, "This incident showed that enemy resistance was by no means ended." Carlson was convinced that a large number of the enemy was left and the surviving Raiders would be at the "tender" mercies of them come daylight.

Carlson called several of his officers together and discussed their predicament—lack of weapons, the almost complete absence of organizational unity, and the plight of the wounded, one of whom was the indomitable "Frenchie" LeFrancois. He decided that the only option was to surrender! The decision did not sit well with the men. Spotts noted in his diary, "The word started around here that we would surrender in the morning [and] this didn't set so very good with anyone . . . but there didn't appear to be any choice. Most of the weapons had been lost in our attempts at getting off." Another Marine remembered, " . . . [N]ot many of us accepted the surrender policy." And Ben Carson said it was " the most terrible message I have ever been given."

Carlson took Captain Coyte aside and ordered him to contact the Japanese commander and arrange for the surrender, but stipulated that only if they would be treated as prisoners of war. "At around 0330, Coyte and Pvt. William McCall . . . set out to the south on their quest for the garrison commander, dressed only in trousers and shoes and unarmed," Peatross recalled. The two stopped in a native hut and were attempting to find out where they might find the enemy commander when an armed Japanese soldier came in and confronted them. "He was most unhappy," Coyte explained, "He kept threatening to shoot me and was sticking the end of the rifle in my stomach. I was so tired and exhausted that it really didn't make much difference. I would push the rifle aside and . . . demand that he take me to his commanding officer."

Peatross noted that, "With the natives' help, Coyte and McCall eventually assuaged the Japanese soldier's injured pride and calmed his anger enough to win his reluctant agreement to carry a note to his commanding officer. It was nearly daylight when Coyte addressed himself to the task of composing the offer to surrender, as ordered by Carlson."

To the Commanding Officer,
Japanese forces, Makin Island

Dear Sir
I am a member of the American forces now on Makin.
  We have suffered severe casualties and wish to make an end of the bloodshed and bombings.
  We wish to surrender according to the rules of military law and be treated as prisoners of war. We would also like to bury our dead and care for our wounded.
  There are approximately sixty of us left. We have all voted to surrender.
  I would like to see you personally as soon as possible to prevent future bloodshed and bombing.
                    /S/ Ralph H. Coyte, Captain, USMCR

The note was passed to the enemy soldier who took it and left. Shortly afterward, Coyte heard a shot and went to investigate. Two Raiders were walking down the road, one holding a smoking pistol. The two proudly announced they had just knocked off a lone Jap. Coyte assumed it was it was the messenger and reported the incident and his inability to contact the Japanese commander to the battalion commander. McCall said, "Carlson told me not to say anything about it." Coyte recalled, " . . . [W]e [officers] had all prepared written reports of the operation as it pertained to our participation. After they had been submitted, they were returned to us by Colonel Carlson who advised us that Admiral Nimitz had told him that we should all re-write our report, deleting all reference to the offer to surrender."

Shortly after daylight another four boats managed to get through the surf after a terrific struggle but further evacuation was stopped by an air raid. Meanwhile, Raider patrols that scoured the island found that, except for a couple of snipers, the Japanese garrison was dead. They counted eighty-three enemy bodies and identified the remains of fourteen dead Raiders (five more bodies were discovered in 1999 when the Army's Central Identification Laboratory recovered all the remains from a common grave). When the patrols returned with the news and supplies of food, recovered Japanese weapons, and ammunition, morale improved and there was no further talk of surrender. That afternoon the men constructed a raft. "[It] was made up of three rubber boats tied together with a seaworthy native fishing boat on either end, the whole thing being lashed securely together," LeFrancois recalled. "The two good motors we had were on the end of the rubber boats. The oars of each native boat were manned by our strongest men. Our wounded occupied the center cross seats of the rubber boats." At 2030 the remaining Raiders shoved the ungainly craft into the water and set sail for the submarines standing by off the lagoon entrance. *Nautilus* reported, " . . . [R]eceived the remainder of the Raider unit on board at 2330. The commanding officer reported to the group commander that he was satisfied that all surviving personnel of his command had been evacuated from the island." The final entry in the *Nautilus* log book for 18 August 1942 read, "2353—headed for Pearl Harbor."

Upon arrival in Hawaii, they were greeted as heroes. "As we sailed up the entrance," Carson said, "Every ship of the line in Pearl Harbor was turned out with formations on deck as we sailed by. . . ." Dr. Stephen Stigler of 2nd Raider Battalion recalled, "It was one of the most thrilling parts of my life. Each ship that we passed gave us a salute. We must have heard the 'Marine Corps Hymn' ten times going through the channel." Admiral Nimitz and other high ranking officers were on hand and personally greeted each Raider. The Admiral's report noted, "Through the courage and endurance of the Marines and cool headed cooperation of submarine personnel, this expedition was successfully carried to completion against and by aid of various chances of fortune . . . considerable damage was inflicted on the Japanese, and at a crucial time in the Solomon Islands operations, they were forced to divert men, ships, and planes to the relief of Makin Island."

Nimitz's report also noted, "Losses were somewhat larger than they should have been. . . ." Unknown to Carlson at the time of the withdrawal, nine Raiders were left behind and captured when the Japanese returned to the island. The men were held on Makin until the end of August when they were transported to Kwajalein in the Marshall Islands. On 16 October, Vice Adm. Koso Abe, the commander of the Marshall Islands ordered the Raiders beheaded. After the war, Abe was found guilty of the crime and hanged as a war criminal.

CHAPTER 8

Edson's Ridge

Petty Officer Second Class Sankichi Kaneda, 81st Guard Unit, was having a bad day. He had barely escaped a Marine attack near the village of Matanikau, when he was summoned to the headquarters of the Guadalcanal Defense Unit headquarters, located in the jungle a half mile southwest of Point Cruz. There he was ordered to guide Col. Akinosuka Oka's 124th Infantry Regiment through dense, almost impenetrable jungle to recapture the airstrip on Lunga plain. They started on 9 September. "The [124th Infantry] unit promptly moved out with two of us in the advanced guard," Kaneda wrote in a diary. "It was pitch black and we moved at a crawl . . . I followed my compass east, pushing and cutting a path. . . . [T]he men could not smoke. . . . [We ate] hardtack. . . . [W]e were tired and we slept like the dead. . . . [W]e finally reached our goal and Colonel Oka gave the order to attack."

Mukade Gata (Centipede Hill)

The Japanese objective was a ridge they called *Mukade Gata* (Centipede Hill) because of its centipede-like shape. It was about a mile south of Henderson field, the Marine airfield and the ultimate prize of the Japanese attack. The ridge not only dominated the surrounding terrain but, more importantly, offered a well-defined avenue of approach to

LIEUTENANT COLONEL MERRITT A. EDSON

Merritt A. Edson's formal military service began in 1915 when he enlisted in the National Guard and served in the Mexican border campaign. After receiving a commission in the Marine Corps in 1917, he was assigned to the 11th Marines in France but arrived too late to see action. Following the end of the war, he served in a variety of posts and stations that qualified him for ever-increasing responsible assignments—among them was service in Nicaragua, where he received the Navy Cross for combat actions against the Sandino-led bandits. During his fourteen months ashore, most of it deep in the interior of the country, he won a reputation as an aggressive, savvy small-unit leader and came away with the nickname "Red Mike" because of his red beard. In 1921 he began a long career in competitive shooting, first as a firing member, then team coach, and finally captain of the Marine Corps national rifle and pistol team. In 1922, he earned his pilot's wings and flew for five years before poor depth perception forced him back into the infantry. In the summer of 1937 he became the operations officer for the 4th Marines in Shanghai, China. The assignment gave

the airfield. Colonel Merrill B. Twinning, division assistant operations officer, said a Japanese approach from that direction would place them, "opposite the weakly defended and highly vulnerable southern approach to the airfield, which was where an attack would be most dangerous to us."

In *Bloody Ridge: The Battle that Saved Guadalcanal*, Michael S. Smith described the ridge as " . . . slender, winding, and grass-covered, with three distinct hillocks—one on both ends and one in the middle—appropriately called Hill 123—was the highest." A second slightly lower height, Hill 80, was located about five hundred yards directly south. A narrow dirt trail ran from Hill 80 along the entire length of the ridge. The trail served as a point of contact for adjacent units and a convenient marker for anyone who became disoriented in the dark or heat of battle. An impassible stagnant lagoon—sixty feet wide and several hundred yards long—was located about two hundred yards west of Hill him an opportunity to observe Japanese combat techniques at close range. In June 1941, he assumed command of the 1st Battalion, 5th Marines. On 16 February 1942, Edson's battalion was redesignated 1st Marine Raider Battalion.

Major Griffith probably knew Edson as well as anyone and described him as someone who "required an awful lot of knowing; he was a quiet, reserved man . . . not by any means a great talker . . . in many ways, a pretty cold man. However, he enjoyed social life in what I'd call a restricted sense of the word . . . he loved to play bridge . . . and liked to drink with the boys but never drinking too much." Griffith never really got to know Edson until Guadalcanal. "He was a great stickler for performance of duty. He insisted that everyone give his best, and Lord knows, Edson always gave his best. He was completely unflappable and admired and respected by everyone." Griffith said he was extremely popular with his men because "he recognized merit and rewarded it." Lieutenant Colonel Jon Hoffman, his biographer, wrote, "His absolute fearlessness in action would steady his hard-pressed men in the face of Japanese onslaughts and give the Marines one of the most important victories in their history."

80. "The lagoon would hamper movement and break the continuity of any defensive disposition in the area," according to Smith. Dense jungle, in some places almost impenetrable, bordered the ridge on all sides.

At the same time Colonel Oka's men started their trek through Guadalcanal's trackless jungle, the ridge was virtually defenseless. The understrength 1st Marine Division was oriented toward the coast. Major General Alexander A. Vandegrift, its commander, was convinced that the Japanese would not attempt a jungle march but would instead move along the more passable coastal route. He was unwilling to refocus the division's orientation, despite the recommendations of Colonel Twinning and his assistant Col. Gerald "Jerry" Thomas, even though the two were in possession of captured maps and documents that offered proof the Japanese intended to approach through the jungle. Captain Sherwood "Pappy" Moran, the division's senior Japanese linguist, had translated the documents and was convinced they were genuine. His opinion was shared by Edson, who had reconnoitered the ridge. "This is the place," he told his runner, Cpl. Walter Burak. "This is the place they'll hit." Major Samuel B. Griffith II, his executive officer, recalled, "I remembered distinctly that we were in the operations' tent, when Edson pointed to where he thought the Japanese were going to come in—and that was the ridge."

Fortunately the return of the 1st Marine Raider Battalion and the 1st Parachute Battalion from Tulagi and Gavutu-Tanambogo offered a viable compromise. "Jerry [Thomas] . . . scored a limited concession," Twinning recalled. "The Raider and Parachute battalions . . . could be sent to a 'rest area' south of the field, where their mere presence would discourage snipers or other minor enemy activity. To this the general agreed, and that is how the ridge acquired its sardonic second name— 'Edson's Rest Area.'" Edson briefed his staff and company commanders on the move but decided to keep the bad news to himself. He told them that, "We're moving our bivouac up to the ridge. It'll be a rest area for us. We'll get out of the V-ring for the Jap bombers." He would later have to eat those words.

The Raiders were in need of a rest according to Griffith. "I would say the battalion was in pretty poor physical shape. It had been really pretty rough on Tulagi, because everybody had dysentery, we had a lot of sleepless nights [and] there had been quite a bit of shelling . . . [T]he Japanese were able in those early days to coast right down in broad daylight and shell the hell out of everybody." The attached casualty-riddled 1st Parachute Battalion was in the same condition after their hard-won Gavutu-Tanambogo victory—exhausted, sickly and malnourished. Several of the officers in both units were on the casualty rosters or sick in the hospital. Lieutenant Colonel Jon T. Hoffman wrote in *Once a Legend: "Red Mike" Edson of the Marine Raiders*, "Many other leadership slots, particularly at the platoon and squad level, also were filled by men fleeting up from lower positions."

On the morning of 10 September 1942, the combined Raider-Parachute force—approximately 800 men, 214 Paratroopers and 600 Raiders—formed up by company in a long column and started the march to the ridge. The men carried everything they owned, including weapons and ammunition—on Guadalcanal, the infantry traveled by "shanks mare" because much of the division's motor transport had been left in Australia. The 80-plus degree temperature and oppressive humidity quickly sapped the men's strength, causing many of the weakened men to drop out. The column trudged on, across the flat open area of the runway toward the distant hilltop. Edson hurried the column along; he knew the first Japanese air raid of the day was due sometime around 1100 and they were right on schedule; the bombers appeared, escorted by fifteen Mitsubishi A6M "Zero" fighters. Edson's men got a ringside seat as four VMF-223 Grumman F4F Wildcats intercepted the formation. The Marine fighters were able to shoot down five of the enemy planes but not before the bombers dropped their ordnance. Fortunately the Raider-Paratrooper column was not their target. Not long after, "Condition Red" announced a second air raid forcing the column to seek cover. The two air raids and the physical condition of the men delayed their arrival on the ridge until mid-afternoon.

Organizing the Killing Ground: 10 September 1942

The men were not allowed to relax. "Edson deployed them as they came up," Griffith explained, "Raiders around the southern knob, the right flank company thinly spread toward the Lunga [River]; Parachutists . . . on the left." The high ground was the key to the defense of the southern sector of the perimeter—and the topography of the ridge left Edson with little choice in the deployment of his joint force. He had to hold the high ground, forcing him to leave his left flank hanging. He simply did not have enough men to extend his lines into the jungle. It was a risky decision; the Japanese could simply outflank his lines. Edson did the best he could with the men available but his men were spread dangerously thin. Corporal Daniel Mulcare's under-strength squad had to cover the entire face of Hill 80. He grumbled that, "You could put a whole platoon between each squad member and still not cover the ridge. We need a whole regiment to defend this area."

Edson placed his three strongest companies on the line—Capt. Justin Duryea's Baker Company Parachutists and two Raider companies, Capt.

John B. Sweeney, (replacing Capt. Louis Monville) assumed command of Baker Company on the thirteenth and Maj. Ken Bailey's Charlie Company, in that order—extending from the jungle on the left flank to the Lunga River on the right flank. Charlie Company, numbering 130 fighters, had one platoon in position on the edge of a swampy lagoon and the other two split into platoon strong points, each of which had an exposed flank. The men had worn a path through the vegetation connecting the outposts. It crossed the lagoon via a slippery fallen log, through Baker Company's wire, up Hill 80 to intersect the ridge trail. Private First Class John W. Mielke worried about it. "We crossed the lagoon on a fallen tree . . . which appeared to be our only exit other than . . . along the river." A single strand of barbed wire ran along the company's eight hundred yard front. The men had laboriously cut fields of fire through the waist-high grass with their bayonets. Its well-liked company commander, Ken Bailey, had just returned from the hospital, where he had been treated for a gunshot wound in the leg he received on Tulagi.

Baker Company (Raider) tied its left flank in with Baker Company (Parachute) on the ridge trail, while its right flank abutted the lagoon. Waist-high kunai grass covered the ground all along its front except for the extreme right flank platoon, whose front extended into the jungle. Nickerson had his men chop down the kunai grass as far as they could to clear fields of fire. The company was able to "beg, borrow or steal" enough wire to construct a double apron fence across most of its front. This was a line of pickets with barbed wire running diagonally down to the ground on either side of the fence. Horizontal barbed wire was attached to the diagonals. The platoon in the jungle could not use the fence, so it looped barbed wire from tree to tree. The ninety-man Baker Company (Parachute) occupied the left third of the line. Its position extended from the ridge trail where it tied in with the Raiders, northeast along a spur of the ridge, then several hundred yards on into the jungle. Its left flank was in the air. There was nothing to the east except empty jungle, which Edson attempted to cover with reconnaissance patrols.

Edson reinforced each of the two Raider companies with four .30-caliber Browning M1919 A4 light machine guns from the weapons company. The extra firepower would prove crucial in the battle. To cover a 1,500 yard front, the three companies could muster only 350 men, too few to effectively stop a massed attack. To provide a defense in depth, Edson echeloned the Parachutists of Capt. Dick Johnson's Charlie Company and Capt. William McKennan's Able Company behind their sister company on the left side of the line. Captain William E. Sperling's understrength Dog Company (Raider) was on the right side of the line and Capt. John A. Antonelli, who replaced the hospitalized Maj. Lew Walt, commanded Able Company (Raider).

Edson's headquarters—battalion aid station, communications and battalion reserve (Headquarters Company and Easy Company, minus its machine gun platoons)—was located in a draw on the western slope of Hill 123, which placed it several hundred yards behind the front lines. "It had no overhead cover, wire, or sandbags. A few telephone lines ran out to his front-line units and another snaked its way back to division head-quarters, less than a thousand yards to the read," George W. Smith wrote in *The Do-Or-Die Men: The 1st Marine Raider Battalion at Guadalcanal*. The 60mm mortar platoon was located about a hundred yards behind Able Company. Edson and a handful of his command group established a forward command post on the crest of Hill 123, where he could better observe and control the battle. The Parachute battalion set up a command post in a draw on the east side of Hill 123. General Vandegrift ordered artillery additional support. "Colonel del Valle moved his 3rd Battalion [11th Marines] with its twelve 105mm howitzer tubes closer to the ridge in direct support," Captain Sweeney said.

The men were ordered to dig in, which was easier said than done. kunai grass, roots, and coral rock, just below the surface of the ground, proved frustrating for men who had only small "T-handle" shovels to dig with. Colonel Joe Alexander noted in *Edson's Raiders, The 1st Marine Raider Battalion in World War II* that "Tiger Erskine, lacking even an e-tool [shovel], spent much of the day scraping a hole with his helmet and a borrowed bayonet. By twilight his hole measured ten inches deep. Able Company's Pfc. Henry Neal gave up in frustration. 'I announced I wasn't digging any more. Just then Sgt. Tom Pollard came by, reached down, jerked me about a foot off the deck, said one word—"DIG!" I dug.' As one Raider sweated in the boiling sun, he exclaimed, 'Rest area, my ass!' "

The men were spurred on by their officers. A report circulated that a large enemy force was approaching. Coastwatcher Martin Clemens wrote in *Alone on Guadalcanal: A Coastwatcher's Story*, "My scouts had reported that an enemy force of five thousand men was moving through the jungle . . . in an arch that would leave it in a commanding position in the hills south of the airfield."

The onset of darkness forced the men to stop working. They had made good progress, but much remained to be done before the defenses were strong enough to repel the expected attack. In the meantime, the men settled in for the night—the watch set all along the line, communication checks performed, ammunition and grenades laid out for immediate use—and the listening posts manned. These lonely three or four man outposts were positioned in front of the lines at night to detect enemy movement. It was not a job for the faint of heart—where every noise, every shadow, every foreign smell might be a lurking Japanese infiltrator. Platoon Sergeant Frank Guidone recalled, "Hot chow was served the first evening and we settled in for a relatively quiet night." The only interruption was the regular nightly Tokyo Express bombardment of the airfield.

As Edson's combined Raider-Parachute force dug in, Maj. Gen. Kiyotake Kawaguchi's two thousand-man assault force was struggling toward them through the jungle. "General Kawaguchi had his overworked 6th Independent Shipping Engineer Regiment cut, with machetes and swords, a sodden jungle trail that ran from Kawaguchi's rear assembly point to the outskirts of the ridge, a path well concealed by the thick tropical growth," Stanley Coleman Jersey wrote. "The muddy, narrow course permitted the men to move only single file, and the march through dense jungle in 110-degree inland heat and no breeze taxed the already exhausted troops." Three infantry battalions comprised the heart of Kawaguchi's force—Maj. Yukichi Kokusho's 1st Battalion, 124th Infantry Regiment; Lt. Col. Kusukichi Watanabe's 3rd Battalion, 124th Infantry Regiment; and Maj. Masao Tamura's 2nd Battalion, 4th Infantry Regiment—a total of approximately 2,500 men, including attached units and several light artillery pieces: 37mm and 75mm.

Kawaguchi's difficult trek through the jungle was complicated by a lack of a good map. The one that he was using did not show the interior of the island and he was forced to rely on a compass, which proved to be extremely difficult in the jungle. His command wasted hours and energy wandering aimlessly through the thick forest before they arrived at their attack position.

11 September 1942

At first light the men were up and working. Guidone recalled, " . . . [O]ur own officers and NCOs [were] constantly pushing us in the laying of barbed wire, digging foxholes, building machine gun emplacements, and cutting fire lanes." Everyone sensed that something big was about to happen. "It was evident from some of the things that we saw going on, [like] artillery forward observers from the 11th Marines looking for observation post locations and plotting likely target areas, staff officers from division headquarters checking out the situation, and observation planes circling over the jungle and ridge lines [that] enemy activity was suspected." Major Griffith noted that, "The division artillery commander, Col. Pedro A. del Valle decided he would take a stroll . . . to the ridge, along with the regimental mapping section." They gathered data for the artillery fire direction center and, " . . . sweated through a long night gridding maps and drawing up fire plans."

Edson tagged Able Company (Raider) to conduct a combat patrol south of the ridge. It got into a firefight not far from the nose of the ridge almost immediately. "We moved out in column on a trail to Charlie Company's front line position, passing through its still under-construction barbed wire and on into the unknown jungle. Our forward progress was slow and cautious," Guidone explained. "Shortly before noon the point halted when the sound of Jap voices was heard along with noises from the chopping of underbrush. As Buntin [Joe, platoon sergeant] and his scouts were sizing up the situation they were taken under fire and a lively firefight quickly developed. . . ." Before the patrol could break contact, the noontime bombing raid arrived. "Suddenly

in the distance we heard the drone of aircraft at high altitude . . .
The enemy formation now appeared to be almost overhead from our
position," Guidone said. "That's when the WHAM, WHAM of the first
bombs could be heard directly ahead of us. As the bombs continued
exploding they walked right up to our location and continued on toward
our battalion positions on the ridge . . . Luckily, no one in the patrol
was injured. What was good about this raid was that the Japanese
ahead of us also got bombed and broke off the firefight." The sudden
devastating air attack left two Marines dead, seven wounded, and the
bivouac area shattered . . . proof positive that the Japanese were coming.
The night passed slowly, broken only by the whispered challenges of
nervous sentries.

12 September 1942

An unknown soldier in Kawaguchi's force wrote in his diary, "By marching
day and night, crossing many steep mountains we neared the enemy
position." First Lieutenant Shotaro Maruo noted, "By the twelfth, we had
marched five kilometers during the morning and were four kilometers
from the enemy lines. At 1430, we reached a point near the position where
preparations for the attack were being made. Second Lieutenant Kobayashi
and four men left on a scouting patrol of the enemy lines. Major Kokusho
assembled all the company commanders with our attack orders."

Kawaguchi had prepared a message to inspire his soldiers before the
attack. "It's the time to offer your life for His Majesty the Emperor.
The flower of Japanese infantrymen is in the bayonet-charge. This is what
the enemy soldiers are most afraid of. The strong point of the enemy is
superiority of firepower. But it will be able to do nothing in the night
and in the jungle. When all-out-attack begins, break through the enemy's
defenses without delay. Recapture our bitterest airfield. Rout, stab, kill,
and exterminate the enemy before daybreak. We are sure of ultimate
victory of the Imperial Army!"

Again, as on the previous day, the ridge swarmed with Marine activity
at first light. Working parties continued to work on clearing fire lanes,
cutting brush and stringing more barbed wire entanglements. The men
knew the wire would not stop the Japanese but it might slow them down

long enough for their rifles and machine guns to kill them. Sometime around noon, "Condition Red" sounded, as a large force of Rabaul-based bombers with their fighter escort paid the ridge a return visit. VMF-223, VMF-224, and VF-5 intercepted the formation and shot down sixteen. However, the Japanese still managed to hit the ridge, causing several Marine casualties. "Repeatedly, well-placed sticks walked along the ridge," Major Griffith wrote. "Quarter-ton high-explosive bombs shattered the bordering jungle; 250-pound 'daisy cutters' stripped clinging vegetation off trees and mowed down-six foot kunai grass." An errant bomb "dropped in the midst of the 1st Company, 124th Infantry, killing one and wounding four," Lieutenant Maruo noted. Private First Class Joe Rushton recalled, "As the long afternoon was drawing to a close it became apparent to even the dim-witted that we were in for big trouble . . ."

Edson called a meeting of his company commanders and staff just before dark to discuss plans for a preemptive attack the next day. He thought it might throw the Japanese off-balance and gain time to strengthen his defenses. Edson planned on leaving only a skeleton force on the ridge and taking everyone else to hit the Japanese, wherever they could be found. The meeting broke up a little after 2130, just as "Louie the Louse" (a cruiser float plane that harassed the Marines) dropped a green flare, the signal for the IJN light cruiser *Sendai* and destroyers *Shikinami, Fubuki,* and *Suzukaze* to bombard the ridge. The shelling was unnerving. "Suddenly," Raider Irv Reynolds recalled, "I heard a noise like a runaway freight train and at the same time saw a bright blue light illuminating the hills to our front." The noise was one of five high explosive shells that hit Edson's command post. Only one exploded but there were no casualties. The blue light was from the cruiser's search light. "It was so bright," Captain Sweeney said, "that I knew the ship's skipper could see me moving on the ridge. I felt naked!" The shelling went on for twenty minutes. Fortunately for the men on the ridge, most of the shells were "overs" that exploded harmlessly in the jungle.

Kawaguchi's units were having a devil of a time moving to their attack positions. A unit report noted, "The battalions . . . lost their sense of direction, almost entirely missed the ridge, and instead drifted into the low, waterlogged swath of jungle between the ridge and the Lunga. Units became lost; lost units became scattered; scattered units became intermingled. Control slipped away from Kawaguchi and his battalion commanders." After the war Kawaguchi said, " . . . [D]ue to the devilish jungle, the forces of the Brigade were scattered all over and was completely beyond control. In my whole life, I have never felt so disappointed and helpless." Despite the confusion and lack of control, "[t]he soldiers advanced toward their objective," a translated diary noted.

Private First Class Robert Youngdeer, a machine gunner on Charlie Company's right flank recalled, "When the enemy shelling stopped [naval bombardment], I distinctly heard splashing in the river, the sound of many people wading and coming in our direction." The lead elements of Major Kokusho's 1st Battalion, 124th Infantry, were working their way around the company's flank. One Japanese soldier wrote, " . . . [A] long file of men straggled out of the bush and formed squads and then platoons. Finally the attack began." Enemy flares rose from the jungle in front of Baker and Charlie Companies (Raiders) and a horde of Japanese burst out of the brush firing rifles and throwing grenades. "The Japanese thought they had found a trail, and they followed it virtually to the muzzle of [Warren Morse's machine] gun," Private First Class Mielke said. "He began firing incessantly. There were cries of pain." The Japanese attacked along both sides of the lagoon and across the Lunga River. Charlie Company's right flank platoon was overrun. Several Raiders were cut off. "I heard someone getting beat up on the left," Youngdeer recalled, "I can still hear the screams. He was begging for mercy." The others were able to make their way to safety by hugging the stream bank and using the overhanging growth as concealment.

The word spread quickly, "Don't be captured, the Japs will torture and kill you." Colonel Alexander wrote, "The Japanese captured one or two Raiders alive, interrogated them, then tortured them brutally with their blades. The screams of their dying comrades that night haunted the Marines crouched in their holes along the ridge, waiting for the storm to break against their sector." Private First Class Thomas D. "T. D." Smith said glumly, "All night we could hear a Marine evidently being tortured out front." Another Raider recalled, "We can hear our buddies in the swamps along the line towards the river. It seems as if a few have been overcome and they must be being tortured by the Japs." A Marine found a Japanese officer's diary which translated: "26 September—discovered and captured two prisoners who escaped last night in the jungle. . . . To prevent their escaping a second time, pistols were fired at their feet. . . . The two prisoners were dissected while still alive by Medical Officer Yamaji and their livers were taken out, and for the first time I saw the internal organs of a human being. It was very informative."

A second machine gun position on the right flank was overrun. "We withdrew with them hot after us," Pfc. Charles Everett said. "We tried to carry the gun [30-pound Browning M1919A light machine gun] but that was impossible so we left it and took off." Everett got separated from his team and was wounded after grenading a Japanese machine gun crew. "My left hand was hit, it sailed away like I'd thrown it . . . they fired another burst and hit both my legs pretty bad." He collapsed, unable to walk, but managed to drag himself into the heavy brush to hide. "I couldn't move my legs," he recalled. "I was bleeding awful, and my shoes were filled with blood." He was all alone in the melee of shot and shell, except for infiltrators who were intent on killing all the Raiders.

The 1st Battalion, 124th Infantry hit Lt. John "Black Jack" Salmon's left flank platoon, scattering it and overrunning his position. Sometime around midnight Salmon and a handful of survivors managed to ford the lagoon by walking over the fallen log. His friend Captain Sweeney was surprised to see him leading several men through an opening in Baker Company's barbed wire fence. Salmon was "visibly shaken, in bad shape, and deeply concerned about several of his men who had been cut off during the withdrawal," Sweeney recalled. Baker Company bent its flank back in an effort to stop the penetration.

Charlie Company's 2nd Platoon manned the center of the line. The Japanese knocked out the two flanking machine gun positions but not before the gun on the right got into action. "[Martin] 'Jeeper' Heitz's

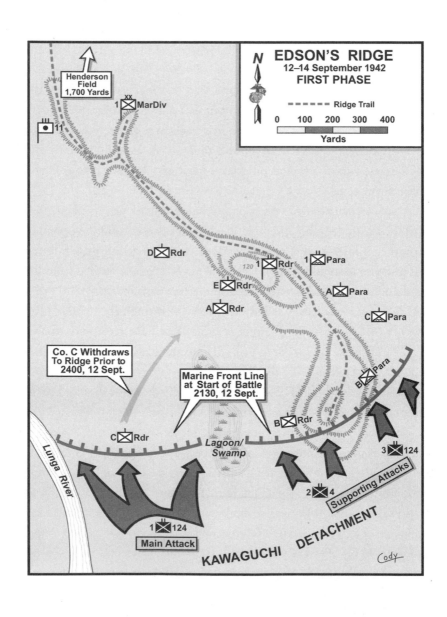

Henderson
Field
1,700 Yards

1 ⊠ MarDiv

⊡ 11

N **EDSON'S RIDGE**
12–14 September 1942
FIRST PHASE

---- Ridge Trail

0   100 200 300 400

Yards

D ⊠ Rdr

120 1 ⊠ Rdr   1 ⊠ Para

E ⊠ Rdr   A ⊠ Para

A ⊠ Rdr   C ⊠ Para

Co. C Withdraws
To Ridge Prior to
2400, 12 Sept.

Marine Front Line
at Start of Battle
2130, 12 Sept.

B ⊠ Para

C ⊠ Rdr   Lagoon/
             Swamp   B ⊠ Rdr   80

Lunga River   3 ⊠ 124

                              2 ⊠ 4   Supporting Attacks

1 ⊠ 124

Main Attack   KAWAGUCHI DETACHMENT

Cody

machine gun crew opened up on them with one hell of a blast which set them screaming and moaning," Raider Joseph Rushton remembered. "Then they started coming in all directions—shouting and yelling—and overran Jeeper's gun." The platoon was forced to give ground. "Shortly," Rushton said, "word came to move out and go back across the log. This was very difficult because of the extreme darkness [rainy, pitch black, no moon] and heavy vegetation. . . . [W]e had to carefully find the comm [communication] wire and follow it along on our hands and knees." Charlie Company's lines were shattered. The survivors were forced to pull back under heavy enemy pressure. The Japanese seemed to be gaining the upper hand—but in truth they were a leaderless mob, for many of their officers and NCOs were early casualties. Without leaders, the disorganized Japanese failed to follow up on their success.

Major Griffith noted, "I was shown a captured map . . . which showed the Japanese plan of attack. . . . It was a three-pronged attack. General Kawaguchi had expected to attack, to deliver his major attack . . . on the 11th, but one of his battalions was not even up yet, it was lost, just hadn't even showed." Griffith said that Kawaguchi "was very, very upset about this. Now if he had, nobody would have been there. He could have walked right in, and there would have been terrible fighting around the airport." As a result, only one battalion attacked on Charlie Company's relatively narrow front. The adjacent Baker Company (Raider) did not see any action. "Although the night of the 12 September was a tense and sleepless one, not a shot was fired in our sector," Captain Sweeney recalled. "It was an eerie and exhausting experience—each man in his foxhole fully expecting to see Japanese soldiers charging out of the jungle to his front at any moment."

13 September 1942

A very somber Edson gathered his officers the next morning. "They'll be back," he said, "But maybe not as many of them." Colonel Alexander wrote, "He [Edson] thought about that for a moment, then shrugged, 'Or maybe more. I want all positions improved, all wire lines paralleled, a hot meal for the men. Today, dig, wire up tight, get some sleep. We'll all need it.' He looked in the faces of each of his company commanders. 'The Nips will be back. I want to surprise them.'"

Kawaguchi lamented that the night's engagement was "a tragedy . . . a miserable failure." He vowed to renew the fight. "On the morning of the thirteenth to the officers of each battalion I sent the order, 'The Brigade will again execute a night attack tonight. The duty of each battalion is same as before.'"

Private First Class Everett, although weak from loss of blood, had survived the night hiding in the brush. "I put on a tourniquet and tried to call for help." At dawn, Pfcs. Robert S. Youngdeer and John D. Simonich went searching for missing Raiders. They heard a weak voice call for help, "Anyone from 'C' Company out there?"

 "We could see a body on the ground lying still," Youngdeer said. "He was dressed in Marine garb and from all appearances was one of us . . . He had removed his belt and used it to wrap around both legs to immobilize them and help cut down the bleeding." Unfortunately, without realizing it, he had been very close to a Japanese machine gun position the entire time. The noise attracted enemy fire and the men were forced to try and drag Everett on a blanket. "Three of us, in a prone position, dragging a limp body, while he groaned and moaned, was no easy task."

The shots attracted two other Marines, John W. Mielke and Leslie R. "Bear" Frink. As they ran to help, Frink pushed through the brush and ran head on into a bayonet-toting Japanese, who stabbed him in the chest. A sniper in a tree then shot Simonich in the leg and as Youngdeer rose to shoot, he was struck by a .25-caliber bullet. The round hit him in the left side of the face and exited under his right ear. He momentarily blacked out. Coming to, he took cover. "My teeth were shattered, my tongue was creased, I could not speak distinctly," he recounted. Mielke took over behind a fallen tree that overlooked the machine gun position. "Their attention was in the direction of the shooting," he explained, "and I had a clear shot at the machine gunner and another man nearest me." In the next few minutes, Mielke expended every round in his cartridge, killing at least six Japanese and saving the wounded men.

Unfortunately Everett's travails were not over. Colonel Joe Alexander wrote, "Everett was too exposed to be rescued—a sad fact which depressed

Youngdeer for four decades—nor could they evacuate Bear Frink's body ... Charlie Everett knew he had been abandoned and understood why, but his spirits sagged. At one point he considered shooting himself—anything to keep the Japanese from capturing him alive. By a small miracle, a Raider patrol eventually found him, barely alive, and carried him out on a blanket." Everett survived and returned home.

Kawaguchi's attack on the twelfth had "alerted the whole division," Major Griffith emphasized. "A battalion of the 5th Marines [2nd Battalion] was moved up behind us, and then the artillery was registered that afternoon, the air was alerted, everything was set for a big attack." Colonel del Valle shifted a four-gun 105mm howitzer battery to a new position that could provide better support. Two artillery observers were sent forward with direct communication with the artillery fire direction center. The stress of combat, coupled with little if any sleep, was bearing heavily on the men. "I went to Edson's command post at mid-afternoon to assess the situation," Colonel Twinning said, "The constant enemy pressure was taking a toll on the hard-pressed Raiders [and Parachutists]. Edson seemed terribly fatigued, but he was in far better shape than anyone else up there. . . . [He] commanded a group of exhausted men. . . ."

Edson decided that something had to be done about the Japanese salient in his lines. The Japanese had dug in and fortified the ground they had seized from Charlie Company. If the lines could not be restored, Edson would be forced to pull back to the more defensible terrain on the slopes of Hill 120. Edson ordered Captain Antonelli to take the combined Able and Dog Companies to regain the lost ground. Antonelli's force moved into the jungle along a dry stream bed. As they neared the front-line positions that had been overrun "we formed a skirmish line with two platoons on line and a platoon in support," Platoon Sergeant Guidone recalled. "As we moved slowly into the jungle, loud, shrill Japanese voices broke the stillness. . . ." The skirmish line froze, holding their breath. It sounded like commands, as if the Japanese officers or NCO were placing their men into position. "I was on line with my squad, trying to stay on line with the squads on our flanks, but the thickness of the jungle made this difficult. We moved forward slowly, since we only had about thirty feet of visibility ahead of us. It was difficult to maintain silence because we were constantly brushing aside long stems and branches. . . . The Japanese were now quiet."

The formation advanced cautiously—tense, expecting any moment to get hit. Suddenly automatic weapons fire erupted from the jungle foliage. "We could actually see the jungle foliage just above our position being moved by the Japanese bullets." The Raiders took cover. "Their initial fire was ineffectual," Guidone said. "We returned fire with our Springfields and BARs [but] there were no targets, we were only firing in the direction of the Japanese positions. We could not move to any upright position or we would have been cut down quickly. I remember off to my left someone tossed a grenade toward the Japanese positions. Suddenly we saw a tail of smoke heading toward us. It was our grenade coming back. We rolled around for cover and fortunately when it exploded no one was hurt. There was sporadic shooting and some more Japanese commands." It was a stalemate. The Raiders did not have enough men to retake the position and the Japanese were satisfied to hold what they had. Captain Antonelli ordered a withdraw.

Edson was forced to reposition his units. "To avoid an exposed right flank, we withdrew our forward elements to the battalion reserve line of the twelfth," Edson explained in a postwar interview. "This actually extended our lines at least five hundred yards, a gap partially filled by Company D, 1st Division Engineers. [I] ordered this realignment about 1500 on the thirteenth when it became definitely apparent we could not regain the position held the night before." Major Griffith thought the positioning, "greatly improved fields of fire for automatic weapons and imposed upon the attacker a trip of about a hundred yards from the jungle's edge before he could physically contact the battle positions. In traversing this open space they could be brought under killing grazing fire."

The realignment positioned the Marine force several hundred yards to the rear with Baker Company (Parachute) tied in with Baker (Raider), Charlie Company (Parachute), and Able Company (Parachute) protecting the exposed left flank. Baker Company (Raider) tied in on the forward slope of Hill 123 with Dog Company (Engineer) on its right. Able Company (Raider) extended from the engineer's position to the Lunga River with the 1st Pioneer Battalion positioned behind them.

Major Griffith was placed in command of the right wing. "I had this little task group, and I was defending a position to the south of the ridge. The Japanese harassed us that night . . . but they didn't cause us any trouble."

Baker Company's Captain Sweeney received a surprise. The company commander and executive officer were evacuated. "As of now," Edson told him, "you're now the B Company commander." At the time, "I had no officers," Sweeney said, "they were all gone, but the NCOs were all strong. At the time I was too tired to realize the situation I was handed, but as the sun was going down, I realized more and more what was given to me." Edson returned just after dark. "John," he told me, "this is it. We are the only ones between the Japs and the airfield. You must hold this position." Night fell. "All was quiet except for the movement of small animals," 1st Platoon's Pfc. Edward Shepherd recalled. "Then we could hear the Japs cautiously advancing. They reached the far edge of the lagoon. The word was passed to hold our fire until they started crossing." Corporal Joe Sweeda in the 2nd Platoon said, "It seemed like only minutes when darkness fell and the jungle seemed to come alive in front of us. We could hear jabbering, then movement in the brush."

Three veteran companies of Major Tamura's 2nd Battalion, 4th Infantry, and Major Kokusho's 1st Battalion, 124th Infantry were crawling through the waist-high kunai grass trying to get as close to the Raider line as possible before starting their attack. Infantrymen from 1st Lt. Yoshimi Onodera's 5th Company, 1st Lt. Tetsuji Isibashi's 7th Company, and 1st Lt.. Kenji Matsumoto's 3rd Company—over four hundred men—were determined to crack the Raider line.

Privates First Class Edgar Shepherd and Frank R. Whittelsey were crouched in a shallow foxhole just off a faint trail leading south along the western edge of the lagoon. The two waited as long as they dared and then Shepherd lobbed a grenade. It was a dud. Just then, First Lieutenant Matsumoto's men opened fire at pointblank range, badly wounding Shepherd in the chest and arms. The Japanese surged forward shouting "*banzai*!" and "*totsugeki*!" (Attack!); some even chanted "Marine, you die!" and "Blood for the Emperor!" Corporal Ira Gilliand of 1st Raider Batallion recalled the terrifying sound. "The Japanese screamed a lot," he

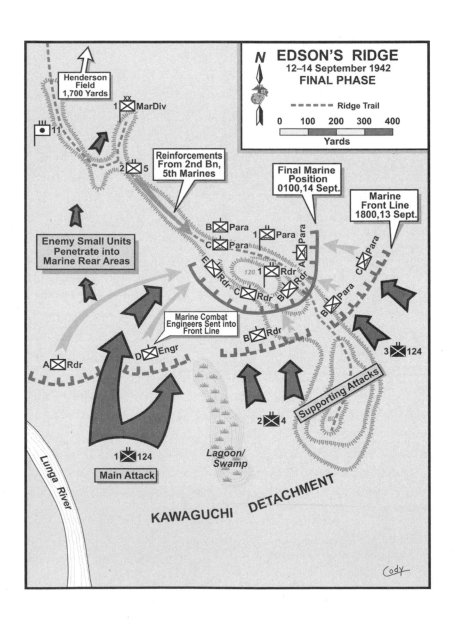

EDSON'S RIDGE
12–14 September 1942
FINAL PHASE

N

- - - - - Ridge Trail

0   100   200   300   400
Yards

Henderson
Field
1,700 Yards

1 ⊠ MarDiv

⊟ 11

2 ⊠ 5

Reinforcements
From 2nd Bn,
5th Marines

Final Marine
Position
0100,14 Sept.

Marine
Front Line
1800,13 Sept.

Enemy Small Units
Penetrate into
Marine Rear Areas

B ⊠ Para

C ⊠ Para

1 ⊠ Para

A ⊠ Para

E ⊠ Rdr

120

1 ⊠ Rdr

A ⊠ Rdr

C ⊠ Rdr

B ⊠ Rdr

B ⊠ Para

C ⊠ Para

Marine Combat
Engineers Sent into
Front Line

A ⊠ Rdr

D ⊠ Engr

B ⊠ Rdr

3 ⊠ 124

Supporting Attacks

2 ⊠ 4

80

1 ⊠ 124

Main Attack

Lagoon/
Swamp

Lunga River

KAWAGUCHI   DETACHMENT

Cody

recalled, "especially when they were charging. It made you alert in a hurry even after being up for two days and you're ready to fall asleep."

Private First Class Whittelsey was able drag Shepherd into the brush before he was shot and killed. Terrified, Shepherd lay quietly in the brush as the Japanese surged past him in the darkness. Weak from loss of blood, he nevertheless crawled painfully though onrushing enemy soldiers to seek help. Pharmacist Mate Third Class Karl B. Coleman found him and assisted him to the forward aid station, located only a few feet from Edson's exposed command post. Major Griffith said it was "a primitive dressing station where two Navy doctors [Lts. Edward P. McLarney and Robert W. Skinner] and their men, flashlight beams shielded by ponchos, applied tourniquets, gave transfusions, cleaned wounds." In all the two doctors and corpsmen, nine of whom received the Navy Cross for extraordinary heroism, treated over two hundred casualties during the night-long battle.

The fierce Japanese assault overran Baker Company's 1st and 2nd Platoons and threatened to cut them off. There was only one place to go and that was up the ridge. "Individuals and squads were scattered and ended up as lonely, scared individuals or in small groups," Sweeney said. "Those lucky enough remained intact as squads. The goal of all was to reach Hill 120." Privates First Class Dave "Tabe" Taber and Herman "Ike" Arnold were communicators attached to Baker Company. "When the Japs attacked, we were throwing grenades," Taber said. "There was a lot of shooting going on, a lot of action: rifle fire, grenades moving fast." Suddenly Arnold said, 'Tabe, I've been hit . . . in the throat.' He no more than said that, and he was dead . . . I looked around, and I was all by myself." Taber decided to "get back and make contact with the others." It was pitch black and difficult to see. At one point, a Japanese hand grenade exploded at his feet, wounding him. "I was a little stunned but got up. I was in shock . . . and walking along slowly [I] heard a Japanese voice behind me . . . I had an .03 rifle and I swung around and shot, and he dropped. I kept on going." Taber made it to the top of the hill and was evacuated the next morning but not without another close call. The truck he was riding in was hit by a hidden machine gunner and two of its passengers were killed.

At the start of the attack Edson's two artillery observers, Staff Sgt. Robert Delanoy and Cpl. Thomas Watson, started calling in devastating artillery fire. Before they were through, the 11th Marines fired almost two thousand rounds of 105mm shells in defense of the ridge. Captain Sweeney recalled, "Colonel del Valle's howitzers went into action with preplanned concentrations when the battle erupted. The initial impact areas were well forward of the action, but as it turned out they did extensive damage to a Japanese battalion in an assembly area preparing to attack Hill 120." Captain Sweeney had 1st Sgt. Brice Maddox call in the artillery. "I handed the radio to Maddox, who had been in mortars and artillery in his career . . . and he relayed it to Corporal Watson, who was on the ridge with Edson. For us it was most effective. He began firing 200 or 300 yards in front of us and fired across until he brought it down to 100 to 150 yards. I remember him saying, 'That's right, now walk it back and forth across the front.' That's what he did. They fired, fired, fired, fired barrages, and that I think broke up the people in front of us that we were almost eyeball to eyeball with."

Sweeney was still in a tough predicament. Two of his platoons had been forced to withdraw and the other was about to be overrun. "About 2230 two red flares arced above the 3rd Platoon position and impacted on Hill 120. The whole area was made plain to the oncoming Japanese at the jungle's edge. Edson, near his forward CP, did not want to use the radio, so he ordered Burak [his runner] to get a message to me. Burak crawled out to the frontline, cupped his hands and yelled, 'John Wolf! This is Burak. Do you hear me?' . . . 'Red Mike says it's OK to withdraw!'" Burak's shout was welcome news but difficult to do in darkness under fire. "I had the first sergeant work with the FO to lay down a covering barrage in front of our company position and await further orders." Sweeney crawled along the lines to notify his squad leaders and then signaled them to withdraw to the reverse slope. " . . . [T]he enemy raked the position with rifle and machine gun fire [but] miraculously none of our Marines were hit." His men threw their remaining hand grenades, took off through the kunai grass to Hill 120. "As we moved, the artillery let loose a hellacious barrage that rolled across the spine of the ridge and into the adjoining jungle not more than a hundred yards forward of the abandoned position."

At the same time as Sweeney's company was undergoing its trial by fire, Baker Company (Parachute) was under heavy pressure from Major Tamura's 2nd Battalion, 4th Infantry. Despite being pummeled by del Valle's artillery, Tamura sent Onodera's and Isibashi's companies into the attack. An intense mortar barrage hit the Parachutists just as the Imperial infantry swept out of the jungle screaming their battle cries. Baker Company reeled under the assault . . . and then gave way. Charlie Company (Parachute) decided its position was also untenable and joined Baker in a withdrawal to a position behind Hill 120. In the darkness and confusion of the battle, the withdrawal quickly became confused and disorganized. Someone yelled "Gas!" after the Japanese threw several smoke grenades. "It contributed to some temporary panic because we didn't have any gas masks," Sweeney said. "Up along the ridge, both para-troopers and Raiders intermingled in the dark. Somehow the word was passed to withdraw and the scramble began."

It appeared that the Marines on the hill were about to break. Raider Mielke described it as "[a] moment of panic." Edson made it known in no uncertain terms that there would be no more "back peddling." Sweeney explained that "[t]he 1st Parachute Battalion had stragglers—not stragglers in the sense they were lagging behind but a few men that were leading a charge to the rear." Colonel del Valle said that, "Sometime after midnight, the artillery forward observers phoned in that the infantry was falling back and they were alone on the ridge, whereupon I ordered them to retire and gave the order for the final protective fires by the 105 battalion," he said. "The twelve howitzers of that battalion covered the front of that ridge, firing so fast that we were afterwards reported by the Japanese to have had automatic artillery. The gun tubes got so hot they had to be swabbed continually."

Captain Sweeney recalled stemming the withdrawal. "That's where Edson, Bailey, myself, and several NCOs were able to quell the panic. . . . We quelled it by shouting, challenging, cursing—'Act like Marines! You call yourself Raiders? Get back in there!' " Bailey was particularly effective according to Colonel Alexander. "Bailey was big enough to collar retreating Marines and shake some sense into them." Another Marine admitted that "[i]t was hard to stop the stampede . . . but Bailey waved his pistol menacingly and the men stopped and went back." At this point,

Edson's final defense was a horseshoe-shaped line wrapped around the slope of Hill 120—three understrength companies arrayed from left to right, Able (Parachutist), Baker (Raider) and Charlie (Raider)—maybe three hundred men in all. Edson called division and told Twinning that he had withdrawn to his final defensive position.

Edson had to do something about the exposed left flank. He couldn't find the parachute commander, so he grabbed fiery Capt. Harry L. Torgerson and ordered him to restore the line. "He told 'Torgy' to counterattack to regain the left flank position," Sweeney recalled, "and to tie in with the Raiders' defensive line on Hill 120." Torgerson reorganized Baker and Charlie Companies (Parachute) and personally led them into the attack against Lieutenant Colonel Watanabe's battalion. "The counterattack by two understrength companies, launched just after midnight, sputtered initially and then gained momentum urged on by Torgerson," Sweeney explained. "The nearly exhausted and bloodied paratroopers soon succeeded in checking and then throwing back the renewed Japanese assault on the left. The fighting was particularly heavy and costly to . . . our paratroopers." Edson noted that 40 percent of Torgerson's men were casualties but completely stopped, "a flanking movement initiated by the enemy which if carried to completion would have resulted in the loss of the battalion reserve line."

Captain William J. McKennan, Baker Company (Parachutist), described the fighting. "The [Japanese] attack was almost constant, like a rain that subsides for a moment and then pours the harder. . . . [W]hen one wave was mowed down—and I mean mowed down— another followed it into death. . . . Some of the Jap rushes were now carrying them into our positions and there was ugly hand-to-hand fighting." Ira Gilliand recalled, "They kept charging, but that's where the grenades came in. We threw grenades all night long. I remember rolling the grenades down. We were up on the hill and they were below us." Lieutenant Onodera's 5th Company tried to infiltrate the line but the Marine fire was too much. Two platoon commanders were struck down and when Onodera continued the attack with his remaining men, he too was killed. Major Kokusho was also killed while leading his men. A Japanese NCO wrote in his diary, "We attacked the American position, but Lieutenant Matsuyama [2nd Company] and about a hundred men of the company were killed."

Edson felt the crisis was near and called Colonel Thomas at the division command center. "About 0430 Edson told me, 'I've been hit hard and I need more men,' " Thomas recalled. "I had a company about a hundred yards from there with Whaling [Lt. Col. William J.], and we started to feed them in . . . to strengthen Edson's line, and they fought there till daybreak." By dawn, Kawaguchi's attack was over, but that didn't mean the killing had stopped. Individuals and small groups of Japanese infiltrators were still active. A badly wounded Raider called for help. Hospital Apprentice First Class Robert L. Smith ran out to help. "The corpsman came over . . . and he got shot right through the heart . . . I grabbed him and carried him down the hill. I didn't think he was going to die. When I got to the aid station, I saw one of the doctors cry—'Smitty was my friend,' he blurted, 'a real nice guy'—I broke down also." Three infiltrators made it to the division command post before being killed.

Edson requested an airstrike on the Japanese position on the southern edge of Hill 80. "There was one little lip about a hundred yards that just dropped off for a hundred feet or so, and the Japs had gotten down underneath there," Thomas recalled. " . . . they couldn't get out nor

MEDAL OF HONOR EXCERPTS
COLONEL EDSON

"During the entire battle, Colonel Edson, continuously exposed to hostile fire of great intensity, personally directed the defense of his position. He displayed such a marked degree of cool leadership and personal courage that the officers and men of his command were constantly inspired by his example, and his personal influence over them kept the men in position throughout the night in the face of fanatical enemy of great superior numbers despite the severest casualties to his own men."

could the Raiders get at them." Three U.S. Army Bell Aircobra P-400s of the 67th Fighter Squadron made several passes with their 20mm cannon, and .30-caliber and .50-caliber machine guns. " . . . [T]he P-400s came in firing right down against that bank . . . and they killed those damned Japs . . . they wiped them out." For all intents, the battle for Edson's ridge was over. "At daybreak, Whaling went in with the rest of his men and took over from Edson," Thomas said. "We pulled the Raiders and the Parachutists, what was left of them, and let them go back down into Whaling's bivouac where they could get some breakfast." The survivors of the 1st Parachute Battalion were evacuated from the island shortly after the battle. In *Battalion of the Damned: The 1st Marine Paratroopers at Gavutu and Bloody Ridge*, James F. Christ wrote that, "On 7 August, they [Parachutists] had numbered 397. Now on 18 September, they had 86." The Raiders suffered 163 casualties—34 men killed in action and 129 men wounded.

Both Lieutenant Colonel Edson and Major Bailey were awarded the Medal of Honor.

Richard Tregaskis saw bullet holes in the colonel's collar and side of his shirt. Captain "Tex" Stiff was close by Edson during the battle. "I can say that if there is such a thing as one man holding a battalion together, Edson did it that night. He stood just behind the front lines—stood, when most of us hugged the ground. . . ." Smith wrote, " . . . [E]ach side had its heroes, but none were bigger than Red Mike Edson. Fearlessly standing erect in his command post with two fresh bullet holes in his shirt, Edson coolly and calmly directed the battle, a mere twenty-five yards behind the front lines. . . ."

CHAPTER 9

Choiseul Coastwatchers

Coastwatchers Lieutenant A. N. A. "Nick" Waddell and Sub-Lieutenant Camden W. Seton, Royal Australian Navy, M-Special Unit, climbed through the deck hatch of the half-submerged USS *Grampus* (SS-207) and made their way aft toward a group of darkened shadows busily launching two rubber boats. After only a whispered "Good luck," the two men climbed down the slippery hull of the submarine and into the heavily laden craft. Holding lines were cast off and the boats floated clear of the sub as it gradually increased speed to clear the area. The two men took a last look at the darkened silhouette and dipped their paddles into the water—no time was to be wasted, daylight was but a few short hours away and they had to be ashore and out of sight .

M-Special Unit— part of the Services Reconnaissance Department, a joint Australian, New Zealand, and British military intelligence unit— was used primarily to gather information on Japanese naval and troop movements around New Guinea and the Solomon Islands. Small teams were inserted along the coast behind enemy lines where they could observe enemy movements and report back via radio. These Australian coastwatchers played decisive roles in the Solomons. Organized under Lt. Cmdr. A. Eric Feldt of the Royal Australian Navy in 1939, by 1941

2ND PARACHUTE BATTALION

In October 1940, the commandant of the Marine Corps solicited volunteers from all units to become paratroopers. Requirements were strict: all volunteers (except officers of rank higher than captain), had to be 21 to 32 years old, be 66 to 74 inches tall, have normal eyesight and blood pressure, and be unmarried. In addition, applications had to include educational records and athletic background. The letter made clear that Parachutists would receive extra pay, although it didn't include exact numbers. Eventually, Congress set the extra pay at $50 per month for enlisted men and $100 for officers. Regular pay at the time was about $36 per month for a private first class and $125 for a second lieutenant. The substantial bonus served as an incentive for volunteers and acknowledged the increased danger for the Marines.

Although they started looking for paratroopers in 1940, the Corps didn't formalize its airborne doctrine until late 1942. The twelve-page manual, "Parachute and Air Troops," stated that airborne forces would deliver "a paralyzing application of power in the initial phase of a landing attack." The manual noted that airborne forces could only hold small critical objectives, such as bridges and airfields, for a short time until joined by overland or seaborne forces. Small units of parachute troops could also gather intelligence and conduct sabotage operations behind enemy lines.

On 23 July 1941, Company "B," 2nd Parachute Battalion was activated under the command of Capt. Charles E. Shepherd Jr.

there were one hundred of them in the island chain. They depended on the natives to help carry their heavy wireless sets, which could broadcast four hundred miles by voice, and up to six hundred miles by key. It was a risky assignment, far from reinforcements. If captured, torture was likely.

Waddell and Seton were on a special mission to set up a coast watching station on the Japanese occupied island of Choiseul in the northern Solomon Islands. Choiseul was located forty-five miles

The company was attached to the 2nd Marine Division Special Troops. Company "A" was organized on 7 February 1942, followed by Company "C" on 3 September 1942. The battalion sailed from San Diego on 20 October 1942, and arrived at Tatahi Bay, fourteen miles north of Wellington, New Zealand, approximately three weeks later. After two months of training, the battalion shipped out for Noumea, New Calendonia, where it joined the 1st Parachute Battalion. On 1 April 1943, the two battalions were incorporated into the newly organized 1st Marine Parachute Regiment, under the command of Lt. Col. Robert H. Williams. Lieutenant Colonel Victor H. Krulak assumed command of the 2nd Battalion. Under the new organization, the 2nd Battalion's letter designation was changed to "Easy," "Fox," and "George" Company. The 2d Parachute Battalion sailed to Guadalcanal in early September and then moved forward to a staging area at Vella Lavella on 1 October, 1943.

On 27 October 1943, the 2d Parachute Battalion, reinforced with a machine gun platoon from Regimental Weapons Company, a boat detachment (4LCP (R) 8s), and an Experimental Rocket Detachment—a lieutenant and eight men with 40 fin-stabilized, 65-pound weapons that had a range of one thousand yards— landed on Choiseul Island. The battalion mustered 725 officers and men.

southeast of Bougainville at the beginning of the slot, a narrow ocean corridor between several Solomon Islands that Japanese warships, known as the "Tokyo Express," traversed to resupply their garrison on Guadalcanal. The two coastwatchers were assigned to provide early warning of Japanese ship movements coming down the slot.

The two men got halfway to shore when they were caught in a strong crosscurrent that began sweeping them down the coast. In *Lonely Vigil: Coastwatchers of the Solomons,* Walter Lord wrote, "It took three hours of hard paddling to reach the reef, and then they couldn't find the opening. Dawn was breaking, and in desperation they finally landed directly on the reef. Soaking wet, stumbling, and falling in holes in the coral, they carried their gear the last fifty yards to shore." Unfortunately the yellow rafts were wedged in the coral. The two men had to hack the boats apart and drag them to cover. They finished just as the Japanese surveillance aircraft flew by on its morning patrol. Within days they had established contact with friendly natives, who assisted them in establishing their camp.

It did not take the two long to set up their radio station called DEL about two miles in from the coast near the little village of Tagatagera on the northern coast, where they had a magnificent view of the Slot. Not only were they able to broadcast alerts—"Six fighters now going southeast, twenty-eight planes passing from north to yours, thirteen fighters going yours"—but they were also active in rescuing downed airmen. Corporal J. E. Hartman, tail gunner on a B-17, Marine SBD pilot H. J. Murphy, and his rear seater, Cpl. G. W. Williamson, were among the many that owed their lives to the coastwatcher/rescue network. In September 1943, American reconnaissance teams arrived on the island and Seton spent most of the month guiding them around. A month later, a new mission was added: the diversionary landing of the 2nd Marine Parachute Battalion on Choiseul Island.

Choiseul Diversion

In mid-October 1943, Maj. James Murray, 1st Marine Amphibious Corps (IMAC) staff secretary raised the possibility of a small-scale landing on Choiseul as part of diversionary effort to confuse the Japanese as to the true objective of the American campaign in the Solomons, the island of Bougainville. Code named "Operation Blissful," the diversionary plan called for the 2nd Parachute Battalion under Lt. Col. Victor H. Krulak to make an amphibious landing near the village of Voza on the northern portion of Choiseul's southwest coast. On 21 October, Lt. Cols. Krulak and Robert Williams, 1st Parachute Regiment were summoned to IMAC headquarters on Guadalcanal where they were briefed on the operation. "I reported to Colonel Thomas [Division G-3], who took me into their

MAJOR BAILEY

Completely reorganized following the severe engagement of the night before, Major Bailey's company, within an hour after taking its assigned position as reserve battalion between the main line and the coveted airport, was threatened on the right flank by the penetration of the enemy into a gap in the main line. In addition to repulsing this threat, while steadily improving his own desperately held position, he used every weapon at his command to cover the forced withdrawal of the main line before a hammering assault by superior enemy forces. After rendering invaluable service to the battalion commander in stemming the retreat, reorganizing the troops and extending the reverse position to the left, Major Bailey, despite a severe head wound, repeatedly led his troops in fierce hand-to-hand combat for a period of ten hours.

planning tent and had Maj. Jim Murray brief me," Krulak recalled. 'We've changed our plan,' Murray said, 'we want to encourage the Japanese to think that we are going to land [on Choiseul]. We want to make it about a week ahead of the Bougainville landing.' " Krulak was told that his battalion's mission was to conduct raids along the northwest coast, select a site for a possible torpedo boat (PT) base, and withdraw after twelve days. "Make a lot of noise," he was told, "but don't get decisively engaged."

Murray and the intelligence staff briefed Krulak on the information that had been gathered by two amphibious reconnaissance patrols that had scouted the island. The patrols estimated that there were four to five thousand Japanese dispersed in small camps along the coast waiting for transportation to Bougainville. Seton verified the estimate volunteering that, "The Japanese are spooked; they're shooting at their own shadows because of the patrol activity." The coastwatcher and two of his best scouts were brought off the island by a PT boat specifically to brief Krulak. The intelligence staff thought the Japanese supply situation was poor, but they still believed they were a potent force possessing infantry weapons, mortars and even light artillery.

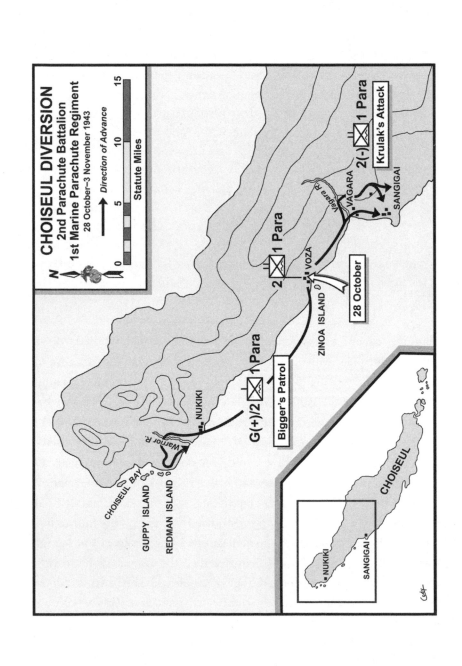

CHOISEUL DIVERSION
2nd Parachute Battalion
1st Marine Parachute Regiment
28 October–3 November 1943

Direction of Advance

Statute Miles
0   5   10   15

Krulak said after the meeting that he "didn't believe anybody went into an operation knowing as much as they needed to know as I did about Choiseul." He was given a great deal of discretion in planning the operation. "I was told that I could select the landing area . . . the Navy didn't have any interest in selecting it, they were just going to haul us over there . . . so I proposed to land where the enemy wasn't, if possible." Following the meeting, General Vandegrift, 1st Marine Division commander, had taken Krulak aside: "I desire an immediate and credible appearance of a large force. Take immediate action . . . [and he emphasized], Get ashore where there are no Japs!"

Lieutenant Colonel Victor H. Krulak was born in 1913 to a family of Russian Jewish immigrants. He was commissioned a Marine second lieutenant upon graduation from the U.S. Naval Academy in May 1934. His early Marine Corps service included sea duty aboard USS *Arizona*, an assignment at the U.S. Naval Academy, and duty with the 6th Marines in San Diego and the 4th Marines in China (1937–1939). During the Second Sino-Japanese War in 1937, Krulak served as an observer in Shanghai, where he took telephoto pictures of a Japanese landing boat with a ramp in the bow. Krulak sent the photographs to Washington, convinced that a similar craft would prove useful to the U.S. armed forces, but at the time the photos were dismissed as being from "some nut out in China." Later Krulak discussed the concept with boat builder Andrew Higgins and even built a model of the Japanese boat to demonstrate the retractable ramp. Higgins incorporated Krulak's thoughts into his design of the Landing Craft, Vehicle, Personnel (LCVP) or "Higgins boat." The LCVP was a critical part of the Normandy landings on D-Day as well as other amphibious assaults across the Pacific.

Upon his return to the United States, he attended the Junior School at Quantico, Virginia, and following completion in 1940 was assigned to the 1st Marine Brigade, FMF, which later became the 1st Marine Division. At the outbreak of World War II, he was a captain serving as aide to the Commanding General, Amphibious Corps, Atlantic Fleet, Gen. Holland M. Smith. He volunteered for parachute training and on completing training was ordered to the Pacific area as commander of the 2d Parachute Battalion, 1st Marine Amphibious Corps.

Now, while waiting for the plane to take him back to Vella Lavella, Krulak " . . . sat down and wrote the operation order on the back of a set of travel orders. I flew up to Vella, got my staff together and set the wheels in motion. We had about seventy-two hours to do it." In *Mustang: A Combat Marine,* Gerald P. Averill, who had been a platoon commander in Easy Company during the landing, wrote that operation was "the kind that everyone wanted to be in on, the kind that movies sometimes were based on. The news set the battalion afire with anticipation!" Camden Seton and two of his native scouts were brought in to provide detailed information to help Krulak in the planning process. "We had about thirty-six hours with the coastwatcher [Seton] and his two guides, who could only speak a tiny bit of pidgin, but they were useful to answer the very questions that we wanted to know. The result was that, while their information was a little stale, they did know a lot. They answered my questions, as it turned out, very accurately." One important item that was not accurate was the maps of the island, which played havoc with navigation once the Parachutists were on the island.

For the next four days, the Parachutists labored to assemble equipment—"The G-4 gave me what I wanted," Krulak said. "They took me to the Navy. I had asked to have some boats attached to my battalion—[and I] got the boats..." The Navy provided eight LCMs and four APDs—*Kilty, Ward, Crosby,* and *McKean*. Krulak had his men organize the supplies and equipment in four separate stacks on the beach to facilitate loading. Late in the afternoon of 27 October the LCMs were loaded, and at dusk, the small craft lay alongside the larger APDs. Parachutist working parties turned to with a vengeance and within forty-five minutes had loaded their supplies and equipment. "One of the requirements was that the APDs . . . could not load until after dark because there were too many Japanese eyes around to see them," Krulak recalled. "It had to be done quickly because they had to sail by about 2300 in order to make it across Vella gulf and conduct the landing under cover of darkness. We had staged and concealed all of our material over the preceding night or two, so it was easy to embark. The four ships got underway in plenty of time."

The four APDs took station under the watchful eye of the destroyer USS *Conway* (DD507) and proceeded in column through the darkness. "It just happened," Krulak said, "to be a very still night, in which the phosphorescence from the ship's wake was very visible." Suddenly, without warning, a Japanese aircraft swooped in and dropped a single bomb near the rearmost APD in the column. The bomb landed close enough to cause the ship to shake but did not do any damage. In *Bougainville and the Northern Solomons,* Maj. John N. Rentz wrote that "[a] young Marine standing near the ship's rail, thinking as many other Marines aboard that the ship's guns were firing, asked, 'What are they shooting at?' 'My boy,' answered one of the battalion's officers, 'you have just been bombed.'" The incident happened so fast that the ship's antiaircraft gunners were not able to get a shot off.

Just prior to midnight, the convoy hove to at a point about two thousand yards off the southwest coast of Choiseul. "We got to the place where we were supposed to go, a place called Voza," Krulak said. "The plan was to send a small reconnaissance detachment ashore to scout out the landing area and guide the battalion ashore by light signal if the beach was clear." Lieutenant Rea E. Duncan, 3rd Platoon, George Company was assigned to lead the patrol. He told his platoon to "[m]ove quickly up the beach to the edge of the jungle. Spread out and set up a beachhead perimeter . . . Somewhere on the beach is the Australian Coastwatcher Nick Waddell and the native guides . . ." On signal, the platoon climbed down the cargo net rigged against the ship's side and into a ramped landing craft (LCP(R)) for the run to the beach. The men tensed as they approached the darkened, jungle lined shore, wondering if the Japanese were waiting in ambush. The noise from the boat's engine was enough to wake the dead!

Suddenly the craft lurched to a stop as the bow slid up on the sandy beach. The ramp dropped and the Parachutists scrambled out and across the narrow beach to the edge of the jungle. Nothing stirred, except the rustle of jungle creatures disturbed by the sudden invasion. Averill wrote that if the beach was secure Duncan "would signal the old Churchillian 'V' for victory signal, dit-dit-dit-da, by shaded light." After listening intently for several minutes, Duncan decided the beach was safe and used

KRULAK PRELIMINARY REPORT, OPERATION BLISSFUL

The Second Parachute Battalion (Reinforced) landed at Voza, Choiseul, British Solomon Islands at 2300, October 27th unopposed, and established a beachhead. Enemy Reconnaissance aircraft discovered the landing and ineffectively bombed the area. At daybreak the battalion moved into the mountain area one mile inland from Voza and established a defensive base position. Patrols were immediately sent out both by foot and boat to determine the location of the nearest enemy installations. These were found to be at Sangigai to the southward, a barge staging and replenishing base, and at Warrior River to the northward the Choiseul Bay outposts.

his flashlight to signal the battalion. Shortly after midnight the first wave of Parachutists landed, and within an hour the entire battalion was ashore with the bulk of its equipment. In the middle of the unloading, a Japanese twin-float plane, code named "Jake," swept in and dropped two bombs that exploded off the port quarter of the *Conway*. Fortunately they did not do any damage, but the bombing certainly lent a sense of urgency to the unloading. The two bombings indicated that the Japanese were alert to the possibility of an American landing and were maintaining aircraft surveillance around the island.

As Krulak's men assembled on the beach, Seton, who had accompanied the battalion, tried to locate the native carriers he and Nick Waddell had recruited to assist the Parachutists. They were supposed to meet him at the abandoned village of Voza but for some reason they were not there. After tromping through the jungle for several minutes, Seton found eighty of the wayward natives and led them back to the beach without incident. Peatross stated, "Before dawn, the battalion, reinforced with native bearers of Seton's coast-watcher group, carrying heavy-duty radio equipment, ammunition, and rations, struggled up the narrow, single-track trail towards the base camp location. It was high ground covered with forest growth, well-concealed from the ground and air, a stream of clear, rushing water sliding around one side of the bluff."

At daylight the beachhead was attacked by several enemy planes, which blindly strafed the area. Fortunately everything had been either moved or camouflaged, so the air raid did not cause any damage. At this point, Krulak knew that the first phase of the operation was successful. The Japanese knew Americans were ashore—but did not know how many there were or their intentions. The first part of the diversion was working. To reinforce the idea of a landing, IMAC headquarters broadcast the news of the landing on Allied radio and told the press that an invasion was underway. In *Silk Chutes and Hard Fighting: U.S. Marine Corps Parachute Units in World War II,* Lt. Col. Jon T. Hoffman wrote, "At least one newspaper illustrated the story with fanciful drawings of parachutists floating down from the sky."

Four Navy LCP(R)s were left behind to provide support. They were taken to a small cove on Zinoa Island, a tiny islet directly off Voza, where they were camouflaged under overhanging mangrove trees. Lieutenant John Richard's 1st Platoon, Easy Company, went along to guard them. Sometime just before dawn, a Japanese plane circled overhead but did not drop any bombs. The men believed they had been spotted and couldn't understand why they weren't bombed. Back at the base camp, Krulak sent out patrols with native guides to gather information. One of the patrols reported that approximately two hundred Japanese were guarding a barge station at Sangigai, about eight miles southeast of the camp and another force was defending an outpost about ten miles northwest at the mouth of the Warrior River. Krulak decided that Sangigai would be the first target and decided to personally scout the objective before launching an attack.

The next day Krulak sent Lieutenant Averill on a reconnaissance patrol to check out the possibility of using Moli Point as a base for PT boats, while he led another to Sangigai. "Yours is a reconnaissance patrol, not a combat patrol," he stressed to Averill. "Don't get into a wrestling match." Lieutenant Junior Grade Richard Keresey (a former PT boat skipper), an Army radar specialist, and a native guide accompanied the patrol. Averill started out in good spirits. His map showed a good trail from Voza to the point, a distance of about six miles. However, he soon learned that he could not rely on its accuracy.

"The maps issued for BLISSFUL were unbelievable, next to useless," Averill complained. "A gridded overprint of aerial photographs of our area of operations, which supplemented these maps, left much to be desired. The jungle growth was so dense that the camera's eye had no more success in penetrating it than did the eye of a human. Trails were inked in and overprinted, pure guesswork, for beneath the umbrella of the rainforest no trails actually could be observed. Native villages and known Japanese installations were overprinted, their locations the most accurate of any on the map. The larger streams and rivers were portrayed with some accuracy also. What were not shown, perhaps not known about at all by the planners of BLISSFUL, were the rocky spurs that extended from the central mountain mass, east and west, projecting into the sea in places. In following the northwest trail along the beach, there was no way to circumvent these spurs except to seaward, so it was up and over—the slow tedious, exhausting method of making headway."

It took Averill's patrol eight physically exhausting hours to cut and claw their way to the Moli Point destination. In *Isolation of Rabaul*, Henry Shaw and Douglas Kane described the island as being, "[f]ully overgrown and choked with rank, impenetrable jungle and rain forest. The mountain ranges in the center of the island extend in long spurs and ridges toward the coasts, thus effectively dividing the island into a series of large compartments." By that time they explored the area and determined that it was impracticable for a PT base it was so late in the day they decided to spend the night—which was anything but uneventful. Just after dark the first of several Japanese barges loaded with troops pulled into the cove near their perimeter. This happened several times but inexplicably the barges all turned back and steamed farther up the coast. At dawn, Averill was about to call the guide when he saw the man beckon. "Jap! Jap! Many! Many!" the guide whispered urgently. Averill was shocked to discover that a large number of enemy soldiers had bivouacked less than a hundred yards from his position and were now between the patrol and the main base camp. Fortunately the native

KRULAK PRELIMINARY REPORT, OPERATION BLISSFUL

On October 30th a combat patrol was dispatched to the southward with the intention of apprising the Japanese of our presence on Choiseul. A Japanese detachment of about ten men was encountered at the Vagara River. In the encounter seven (7) Japs were killed and a landing barge which these men were using was destroyed. There were no Marine casualties. On October 30 a combat patrol accompanied by a PT base reconnaissance party proceeded up the beach as far as Moli Island and returned without event. On the night of October 30th plans were prepared and orders issued for a coordinated attack with the two-fold mission of destroying the Sangigai base and impressing the enemy with the strength of our forces.

guide was able to show them a way around the large Japanese force and they were able to successfully make it back to the camp by mid-morning. When he returned, he found that Krulak had not yet returned from the patrol to Sangigai.

Krulak's reconnaissance patrol, consisting of two officers, seventeen enlisted men, and five native guides, left at first light. They followed a fairly well-defined trail southeast toward the objective. Within a short distance, the patrol discovered evidence that the Japanese had been in the area—lean-tos, discarded equipment, log bunkers—fairly recently. The patrol continued to the Vagara River where Krulak had Platoon Sgt. Frank J. Mullins, a detail of three Marines, and four native guides, split off from the main body and move inland to the high ground behind Sangigai. He told Mullins to make panoramic sketches of the Japanese positions and to calculate the time it took him to reach the high ground. Krulak intended to use the information to brief the battalion for the attack.

The main body of the patrol continued toward the mouth of the river, paralleling the beach, just inside the jungle. About a mile and a half farther on, the point man signaled "enemy in sight" after spotting ten unsuspecting Japanese soldiers unloading a landing barge no more than seventy yards away. Krulak immediately decided to take them on and moved the men into firing positions. "Pick out individual targets," he whispered. "When I give the word, kill them all!" In the ensuing burst of gunfire, seven of the Japanese were killed but the others managed to escape into the jungle. The barge was destroyed with demolitions and, having announced its presence to the Japanese, the patrol returned to camp without incident. Krulak was pleased. The first round of his "hit and run" strategy was paying off. Later that same afternoon, the Miller patrol returned after an exhausting trek through the jungle. They received a well done for the "complete and accurate" sketches they had made.

Late in the afternoon, Sgt. Norman F. Law and a squad of Marines from Fox Company were sent to set up an overnight ambush position near the Vagara River. They had hardly left the perimeter before they ran head-on into a platoon-sized Japanese unit. Both sides immediately opened fire and in the brief fire fight that resulted, the enemy patrol was driven off. The Parachutists claimed seven enemy killed in action. Sergeant Law and two men returned to the camp to brief Krulak while the others hunkered down for the night.

Sangigai

The village of Sangigai had been in Marine sights since mid-October when the plan for the diversion was first considered. It was an important replenishing point for the Japanese coastal barge traffic and its loss might cause the enemy to react to the threat posed by the raiding force, which is just what Krulak wanted. He hoped that a successful attack would make the Japanese believe the Americans were on the island in force and might transfer troops from Bougainville. As a secondary objective, Krulak intended to destroy the Japanese headquarters and the supplies they had stored there.

Upon his return from the patrol, Krulak gathered his key personnel to issue the attack order. He planned for a two-company attack. The companies, reinforced with a section of machine guns, two rocket teams, and twenty native carriers, were to be transported by LCP(R) to the mouth of the Vagara River, where they would disembark and move to their assigned positions. Easy Company was to proceed along the coast to an attack position north of the village, while Fox Company

KRULAK SANGIGAI ATTACK ORDER

- There are between 100 and 200 Japs at Sangigai, guarding a barge station and attempting to locate and destroy coastwatchers in that area.
- This battalion attacks Sangigai about 1400 tomorrow. Destroys garrison and installations, captures material and withdraws to base.
- Company "E," attached; one machine gun section regimental weapons, two rocket teams, twenty bearers, take departure from Vagara River down beach 30 minutes after "F" Company passes its left flank. Hit Sangigai on northwest flank, destroy all installations, assist "F" Company. Withdraw on order.
- Company "F," attached; one machine gun section regimental weapons, two rocket teams, one TBA transmitter, twenty bearers; move to Vagara by boat, pass left of Company "G," move wide around north and east of Sangigai. Attack in westerly direction on hearing "E" Company firing. Prevent enemy withdrawal into mountains. Withdraw on order.
- Remainder of battalion set up perimeter defense of base, prepared to move to Sangigai area if required or so directed.
- Re-embark at Vagara in withdrawal.
- Prisoners and captured material to Bn-2.
- Take one K meal.
- One unit of fire for all weapons, 10 rounds per rocket gun.
- TBX make contact at halts with base.
- Open voice net at 1200.
- I will be with Company "F."

circled around through the jungle to the high ground behind the village. At H-hour (1400), Easy Company would assault the village behind a barrage of mortar and rocket fire and drive the surviving enemy into Fox Company's killing zone. The attack was to be proceeded by an early morning air strike. George Company was designated camp security and to be a reaction force, if needed.

The attack force left the perimeter at 0400 and made its way to the beach to meet the LCP(R)s. The early morning air strike arrived on schedule and proceeded to bomb and strafe Sangigai. Much to Krulak's chagrin four of the planes mistook the boats on Zinoa as enemy and strafed them. As the aircraft came around for a second pass, one of the Marines waved an American flag and they pulled off without firing. Fortunately there were no casualties but three of the boats were damaged and could not be used for the attack, forcing the battalion to set out on foot. After a tiring five-hour forced march the battalion's lead element approached the Vagara River where it ran into an enemy outpost. After a brief fire fight the enemy withdrew. At this point, Krulak split the force per his plan—Easy Company continued along the coast, while Fox Company circled inland.

Fox Company

Fox Company had the most difficult route through heavy rain forest. Christ wrote, "They waded through countless streams, climbed huge roots, and crawled under fallen trees. Everything seemed to snag on their shirts, belts, and straps, slowing them down. The terrain was an unforgiving wallow. . . . Men tripped and slid in the mud, their arms flailing to grab branches or something to stop their fall." H-hour was fast approaching and they were still a considerable distance from their assault position. Krulak was worried. Shortly after 1400 he heard Easy Company open fire with its mortars and rockets. Moments later, the native scouts at the front of the column signaled "enemy ahead."

Almost immediately the column came under fire from Japanese snipers in trees, rifle pits, and bunkers constructed in the roots of banyan trees, which were almost impossible to spot. There was momentary confusion as the men adjusted to the sudden ambush. For many of the young Parachutists it was their first time under fire and they hesitated to shoot for lack of a target. It wasn't long before that misconception was cleared up by the old timers, some of whom were veterans of previous fire fights. By fire teams and squads the men rushed forward, building up a firing line that quickly gained superiority. Two of the attached machine gun teams worked their way forward and began laying down suppressive fire, while Lt. W. E. King's 2nd Platoon enveloped the enemy's left flank. The maneuver worked and the Japanese were forced to pull back and regroup. In the initial burst of fire, Capt. Spencer H. Pratt, the company commander was wounded in the shoulder, and Krulak was hit with shrapnel in the cheek, but remained in action.

As the Japanese fire momentarily died down, the Marines could hear them working themselves into frenzy, preparatory to launching a full scale assault. "The Japanese on the ridge above had kept up a constant barrage of screams and curses that began to grow still louder," Christ wrote, describing the moments before the onslaught. "The noise was bloodcurdling and eerily high pitched. Suddenly, with a final, '*Totsugeki*! *Totsugeki*!' (attack, attack) the Japanese poured out of the jungle with bayonets fixed, aching for the opportunity to close with the Americans. The Parachutists opened with a deafening blast of automatic weapons fire that staggered the Japanese assault. . . . [M]en were hit multiple times and collapsed; others ran a few steps before falling . . . but some kept advancing despite the rain of steel, throwing grenades and firing on the run. But flesh can only stand so much . . . and the survivors fled back to the relative safety of the jungle. The Parachutists heaved a sigh of relief. . . . [A] Japanese banzai attack is a terrifying experience."

Now and again, a single shot rang out as a Japanese sniper singled out a Marine for special attention but for the most part the battlefield was quiet. Cordite hung in the air, mixed with the cloying smell of blood from the bodies that littered the jungle floor. Blackened circles and shredded undergrowth marked the explosive power of the hand grenades that were traded back and forth. Here and there along the Parachutist line, the battalion surgeon and his corpsmen ministered to the wounded. Several forms lay in that impossibly limp pose that only the dead can assume. Suddenly the silence was broken by the "pre-assault warm up." The surviving Japanese burst out of the jungle, although not nearly as many as before. It was a half-hearted effort that was almost over before it really began. Lieutenant W. F. Naylor's 3rd Platoon picked up and moved on the enemy's right flank in an effort to box them in. Their effort was only partially successful, as some forty Japanese survivors were observed fleeing into the jungle "in a most non-Samurai fashion." Krulak later wrote, "The outcome appeared to be in question until the Japs destroyed their chances by an uncoordinated banzai charge which was badly cut up by our machine guns. . . ."

After the Japanese fled, Fox Company buried its dead, which were later exhumed by the natives and reburied on the beach near Vagara. The company then pulled back to the Vagara River. The trek back was a test of endurance. The men were physically and mentally drained from the close combat and the struggle to carry twelve wounded on makeshift stretchers through the jungle. It was after dark when the exhausted Paratroopers finally arrived at the river. Krulak decided to remain there overnight rather than risk a night march. Shortly after dawn on 31 October the LCP(R)s arrived and by 0730 Fox Company was safely back at the mountain camp.

Easy Company

Easy Company reached its attack position and, shortly after 1400, opened fire with its mortars and rockets into the enemy positions located on the high ground about five hundred yards northwest of Sangigai. Immediately after the bombardment the company moved into the village and found it deserted. The enemy had fled inland toward Fox Company. The Parachutists began a search of the village. Platoon Sergeant Vernon Hammons found a treasure trove of documents and charts. Averill wrote, "Hammons came across a gold mine. Hydrographic charts of the Bougainville-Shortland-Fauro Island group showed the routes used by the barges evacuating troops from the Central Solomons to the staging areas of Choiseul and onto Bougainville. Others contained exact plots of the Japanese mine fields laid to protect the approaches to the Northern Solomons."

Krulak recalled, "The one that fascinated me most was a chart that portrayed the minefields. . . . When I reported this, the night after the Sangigai attack, I saw my first 'flash' message. . . . 'Transmit at once the coordinates of the limits of the minefields and all channels going through it'. . . . So we laboriously encoded the critical locations and sent them off. . . . Halsey sent in a minelayer and dropped mines in the entrance

KRULAK PRELIMINARY REPORT, OPERATION BLISSFUL

The Sangigai operation commenced with outpost activity in the vicinity of Vagara Village at 1100, October 30th. The enemy outpost was driven into Sangigai by a force moving down the coast while another force moved inland through the mountains and swung west to attack the Japanese rear. The main force was struck at about 1400. It quickly abandoned Sangigai almost to a man, withdrawing into the mountains directly in the face of the enveloping force. Contact was made by the enveloping force at 1420 when the Japs were struck from two sides. This phase of the action, which lasted for forty-five minutes, was a firefight of the most vigorous sort. During its progress the Japs undertook two of their customary Bonzai counterattacks, during which their losses were great, and the failure of which caused their defeat. About 40 ran in a most un-Samurai fashion and escaped southward. Seventy-two dead Jap Marines were counted. Our casualties were six killed, one missing, and 12 wounded. Following destruction or dispersal of the defending force, the base installation, which consisted of permanent buildings, a field hospital and the barge-repair and staging areas, was destroyed.

. . . and they got two Japanese ships." After completing the search, the village was destroyed, including a new barge. Upon completing the destruction, the company pulled back to the Vagara River, where it boarded LCP(R)s that had been repaired and returned to Voza.

Continuing Operations

Having struck hard at Japanese operations on the southeast coast, Krulak felt it was time to "destroy the southern outposts of Choiseul Bay and if possible to shell the Jap supply depot on Guppy Island." He tasked Maj. Warner T. Bigger, the battalion executive officer, and the well-rested George Company, minus one platoon, for the assignment. Before dawn on 1 November, the eighty-seven man combat patrol, dubbed the "Northwest Task Force" by its leader struck out in three LCP(R)s for the Warrior River, reaching it without difficulty by mid-morning. However, once at the river's mouth, the boats kept grounding, preventing them from going farther, so Bigger decided to send them back down the coast to wait until they were needed. He also decided to leave the heavy, cumbersome TBS radio on the river's east bank with a squad-sized security detail. After distributing the 60mm mortar ammunition, the patrol, led by two native guides, began an overland march along the eastern bank of the river. By mid-afternoon, Bigger realized that the natives were lost—they were from another part of the island and not familiar with this area—so he decided to bivouac for the night. Unfortunately the site was in the middle of a swamp.

Major Bigger sent Lieutenant Duncan and a ten-man squad back to the radio site to brief Krulak. The patrol reached the site late in the afternoon and found that the radio was not working. It was too late to travel farther, so Duncan decided to stay there. Meanwhile back at the mountain camp, Seton found out about the lost guides and sent another who was familiar with the area, but he would not arrive until the next day. The next morning Duncan discovered that a large Japanese force was hot on his trail and was about to surround him. The Parachutists were able to fight their way out and make their way back to the small coastal village of Nukiki, where they were picked up by the LCP(R)s. The boats took them to Voza where Duncan briefed Krulak. Krulak immediately requested air and PT boat support for the LCP(R)s that were to evacuate Bigger's force.

Because Bigger was out of communication, he was unaware that a Japanese battalion was behind him and continued the mission. By this time the new guide had reached the patrol and led them to the coast. At this point, another small detail, under Sgt. Rahland Wilson, was sent back to the radio site to pass instructions for the boats to pick up the Bigger force that afternoon. Wilson could not find the radio detail and sent Cpl. Winston Gallaher across the river to find them. Gallaher swam across the river but just as he reached the opposite shore, several Japanese soldiers sprang out of the jungle and grabbed him before the patrol could do anything. Wilson was left with no recourse but to cross the river at a low spot and work his way back in an attempt to rescue Gallaher. It took the detail some time to work their way back. Archivist Greg Bradsher wrote that, "They found the missing Marine, stripped naked, tied to a tree, and dead, having been used for bayonet practice. Continuing on to the coast, they spotted five Japanese, apparently the ones who had killed their colleague. They immediately opened fire, instantly killing them." The detail was able to flag down the LCP(R)s carrying Lieutenant Duncan on the way to rejoin the Northwest Task Force and escape.

The Bigger force had proceeded as far as the southern tip of Redman Island, the southern-most island in the chain stretching across the front of Choiseul Bay, when it ran into a Japanese outpost. In the short firefight that followed, three of the enemy were killed but a fourth managed to get away. Bigger felt the enemy was now alert to their presence and opted to hit the secondary target, Guppy Island, the barge replenishing center and fuel base for the Choiseul area. The patrol came within range of their small 60mm mortars. Overhanging vegetation forced the gunners to set up in the water, with only the muzzles protruding. Within minutes they fired 143 rounds of high explosive, "causing huge fires in a fuel dump and detonating ammunition and explosives stored on the island," according to Gerald Averill. The patrol immediately turned around and headed as fast as they could for the Warrior River, arriving there approximately 1600.

Major Bigger, still unaware that the Japanese were in the area, gave permission for some of the men to cool off in the river while waiting for the boats. They had no sooner entered the water when they were taken under fire, sparking a fire fight that resulted in several Japanese casualties before the enemy withdrew. Bigger realized the boats could not pick his force in the river itself and sent three men across the river to bring the boats to the east bank when they arrived. The moment one of the men reached the bank the Japanese opened fire. One Marine was killed in the water, another was wounded but managed to make it back to the friendly side of the river, and the third was wounded and captured.

The Japanese shifted their fire to Bigger's force, precipitating an all-out engagement that left Cpl. Edward J. Schnell critically wounded and several of the enemy dead. During the action, the boats arrived

WARRIOR RIVER INCIDENT

First Lieutenant Samuel M. Johnston, Platoon Sgt. Frank J. Muller, and Cpl. Paul Pare were sent across the Warrior River to contact the LCP(R)s and bring them to the east bank to embark the Bigger force. That part of the incident has been established as fact. What happened after the men entered the water remains a question. Bigger stated that the Japanese fired on the three volunteers as they approached the east bank of the river. Muller was killed instantly and sank beneath the water, and Johnston and Pare were both wounded. Pare managed to escape back to the west bank. He stated that two Japanese ran into the water and captured Johnston. However, official records indicate that Johnston swam over alone, contacted Andrew Sivokana (a native of the coastwatcher group), and reconnoitered the Japanese positions. He then proceeded toward Nukiki and was suddenly confronted en route by a party of Japanese to whom he surrendered.

Regardless of which version of the incident is true, Lieutenant Seton reported that two Marine bodies were found on the east side of the river and buried. The only identification he found was "Galla" stenciled on the jacket of one of the bodies. Marine Corps headquarters assumed that this was Cpl. Winston Gallaher, killed earlier, and since Johnston was the only other Marine known to have gotten across the river (Muller's body sank), the second body must have been his. Coastwatcher Sivokana's statement seems to corroborate the official version of the story when he told the Marines that Johnston was captured.

and added their firepower to the fight. They started taking fire. Author Christ noted that a Navy officer ordered the boats to stand out to sea, but Duncan drew his pistol on the officer. "This boat is going in there," stated Duncan, "with or without your head." The boats were unable to cross the coral reef and had to stand out in the heavy surf, forcing Bigger's men to wade over a hundred yards through sporadic Japanese fire. In the process of embarking the men, both of the LCP(R)s were damaged on the coral. One had a bent rudder and the other started taking on water, causing its engine to flood out. The high wind drove the boat toward the enemy-held beach.

Suddenly the two PT boats (PT-59 and PT-236) that Krulak had requested appeared out of the rainsquall. PT-59, skippered by Lt. John F. Kennedy, who would later become the thirty-fifth president of the United States, came alongside the rapidly sinking boat and took the men off, including Corporal Schnell, who was placed in Kennedy's bunk. As the men scrambled aboard the torpedo boat, three U.S. aircraft strafed the shoreline. At 2130, Kennedy's badly overloaded PT boat safely arrived at Voza. The operation cost the patrol two men killed, including Corporal Schnell who died aboard the PT boat, one wounded, and two missing, presumed dead. In addition to the damage done to the Guppy Island base, Bigger estimated that forty-two Japanese died and an undetermined number were wounded during the successful patrol.

During the two-day Bigger patrol, Krulak also conducted several platoon-sized patrols, which resulted in more than a dozen Japanese losses at a cost of one Marine killed in action. Intelligence indicated that the Japanese were closing in on Krulak's mountain base, having finally realized how small the American force was. Krulak reported, "By November 2 the ruse was plain to the Japs, and they began running troops on both flanks and scouting the mountain front of our perimeter . . . their activities were becoming more aggressive." The enemy was now within striking distance and Krulak expected an attack within forty-eight hours. Headquarters considered the information and sent a message ending with, " . . . feel your mission accomplished." Based on this assessment, Krulak recommended that the parachute battalion be withdrawn during the night of 3–4 November.

On the afternoon of 3 November, Krulak moved the battalion to the beach at Voza to await the nighttime arrival of four landing craft infantry (LCI), one configured as a gunboat to provide covering fire. The demolition platoon set about preparing a nasty surprise for the Japanese. The platoon laid two mine fields and placed over two hundred booby traps on likely avenues of approach. Sometime after midnight the landing craft arrived and within twelve minutes the battalion was safely aboard with all

KRULAK NAVY CROSS

The President of the United States of America takes pleasure in presenting the Navy Cross to Lieutenant Colonel Victor Harold Krulak (MCSN: 0-4990), United States Marine Corps, for extraordinary heroism and distinguished service as Commanding Officer of the Second Battalion, FIRST Marine Parachute Regiment, during operations on Choiseul Island, Solomon Islands, 28 October 1943 to 3 November 1943. Assigned the task of diverting hostile attention from the movements of our main attack force en route to Empress Augusta Bay, Bougainville Island, Lieutenant Colonel Krulak landed at Choiseul and daringly directed the attack of his battalion against the Japanese, destroying hundreds of tons of supplies and burning camps and landing barges. Although wounded during the assault on 30 October he repeatedly refused to relinquish his command and with dauntless courage and tenacious devotion to duty, continued to lead his battalion against the numerically superior Japanese forces. His brilliant leadership and indomitable fighting spirit assured the success of this vital mission and were in keeping with the highest traditions of the United States Naval Service.

its supplies and equipment, minus rations. They were left behind for the native carriers, who had done such a magnificent job for the force. Krulak was the last man aboard and as he left, he urged Seton to come along but the coastwatcher declined. His post, he declared, was on the island and the natives needed him.

By 0730 4 November, the battalion was back at Vella Lavella, having accomplished its mission in "conformity with the highest traditions of the Marine Corps," as spelled out in a commendatory letter written by General Vandegrift. "And so we came back across The Slot, the sunrise behind us, on a beautiful November morning," Gerald Averill wrote. "The colonel [Krulak], his face wound freshly bandaged, rode in on the LCI like a baron returning from the Crusades. The regimental commander, his staff, the battalion commanders of the other two parachute battalions, and selected members of the I Marine Corps Amphibious Corps staff were on the beach to greet him . . . a section of the band played marches and martial airs."

On 9 November Lieutenant Colonel Krulak was awarded the Navy Cross by Adm. William Halsey.

CHAPTER 10

Spy Catcher

Marine Captain Francis Thomas "Frank" Ferrell stood in the open door of the Army Air Corps C-47 waiting for the "green light," the signal to leap into space on a mission that could mean life or death for hundreds, perhaps thousands, of people. He and a hand-picked team were parachuting into the Japanese-held city of Canton, China, to hammer out the details of the Japanese surrender, only two days after Emperor Hirohito capitulated. They also had orders to rescue Allied POWs and investigate cases of possible war crimes. Captain Ferrell had served with the First Marine Division during the Guadalcanal and Peleliu operations and was well aware of how fanatical the Japanese could be. Thousands upon thousands of heavily armed Imperial soldiers occupied the city spread out below him. The question in his mind was, would they obey the Emperor and surrender, or would they disobey and fight? The light flashed green and Farrell stepped into the slip stream in a leap of faith.

Frank Farrell was twenty-nine years old and the feature editor of the *New York World Telegram* when the war broke out. In a burst of patriotic fervor he attempted to join the Navy but was turned down because of high blood pressure. Disappointed, he turned to an influential old friend, "Wild Bill" Donovan, at the time the driving force behind COI, and asked him to intercede on his behalf to gain a commission in the Marine Corps. Donovan agreed, if Farrell would help him sometime in the future. Farrell agreed. After attending officer training, he was commissioned and assigned to the 1st Battalion, 7th Marines, 1st Marine Division as an intelligence officer.

On 7 August 1942, the 1st Marine Division landed on Guadalcanal, in the first ground offensive operation of the war. Farrell led many small jungle patrols, becoming adept at surviving the deadly close encounters and ambushes of the bush-wise Japanese soldiers. The experience was a great training ground. It hardened him to the rigors of leading men in combat and gave him confidence and the mental toughness to operate independently, attributes that stood him in good stead during his pursuit of Nazi spies three year later. His regimental commander called him "the finest young officer I ever knew."

After Guadalcanal, Farrell took part in two more island campaigns, Cape Gloucester and Peleliu, where he was awarded the Silver Star Medal for conspicuous gallantry. The award citation noted that he voluntarily led numerous small patrols into hostile territory to secure vital information on the enemy at great risk of his life. On one occasion, he was pinned down by hostile fire for more than forty minutes, and on another, a Japanese ammunition dump exploded in a cave that he was searching.

Farrell returned to the United States and was assigned to the Special Services Unit of the OSS. In May 1945, he received orders for Kumming, China, and special temporary duty as commander of the "Buick" mission, a reconnaissance of Japanese forces in the coastal areas of South China. The mission was so successful that he was awarded the Bronze Star Medal for meritorious service. The citation noted, "On numerous occasions Captain Farrell was compelled to make rapid decisions which concerned the lives and safety of his men who were operating as agents behind enemy lines. His decisions proved sound and showed evidence of thorough knowledge of combat and infiltration work."

As Farrell neared the ground of Canton, he saw a number of armed Japanese pointing at his rapidly descending parachute and gesturing excitedly. Immediately upon landing, he and his team were surrounded by soldiers brandishing bayonet-tipped rifles. An officer's sharp command brought the onslaught to a halt, giving Ferrell an opportunity to talk to the English-speaking officer. The officer knew of the Emperor's decision and told Farrell that his orders were to take him and his team to the Swiss Embassy. The team languished in the embassy for two days before the Japanese commander summoned Ferrell and told him that his troops would lay down their arms. Ferrell immediately notified General Chang Fa Kwai, commander-in-chief, 2nd Chinese Army Group, to which his OSS field intelligence team was attached. On 18 August 1945, Farrell and his team welcomed elements of the Chinese First Army as they entered the city to accept the Japanese surrender.

Germany's Interest in China

For decades Germany had had an extensive commercial interest in China, and over the course of many years leading up to World War II, had cultivated excellent diplomatic relations with the Chinese Nationalist Government, led by Chiang Kai-shek. There were fairly large German communities in the major port cities where they enjoyed a high standard of living. Trade was particularly encouraged by the German War Department, hoping to develop a source of scarce raw materials. The German Army even furnished advisers to train Chiang Kai-shek's army, an arrangement that lasted until Hitler withdrew the advisers in 1938 when he was shifting his support to Japan, then at war with China.

The German Government's interests in China was represented by the Diplomatic Service whose embassy was in Nanking with branches in Shanghai and Peking. In the late 1930s, the German ambassador opposed the Nazis' pro-Japanese policy and was recalled in 1938. During the critical years that followed there was little if any coordination of German political affairs in China. However, the embassy continued to maintain a radio station (XGRS) that beamed propaganda in six languages throughout China and supported a listening post that monitored Allied broadcasts, which was used by the Nazi Party's propaganda office, as well as the German War Department's Intelligence Bureau.

The Nazi Party in China had its headquarters in Shanghai but was directly subordinate to Berlin through the National Socialist

Organization for Germans in Foreign Countries (AO). AO's principal aim was to penetrate the existing German societies abroad, to gain control over public and private institutions, and to have trusted members appointed to consular and diplomatic posts. The Nazi Party exercised considerable control over all German nationals living in China. Any party member who did not obey orders was subject to disciplinary action. There was even a local Gestapo office in Shanghai, acting under the direct orders of the Gestapo Chief of the Far East, Col. Joseph Meisinger, the "Butcher of the Warsaw Ghetto." The Nazi Party oversaw various organizations in Shanghai—satellites of the Storm Troopers (SA), German Labor Front (DAF), League of German Girls (BDM), and the Hitler Youth (Hitler Jugend) organizations. There was even an offshoot of Goebbels's Propaganda Ministry, operating under the cover name, "German Bureau of Information" (DISS), under Baron Jesco von Puttkamer, an ardent Nazi and member of the German upper class. His Shanghai Park Hotel office became the focal point for propaganda in the Far East, even penetrating into North and South American and Europe.

The most important German organization to penetrate China was the Intelligence Department of the German War Office, the *Amt Auslands und Abwehr*. The Abwehr responsible for secret military intelligence and covert operations, and was an integral part of the German High Command. All its affiliations were with the Wehrmacht, not with the Party or Party formations. In neutral countries, covert Abwehr offices called the *Kriegsorganisation* (KO) often worked within embassies and consulates under diplomatic cover. The first KO was established in Shanghai in 1940. Its leader, Navy Capt. Louis Theodor Siefken, recruited agents from the German community, relying on their connections to expand operations throughout China and the Far East. Its mission was to gather military and economic intelligence through the use of agents acting under the guise of journalists, doctors, technicians, diplomats, and businessmen. The KO's principal agents were German but there were also subagents of various nationalities—Chinese, Japanese, Russian, French, Portuguese, Italian—involved in the spy network. The head of the organization worked out of the embassy office in Shanghai. This provided diplomatic "cover" for him, but raised the hackles of the "official foreign-service" types. Siefken used the embassy radio transmission to send reports back to Berlin, causing additional friction because he used his own codes, which was undecipherable by the diplomats. The KO also established listening posts to monitor Allied broadcasts. It broke one of the U.S. Coast Guard's codes, enabling it to identify ships' locations for German submarines. By 1942 another KO had been set up in Shanghai.

On the Hunt

Farrell reported the discovery of the transmitting station to the OSS, which ordered him to continue the investigation. In December 1945, Dr. Erich Kordt, Consul General of the German Embassies in Tokyo, Nanking, and Shanghai, was interrogated by OSS agents. Farrell was provided the interrogation report, that outlined the extent of German penetration into China and also revealed the internal conflicts which hindered cooperation among the different German governmental agencies—the diplomatic department, the Nazi party, and the intelligence department of the German War Office—by fostering conflicting agendas and encouraging personality conflicts. Dr. Kordt had been involved in the German resistance to Hitler's regime in the late 1930s and had been an agent for the Soviet spy Richard Sorge until 1944. Based on the report, Farrell became convinced that German officials continued to furnish aid to the Japanese until their surrender. The OSS directed Farrell to brief the Chinese on the extent of his findings. As a result of his investigation, he was appointed as a member of the War Crimes Investigation Board of Chiang Kai-shek's Military Council, Canton Branch.

Farrell realized that he had to act quickly. He had evidence that the key suspects, Lt. Col. Lothar Eisentraeger, alias Col. Ludwig Ehrhardt, head of the German War Office Intelligence Department in China; Baron Jesco von Puttkamer, head of the German Bureau of Information; SS Col. Joseph Meisinger, Gestapo Chief of the Far East; and others of their ilk, were "going to ground" in an effort to escape Allied counterespionage efforts. In addition, vital witnesses, many of whom were former Japanese intelligence operatives, were being repatriated back to the home islands or were in danger of being lost in the confusion of war-torn China.

COLONEL JOSEPH MEISINGER

SS-*Standartenführer* (Col.) Joseph Albert Meisinger, a long-time member of the SS, was ordered to the Tokyo Embassy early in 1941 after a series of failed assignments and charges of brutality. His personnel file noted him to be "so utterly bestial and corrupt as to be practically inhuman." He was notorious for ordering the execution of hundreds of Polish Jews, earning the sobriquet "Butcher of Warsaw." In Japan he continued to campaign for the extermination of Jews, while purging the German community of enemies of the Third Reich. He also worked closely with the Kempeitai, the Japanese Secret Intelligence Service. At the end of the war, he turned himself in to American counterintelligence and was eventually turned over to the Polish government as a war criminal. Meisinger was convicted and sentenced to death. The sentence was carried out on 7 March 1947.

Armed with the authority of the Military Council and backed by the OSS, Farrell used the extensive resources of the X-2 Counter-Espionage Section Branch to assist Chinese police in locating, arresting, and interrogating suspected war criminals. In some cases he accompanied Chinese police on the arrests.

X-2 had been created in June 1943 by Colonel Donovan to work with the British on their "Ultra" program breaking German encrypted communications. Donovan picked an old friend, Washington attorney James Murphy, to head the branch. Its officers could veto operations proposed by Special Operations and Secret Intelligence no questions asked, and all sections of the OSS were instructed to give full cooperation and support to X-2. By the end of World War II, the X-2 had 650 personnel assigned in its various locations and had exposed some three thousand enemy agents.

As Farrell and his team identified suspects and evidence of illegal activities beyond the Canton-Shanghai area, field detachments from the Strategic Services Unit (SSU) were tasked to provide support. Their investigations uncovered evidence of the execution of American flyers, the mistreatment of Allied prisoners of war, the collaboration of Americans and other foreign nationals, as well as the post-surrender operations of Bureau Ehrhardt. Farrell quickly discovered that his investigation could be compared to peeling on onion—each layer exposing another, adding to his store of information and forming a picture of German subversive activities.

The sixty-year old Ehrhardt (Eisentraeger) was described by Farrell "as a close personal friend of Hitler. He was a somewhat nondescript, balding man with a high 'widow's peak,' prominent chin, and stern countenance, leaving one with the impression of firm authority. He was an extrovert, who enjoyed the 'good life' and the companionship of everyone willing to keep him company and listen to his boastful tales." During the war, Bureau Ehrhardt was a unit of the German High Command and operated under the auspices of the German Embassy. Its offices were located in Shanghai, with branch offices in Canton (Bureau Heise) and Peiping (Fuellkrug)—named after their leaders, Erich Heise and Siegfried Fuellkrug. Under Ehrhardt's leadership the organization flourished, recruiting agents, expanding operations, and developing sources within the Japanese military hierarchy.

By 1945, however, the German military situation at home was desperate. The Allies were pressing on all fronts and it was only a matter of time until Hitler's forces were totally defeated. Ehrhardt clearly understood that his organization's status was precarious at best and, after repeated requests for instructions to Germany went unanswered, he ordered, on his own initiative, the files containing information about the Japanese burned. He did not want them to see what his organization had learned about them, in case Germany surrendered and the files fell into Japanese hands. On 8 May the German High Command unconditionally surrendered and ordered all German military, naval, and air forces, and all forces under German control to cease active operations. Paragraph five of the order specifically stated: "In the event of the German High Command or any of the forces under their control failing to act in accordance with this act of surrender, the Supreme Commander, Allied Expeditionary Force and the Soviet High Command will take such punitive or other action as they deem appropriate."

FUNCTIONS OF THE COUNTER ESPIONAGE BRANCH

1. To collect from every authorized source appropriate intelligence data concerning espionage and subversive activities of the enemy.
2. To analyze and process such intelligence in order to take appropriate action, and to exchange such intelligence with appropriate authorized agencies.
3. To institute such measures as may be necessary to protect the operational security of OSS, and to prevent the penetration of our espionage and other secret activities.
4. To cooperate with the counterintelligence agencies of the United States and our allies, and afford them timely information of enemy attempts at penetration or subversive action from areas in which X-2 is authorized to operate.
5. To prepare secret lists of subversive personalities in foreign areas for the theater commanders and other such government agencies as the director may prescribe.

Ehrhardt was informed of the order and sent a telegram through the German Embassy to all agencies and sub-offices of his organization notifying them of the surrender and directing them to cease operations. However, he worded the telegram in such a way as to suggest that continued cooperation with the Japanese was desirable. As a result of his suggestion, the members of the bureau and the German Information Bureau in Shanghai signed contracts to provide military information to the Japanese, violating the surrender agreement. On 20 May, an intelligence officer of the Japanese High Command at Nanking visited Ehrhardt on orders from the Japanese Supreme Command in Tokyo. He conveyed to him that the Japanese government was anxious to use the bureau "to the greatest extent possible." He also encouraged the bureau to continue forwarding Allied radio call signs and wave lengths. The bureau complied, sending the intercepted messages to the Supreme Command at Nanking once or twice a week.

Getting the Goods on the Evil Doers

Heise Bureau

During the investigation of possible war crimes, Farrell reported receiving information regarding a German-run transmitting station located in Shameen, the European section of Canton. "Investigations were made concerning the inhabitants of this place [30 Chu Kong Road] and the significance of the aerials on the roof of the building," he noted. On the morning of 13 September 1945, Farrell and two members of his team entered the building and found two German nationals, Oswald Ulbricht and Hanz Niemann. Farrell and his fellow agent, U.S. Army Staff Sgt. Marvin M. Gray, interrogated them. The men reported that, "The operation of the station was planned in Shanghai by Lothar Eisentraeger out of an office in the German Embassy known as the Bureau Ehrhardt." The two indicated that Erich Heise and themselves were assigned to operate the station. They identified Heise as the head of the Canton organization. They also provided information that laid out Heise's post-surrender activities but remained silent about their own actions. Ulbricht swore that the station was in operation only until Germany's surrender on 8 May 1945. Farrell noted however, "I suspect that under cover, the station was still functioning up until . . . the Japanese surrendered [in mid-August 1945]."

Farrell learned that Hajimu Masuda, a Nisei born in Los Angeles, was being held in the Ward Road Jail, Shanghai for having served in the Japanese Army. Farrell notified headquarters that, "If we receive confirmation that Masuda is an American citizen as he claims, I am going to arrest him for treason and demand the death penalty." Under interrogation, Masuda admitted being a radio interceptor in the Heise organization after the surrender. "I monitored certain broadcast bands of the United States and Chinese Air Forces. My job was to take down word for word the conversations concerning take-offs, plane numbers, how many planes in flight, cargoes they carried, and landing times and places. I came to know that we were plotting all the American and Chinese plane movements, cargo movements and troop traffic which were coming over the Hump from India into China."

Masuda implicated Ulbright and Niemann as continuing to work after the surrender.

Next Farrell had Maj. Gen. Tomita Naosuke, chief of staff of the Japanese 23rd Army questioned. Staff Sergeant Gray took his deposition at the Honan Japanese Internment Camp. Naosuke swore that, "Erich Heise and his office staff (including Ulbricht and Niemann) continued operations with the Japanese after the surrender of Germany. . . ." Gray also interviewed Heise's Chinese interpreter, D. M. Shaw. "He made me continue to help in the work he was doing . . . despite the German surrender." Based on their testimony, Farrell had Heise arrested. After being confronted with the evidence, Heise caved in and provided Farrell with a chart of the German organizational structure in China, implicating Ehrhardt as the head of the German War Office Intelligence Department, the KO as well as the individual responsible for "suggesting" to continue providing intelligence information to the Japanese.

Farrell continued pressuring Heise, who admitted receiving a monthly salary of between two and five million dollars CRB (Central Reserve Bank of China) from the Japanese for information. He implicated Ulbricht and Niemann in an ongoing effort to monitor U.S. wireless communication and intercept warning net messages during the battle for Okinawa. He also "fingered" Franz Siebert, the Canton Consul General. According to Heise, Siebert continued to act as the German government representative and did nothing to stop Ehrhardt's activities even though he knew they were in violation of the surrender protocols. After his office was closed, he continued to exercise consular prerogatives and ordered German nationals to actively assist the Japanese. In June 1945, Siebert gave the Japanese detailed lists of war materials held by German firms in Canton because "he considered it his duty."

As a result of Heise's admission, Farrell had him jailed, along with his two confederates, Ulbright and Niemann; Dr. Johannes Otto, head of the Nazi party in China, Siebert; and all members of the consulate, who were stripped of their diplomatic immunity. One night while pursuing leads, Farrell was ambushed near his hotel by a lone gunman, who fired one shot at a distance of ten feet, just missing—but Farrell felt the round pass his head! Farrell pulled his pistol but the flash from the gunman's pistol had

HEISE BUREAU-JAPANESE INTELLIGENCE

Farrell and Gray interviewed a number of Japanese intelligence officers to determine the relationship between the Heise Bureau and the intelligence office of the 23rd Army, which was responsible for the Canton area.

- Captain Aoyama, Japanese intelligence liaison officer to the Heise Office stated that, "The Heise had been detailed from the Bureau Ehrhardt, headquarters of the German espionage system for all China in Shanghai, to open a sub-office for South China in Canton. Heise was told to monitor broadcasts from Kunming and other related ATC [Air Traffic Control] bases. Since March 1944, the Heise office provided intelligence to two Japanese units, Kagami and Misumi, named for their commanders. After the German surrender, the Heise office received technical assistance for the interception of U.S. naval broadcasts, 2730 kilocycles, under orders from General Headquarters in Nanking. Heise told me that he had received a telegram from Shanghai at the time of the German surrender, ordering him to continue to work."
- Major Kobayashi Kazuo, staff intelligence officer with the 23rd Army stated, "I remember two remittances of money that came for the Heise office from Shanghai . . . that had been sent from Lt. Col. Ehrhardt."
- Captain Taizo Oka, a staff officer in the political department of the 23rd Army stated, "The Heise office was connected to Lt. Col. Ehrhardt in Shanghai. The office collected information about the air force from Chungking and relayed the information to their home country. The 23rd Army helped them in the gathering of this information."

blinded him, so he was unable to get off a shot or identify the assailant. Not long after this incident, an intruder broke into his hotel room but was scared off by Farrell and Gray who brandished their .45-caliber service automatics. The two incidents convinced Farrell that he was on the right track, for attacking an OSS agent was an act of desperation that would bring the entire weight of the American counterespionage effort down on the assailants.

The December 1946 SSU War Crimes Intelligence Section commended Farrell and Gray. " . . . Captain Frank Farrell and Sgt. Gray have done an excellent job in revealing the workings of the Canton Branch of the German espionage system operating under the Ehrhardt Bureau in Shanghai. Reports and signed statements confirm beyond doubt the operations in Canton of German espionage activity directed against America, following the capitulation of Germany, and hence conducted in violation of the surrender terms to which Germany subscribed. Interrogations of high-ranking Japanese officers of the Twenty-Third Army carried out in this area, and signed statements obtained from them, go far towards establishing the degree of relative responsibility of the various army and Gendarmerie units and individual officers for the acts of atrocity committed in the extensive area occupied by the South China Expeditionary Forces."

Bureau Fuellkrug

The Heise investigation uncovered the espionage activities of the four members of the Bureau Fuellkrug in Peking who were providing intelligence information to the Japanese North China Army. In late July, Staff Sergeant Gray interviewed Hans Menien, manager and editor of the Transocean News Service, regarding an agreement to provide intelligence information to the Japanese. "Fuellkrug signed on behalf of his intelligence organization," he said. Farrell interrogated Col. Tomiaki Hidaka, the senior Japanese intelligence officer in Peking, who testified that Fuellkrug and his subordinates, Maria Muller, August Stock, and Walter Heissig, provided important information to him at private conferences and weekly intelligence briefings. As a result of this information, Farrell had the four quickly rounded up by the Chinese police and jailed.

Bureau Ehrhardt

Having rolled up the Canton and Peking branches of the KO, Farrell and Gray moved their base of operations to Shanghai in an effort to prove their case against Ehrhardt and bring him and his cohorts to justice. Using the Heise organizational chart, they scoured the Shanghai area, finding that most of the individuals lived in and around the city. A few of the former Ehrhardt bureau were willing to testify against their former boss to gain clemency from prosecution; however, others stonewalled, refusing to admit any complicity in post-surrender espionage. Hans Dethleffs, a bureau member, swore, "I know that we stopped here [Shanghai] completely; with the day of the German collapse, we did not work anymore." Another, Ingward Rudloff, stated, "I have sworn on the Gospel before Captain Farrell that to the best of my knowledge nobody of the Ehrhardt Bureau worked for the Japanese after the German surrender." Heinz Peerschke said, with a perfectly straight face, that he "simply studied languages after the surrender, occasionally venturing out to get ice-water to take home." Farrell, ever the hard-nosed skeptic, had them all arrested.

Farrell expanded his search to include former Japanese intelligence officers, most of whom were waiting for transportation back to Japan in the Honam Japanese Internment Camp. "They were happy to oblige," he explained, "hoping their cooperation might speed up their return home." Lieutenant Colonel Akira Mori*, the senior Japanese intelligence officer in Shanghai, was one of the first that Farrell interviewed. Mori volunteered that, "Ehrhardt told me that he would continue to help us and he would pass that message on to the other members of his organization, all of whom signed a statement indicating they would help us." Mori indicated that the Japanese High Command was particularly anxious for the Ehrhardt Bureau to continue its efforts because it was providing important tactical information on U.S. Navy operations during the battle of Okinawa, where U.S. forces were engaged in a bloody battle at sea with Japanese *kamikazes*—suicide pilots. Gray interviewed Kobayshi Kazuo, a staff officer in the 23rd Army, who testified that he saw a telegram in late May 1945 from Shanghai stating that Ehrhardt would continue working for the Japanese. Furthermore, he remembered two large remittances of money, in local currency, that were paid to Ehrhardt, as well as payments in small two-ounce gold bars called "peanuts" for this work.

*Mori was charged with "Stealing POW food" and using harsh "collective punishment" against the POWs.

The Japanese Foreign Affairs Section of the 23rd Army outlined their use of agents and spies to gather intelligence, two of whom Farrell personally tracked down. One agent, Tam Ping Kuo, alias Bianca Tam, alias Bianca Sannino, he compared to Mata Hari, the notorious international spy of World War I. Tam was arrested for being a Japanese spy, collaborator, extortionist, perjurer, prostitute, and procuress. Tam, an Italian, the daughter of a highly respected naval family, married a Chinese officer and, after the war started, left him for the life of a Japanese agent. During that time, she lived with several men, including the Vichy French Consul in Canton, who was a notorious Japanese collaborator. Tam ended her relationship when the man either ran out of money or information. When the war ended, she tried to entice American officers with sexual favors to fly her out of China but instead ended up in a Chinese stockade after Farrell had her arrested. The other spy, Rosaline Wong, was convicted by a Chinese court and executed.

Farrell found that those who had been persecuted by the Nazis, particularly Shanghai's Jews, were more than happy to testify and gain retribution for past injustices. Included in this category were several diplomats who had an ax to grind because of the way they had been treated. Captain Siefken was more than willing to assist in the investigation. Ehrhardt had convinced the Abwehr to dismiss him from the KO for being a homosexual, which Siefken swore was a trumped-up charge. The disaffected officer described Eisentraeger, alias Ehrhardt, alias Count Schwerin, as a "secretive professional spy master and dedicated Nazi."

Satisfied that he had enough evidence for a conviction, Farrell swore out a warrant and accompanied Chinese Army officers to arrest Ehrhardt and his confederates. The arrest went without incident, almost a letdown considering the power these men had wielded during the heyday of the Third Reich. On April 16, 1946, the Mason City (Iowa) *Globe-Gazette* reported:

Intelligence officers Tuesday jailed six more alleged Nazis in connection with operations of Bureau Ehrhardt which operated a German espionage network in China long after VE day in violation of surrender terms. It was announced also that seven other persons

LOTHAR EISENTRAGER, ALIAS LUDWIG EHRHARDT

Lothar Eisentraeger had been an officer in World War I and had been wounded several times. In 1932, he joined the Nazi party entering the German military intelligence in the mid-1930s, where he rose to the rank of major. As a friend and protégé of Adm. Wilhelm Canaris, the German military intelligence chief, he was offered the opportunity to head an organization in China. In 1941, he slipped across the Chinese–Soviet border posing as a businessman and set up an office in the Shanghai embassy. Irmagard Zech, an embassy secretary, said, "Ehrhardt was assigned as a special adviser, whose work consisted of collecting all types of intelligence in the Far Eastern and Pacific Theaters of war." In a deposition to Farrell, Eisentraeger stated that the main tasks of his bureau was to spy on the Soviet Union, observe Japanese activities, and gather information about raw materials in the Far East. He deliberately omitted any mention of spying on the United States.

In a report to OSS headquarters, Farrell described Eisentraeger as "arrogant and jealous of all possible rivals to his authority . . . and tried hard to look and act like a Prussian officer, but it is also said that he does not quite succeed in this." His secretary, Gerda Kocher, told Farrell that he is "a jolly fellow and he likes a good drink, good food, and to enjoy life. His house was open to everybody who wanted to have a drink and was willing to keep him company. He hated to be alone and therefore he was almost always out or had somebody at this place. He was very talkative, especially when he had drunk one too many." Kocher could not understand how "such a man could be appointed to this job."

including three German officials have been held in Canton since Oct 18 1945 as participants in the Ehrhardt network or as material witnesses. Eleven alleged members of the office, including Lt. Col. Ludwig Ehrhardt, the leader, were arrested here Monday and were charged with war crimes. American officers said they carried on war against the United States after the German capitulation. The

Americans are [also] holding the head the Ehrhardt network for south China, a former Captain Heise of the Germany artillery, Oswald Ulbricht, former radio expert for the Urasia German airline, and Hanz Niemann, one time radioman aboard the pocket battleship Lützow. Also in custody in Canton are Dr. Franz Siebert, German consul general at Canton, Vice Consul Herbert, and Second Vice Consul Johannes Bresan; Dr. Johannes Otto, longtime German resident of Canton and the head of the Nazi party in south China, is being held as a material witness.

German Information Bureau/German News Service

The Ehrhardt investigation led directly to German aristocrat Baron Jesco von Puttkamer, who headed the German Information Bureau in Shanghai, the largest Nazi public relations headquarters outside Germany. He was a friend and protégé of Dr. Paul Joseph Goebbels, Hitler's Reich minister of propaganda. Under Puttkamer, known as the "Goebbels of the Far East," the bureau became the center of the German propaganda effort in the Far East. It operated under the German Propaganda Ministry, working closely with the Bureau Ehrhardt. The Information Bureau, located in a swanky villa in the European section of the city, produced a stream of propaganda broadcasts and leaflets, through a system of cut-outs and front organizations that targeted the British and American war efforts. Its propaganda material was sent not only throughout China but to the Philippines, the Dutch East Indies—and even North and South America and Europe. The German News Service provided a news agency for the Japanese forces in China.

Puttkamer was an ardent Nazi, who joined the party in 1932 and became part of an economic espionage unit of the German military intelligence. Later he switched to the foreign ministry's propaganda section. After the war broke out in 1939, Berlin assigned him to Shanghai. In *Secret War in Shanghai: Treachery, Subversion and Collaboration in the Second World War*, Bernard Wasserstein described Puttkamer as "A handsome, stocky man with a wide, toothy smile, he traveled through the town with his Korean bodyguard in a horse-drawn carriage." During an OSS interrogation, Puttkamer tried to play down his role but Farrell

WAR CRIMES INTELLIGENCE REPORT, 15-31 DECEMBER 1945

Regarding the Germans, only a handful of the SS, NSDAF, Gestapo, and espionage and propaganda agents have been interned and against them no formal war crimes charges have been announced by the Chinese or the United States Governments. [However] SSU/CT continues to amass evidence on war-criminal and collaborationist activities and is already well prepared to implement any concerted Allied war crimes progress should such a program be authorized.

learned from a Chinese printer named T. H. Chow that he continued his post-surrender operations. "The German Information Office sent in a printing order once or twice a month, even after the German surrender." Chow said that when the printing was done his orders were to send them directly to Japanese military headquarters. Based on the printer's testimony Farrell swore out a warrant and Puttkamer was arrested by Chinese authorities and taken to the Ward Road Jail, along with the three men from the German News Service—Herbert Muller, Felix Altenburg, and Alfred Romain—who continued to provide news to the Japanese after the surrender.

The Spokesman-Review of Seattle, Washington, reported on April 17, 1946:

Marine Capt. Frank Farrell New York who led an investigation of Bureau Ehrhardt said von Puttkamer was appointed by propaganda chief Joachim von Ribbentrop to head the German information bureau which propagandized the far east in hopes of splitting the United States from China and dividing the Chinese government and communist leaders. The "master propagandist" was said to have received a salary of $2,500 monthly as head of the German Information Bureau which propagandized the Far East in hopes of fermenting dissension between the US and China. It continued to produce propaganda right up to the Japanese surrender.

Time to Pay the Piper

In October 1946, the United States Military Commission in Shanghai brought the men to trial. In all, twenty-seven German nationals were prosecuted as a result of Farrell's investigation, of whom twenty-one were convicted. Ehrhardt was sentenced to life imprisonment, von Puttkamer to thirty years at hard labor, and the remainder received terms from five to twenty years.

Findings and Sentences

The following were sentenced to the terms of imprisonment indicated:

Lothar Eisentraeger, alias Ludwig Ehrhardt: life
Ingward Rudloff: ten years
Bodo Habenicht: ten years
Hans Dethleffs: ten years
Heinz Peerschke: five years
Mans Mosberg: twenty years
Johannes Rathje: fifteen years
Walter Richter: ten years
Hermann Jaeger: ten years
Jesco von Puttkamer: thirty years
Alfred Romain: thirty years, reduced to twenty years by the
    Reviewing Authorities
Franz Siebert: five years
Erich Heise: twenty years
Oswald Ulbricht: five years
Hanz Niemann: five years
Felix Altenburg: eight years
Herbert Mueller: ten years
Siegfried Fuellkrug: twenty years
Walter Heissig: twenty years
August Stoc: five years, reduced to two years by the
    Reviewing Authorities
Maria Muller: five years, reduced to two years by the
    Reviewing Authorities

LEGION OF MERIT EXCERPTS

For exceptionally meritorious service in the performance of duties of great responsibility during the period 7 September 1945 to 15 November 1946 . . . as members of a two-man team, Capt. Farrell's record is especially noteworthy for the unusual productivity and resourcefulness displayed in investigating enemy espionage activities in the Far East after the formal surrender of Germany. Of paramount importance to the Allied Governments was the discovery by Capt. Farrell and his co-investigator of conclusive evidence that a German espionage ring, known as the Bureau Ehrhardt, had continued operations and assisted the Japanese . . . it was substantially proved that this ring operated from Manchuria to Java, centering its activities in Peiping, Shanghai, and Canton, China. . . . Their extensive knowledge of the backgrounds of witnesses, the sources of information, and the framework and history of the Nazi Government organs and operations in China rendered invaluable assistance in securing [convictions]. The resounding success of the investigation and prosecution of the trial lent much prestige to the American war effort in China and reflects great personal credit upon Captain Farrell and the Army of the United States.

Six of the accused were acquitted: Herbert Glietsch, Johannes Otto, Wolf Schenke, Ernst Woermann, Wilhelm Stoller, and Elgar von Randow.

Farrell and Marvin Gray were awarded a Legion of Merit, a singular honor as this award was normally presented to very senior officers. The accompanying citation noted his especially noteworthy performance in securing information necessary for the war crimes trials and the resourcefulness he displayed in carrying out those responsibilities. The Chinese government awarded him the Breast Order of the Cloud and Banner, Seventh Grade, one of their highest military decorations.

On 5 March 1947, Farrell received orders home and demobilization, having carried out one of the most demanding independent assignments for any officer of his rank and experience in the annals of the Marine Corps. Operating independently for two years, he almost single-handedly broke up and brought to trial a major enemy spy ring. He interrogated more than a thousand witnesses, examined an even greater number of documents in various foreign languages, literally covering most of the five thousand Germans in China. Arriving home, he picked up where he left off, going on to become a celebrity in his own right as a columnist with the *New York World Telegram*, a talk show host, and a colonel in the Marine Corps Reserve.

Bibliography

Alcott, Carroll. *My War with Japan.* (New York: Henry Holt and Company, 1943).

Alexander, Joseph H. *Edson's Raiders, The 1st Marine Raider Battalion in World War II.* (Limited Edition by Joseph H. Alexander).

Alsop, Stewart, and Thomas Braden. *Sub Rosa : The O.S.S. and American Espionage.* (New York: Harcourt, 1964).

Atkinson, Rick. *An Army at Dawn, The War in North Africa, 1942–1943.* (New York: Henry Holt Company, 2002).

Averill, Gerald P. *Mustang: A Combat Marine.* (Novato, CA: Presidio Press, 1987).

Blankfort, Michael. *The Big Yankee: The Life of Carlson of the Raiders.* (Boston: Little, Brown and Company, 1947).

Brown, Anthony Cave. *Wild Bill Donovan: The Last Hero.* (New York: Times Books, 1982).

Chambers, John Whiteclay. *OSS Training in the National Parks and Service Abroad in World War II.* (Washington: U.S. National Park Service, 2008).

Christ, James F. *Battalion of the Damned: The 1st Marine Paratroopers at Gavutu and Bloody Ridge.* (Annapolis: Naval Institute Press, 2007).

Christ, James F. *Mission Raise Hell: The U.S. Marines on Choiseul, October-November 1943.* (Annapolis: Naval Institute Press, 2006).

Clark, Mark W. *Calculated Risk.* (New York: Harper & Brothers Publishing, 1950).

Clemens, Martin. *Alone on Guadalcanal: A Coastwatcher's Story.* (Annapolis: Naval Institute Press, 1998).

Coon, Carleton. *Adventures and Discoveries*. (New Jersey: Prentice Hill, Inc., 1981).

Coram, Robert. *Brute: The Life of Victor Krulak, U.S. Marine*. (New York: Little, Brown and Company, 2010).

Dougherty, Leo J. *The Fighting Techniques of a Japanese Infantryman 1941-1945, Training, Techniques and Weapons*. (St. Paul: MBI, 2002).

Drea, Edward J. *Japan's Imperial Army: Its Rise and Fall, 1853-1945*. (Kansas: University Press of Kansas, 2009).

Frank, Richard B. *Guadalcanal: The Definitive Account of the Landmark Battle*. (New York: Penguin Books, 1990).

Funk, Arthur Layton. *The Politics of Torch, The Allied Landings and the Algiers Putsch, 1942*. (Kansas: University Press of Kansas, 1974).

Gailey, Harry A. *Bougainville, 1943–1945: The Forgotten Campaign*. (Kentucky: University Press of Kentucky, 2003).

Griffith, Samuel B. II. *The Battle for Guadalcanal*. (New York: J.B. Lippicott Company, 1963).

Hammel, Eric. *Guadalcanal: Starvation Island*. (New York: Crown Publishers, Inc., 1987).

Hoffman, Jon T. *Once a Legend: "Red Mike" Edson of the Marine Raiders*. (California: Presidio, 1994).

Hoffman, Jon T. *Silk Chutes and Hard Fighting: U.S. Marine Corps Parachute Units in World War II*. (Washington: Marine Corps History Division, 1999).

Howe, George F. *U.S. Army in World War II: The Mediterranean Theater of Operations, Northwest Africa: Seizing the Initiate in the West*. (Washington: Department of the Army, 1957).

Isely, Jeter A., and Philip A. Crowl. *The U.S. Marines and Amphibious War, Its Theory, and Its Practice in the Pacific*. (New Jersey: Princeton University Press, 1951).

Jersey, Stanley Coleman. *Hell's Islands: The Untold Story of Guadalcanal*. (College Station: Texas A & M Press, 2008).

Johnson, Richard W. *Follow Me: The Story of the Second Marine Division in World War II*. (New York: Random House, 1948).

Kane, Henry I. Jr., and Douglas T. Shaw. *Isolation of Rabul: History of U.S. Marine Corp in World War II, Volume II*. (Washington: U.S. Government Printing Office, 1989).

Leckie, Robert. *Challenge for the Pacific: The Story of the Incredible Hundred Days in which the Americans Seized the Offensive from the*

Japanese at Guadalcanal. (New York: Doubleday & Company, Inc., 1965).

Lee, Robert Edward. *Victory at Guadalcanal.* (Novato: Presidio Press, 1981).

Lees, Michael. *The Rape of Serbia: The British Role in Tito's Grab for Power 1943–1944.* (New York: Harcourt Brace Jovanovich, 1990).

Lippman, Thomas W. *Arabian Knight: Colonel Bill Eddy USMC and the Rise of American Power in the Middle East.* (California: Selwa Press, 2008).

Lord, Walter. *Lonely Vigil: Coastwatchers of the Solomons.* (New York: The Viking Press, 1977).

Lundstrom, John B. *The First Team and the Guadalcanal Campaign: Naval Fighter Combat from August to November 1942.* (Annapolis: Naval Institute Press, 1994).

McMillan, George. *The Old Breed: A History of the First Marine Division in World War II.* (Washington: Infantry Journal Press, 1949).

Merillat, Herbert Christian. *Guadalcanal Remembered.* (New York: Dodd, Mead & Company, 1982).

Meyers, Bruce. *Swift, Silent, and Deadly: Marine Amphibious Reconnaissance in the Pacific, 1942–1945.* (Annapolis: Naval Institute Press, 2004).

Morison, Samuel Eliot. *History of U.S. Naval Operations in World War II: Operations in North African Waters, October 1942–June 1943.* (Boston: Little, Brown and Company, 1947).

Murphy, Robert. *Diplomat Among Warriors.* (New York: Doubleday & Company, Inc., 1964).

O'Donnell, Patrick K. *Operatives, Spies, and Saboteurs: The Unknown Story of the Men and Women of WW II's OSS.* (New York: Free Press, 2004).

O'Donnell, Patrick K. *Into the Rising Sun: In Their Own Words, World War II's Pacific Veterans Reveal the Heart of Combat.* (New York: Free Press, 2002).

Peatross, Oscar F. *Bless 'em All: The Raider Marines of World War II.* (Irvine, California: ReView Publications, 1995).

Roosevelt, Kermit. *War Report of the OSS (Office of Strategic Services).* (New York: Walker and Company, 1976).

Shores, Christopher, Ikuhiko Hata, Yasuho Izawa. *Japanese Naval Air Force Fighter Units and Their Aces 1932-1945.* (London: Grub Street, 2011).

Smith, George W. *Carlson's Raid: The Daring Marine Assault on Makin.* (California: Presidio, 2001).

Smith, George W. *Do-Or-Die Men: The 1st Marine Raider Battalion at Guadalcanal.* (New York: Simon and Schuster, 2003).

Smith, Michael S. *Bloody Ridge: The Battle that Saved Guadalcanal.* (California: Presidio, 2000).

Smith, Richard Harris. *OSS: The Secret History of America's First Central Intelligence Agency.* (Berkley: University of California Press, 1972).

Smith, S. E. *The United States Marine Corps in World War II.* (New York: Random House, 1969).

Tregaskis, Richard. *Guadalcanal Diary.* (New York: Blue Ribbon Books, 1943).

Twinning, Merrill B. *No Bended Knee: The Battle for Guadalcanal.* (Navato: Presidio, 1996).

Vaughan, Hal. *FDR's 12 Apostles: The Spies who Paved the Way for the Invasion of North Africa.* (Connecticut: The Lyon Press, 2006).

Wasserstein, Bernard. *Secret War in Shanghai: Treachery, Subversion and Collaboration in the Second World War.* (London: Profile Books, 1998).

Willard, W. Wyeth. *The Leathernecks Come Through.* (New York: Fleming H. Revell Company, 1944).

Winks, Robin W. *Cloak & Gown: Scholars in the Secret War, 1939–1961.* (New York: William Morrow and Company, Inc., 1987).

Wukovits, John. *American Commando: Evans Carlson, His WWII Marine Raiders, and America's First Special Forces Mission.* (New York: NAL Caliber, 2009).

OSS Documents in Author's Possession

Captain Peter J. Ortiz, Memorandum for General Donovan, dated 15 May, 1943 (copy)

OSS X-2 Branch report, Shanghai, 15 November 1945, *German Organizations in Shanghai.* Author's collection.

War Crimes Intelligent *Report for 15–31 December 1945.* Author's collection.

OSS X-2 Branch report, Canton, 20 September 1945, German Transmitting Station in Canton. Author's collection.

Statement of Interview with Dr. Franz Siebert, 19 January 1946 and June 28, 1946.

Statement of Interview with Saski Tomotsune, 13 January 1946.

Statement of Interview with Capt. Taizo Oka, 6 November 1945. Author's collection.

Statement of Interview with Kobayashi Kazuo, 14 January 1946. Author's collection.

Statement of Interview with Hajimu Masuda, 13 March 1946.

Statement of Interview with D. M. Shaw, 22 September 1945.

Statement of Interview with Tomita Naosuke, 14 January 1946.

Statement of Interview with Aoyama Harumitsu, 13 January 1946.

Statement of Interview with Col. Yoshimasa Okada, 20 March 1946.

Statement of Interview with Oswald Ulbricht, 19 January 1946.

Statement of Capt. Frank Farrell and Staff Sgt. Marvin Gray, 25 December 1945, Conversation of Erich Heise with Captain Aoyama about the transfer of Gen. Ho Yin Chin.

Statement of Capt. Frank Farrell and Staff Sgt. Marvin Gray, 11 November 1945, Hajimu Masuda, who claims U.S. citizenship, a collaborator with the Japanese in Office Heise, the Canton office of Bureau Ehrhardt.

Statement of Capt. Frank Farrell and Staff Sgt. Marvin Gray, 4 December 1945, Heise Office, Further details.

Unpublished Sources

Platoon Sergeant Francis C. Pettus unpublished manuscript, "Observation on Tulagi."

Marine Corps University Archives and Marine Corps History Division

Banks, Brig. Gen. Charles L., Marine Corps Historical Division. Oral History Interview, 1974.

Chambers, Col. Justice M., Marine Corps Historical Division. Oral History Interview, 1988.

Griffith, Brig. Gen. Samuel B. II, Marine Corps Historical Division. Oral History Interview, 1976.

Krulak, Lt. Gen. Victor H., Marine Corps Historical Division. Oral History Interview, 1973.

Peatross, Maj. Gen. Oscar F., Marine Corps Historical Division. Oral History Interview, 1975.

Thomas, Lt. Gen. Gerald C., Marine Corps Historical Division. Oral History Interview, 1973.

Twining, Lt. Gen. Merrill B., Marine Corps Historical Division. Oral History Interview, 1975.

U.S. Government

Department of the Navy. *The Landing in the Solomons 7–8 August 1942.* (Washington: Naval Historical Center, 1994).

1st Marine Parachute Battalion Operations Reports. (13 September to 14 September 1942)

Headquarters U.S. Marine Corps. *Bougainville and the Northern Solomons.* (Washington: Historical Section, Division of Public Information, 1948).

Headquarters U.S. Marine Corps. *The Guadalcanal Campaign.* (Washington: Historical Division, 1949).

OSS X-2 Branch report, Shanghai, 11 October 1945, NARA, RG 226, entry 182, box 16. Folder 182.

Office of Naval Intelligence. *The Landing in the Solomons, 7–8 August 1942.* (Washington, D.C.: Publications Branch, U.S. Navy, 1943).

Office of Naval Intelligence. *Miscellaneous Actions in the South Pacific, 8 August 1942–22 January 1943.* (Washington, D.C.: Publications Branch, U.S. Navy, 1943).

Office of Naval Intelligence. *The Landings in North Africa, November 1942.* (Washington, D.C.: Publications Branch, U.S. Navy, 1943).

Bureau of Naval Personnel. *Information Bulletin No. 306.* (Washington, D.C.: Department of the Navy, 1942)

War Department. *Handbook on Japanese Military Forces.* (Washington, D.C.: U.S. Government Printing Office, 1944).

Articles

Cooke, F. O. "They Took Thirty Marines," *Leatherneck*: July 1943; 26, 7; pg. 26-57.

Le Francois, W.S. "We Mopped up Makin Island," *Saturday Evening Post*, Part I—December 4, 1943, pp. 20-21, 109-110; Part II—December 11, 1943, pp. 28-29, 41, 43, 45, 48.

Mansfield, Walter. "Marine with the Chetniks." *Marine Corps Gazette*: Part I—Jan. 1946, pp. 2-9; Part II Feb. 1946.

Mattingly, Maj. Robert E. "Who Knew Not Fear," *Studies in Intelligence*, Summer 1982.

Walling, Michael G. *Oran Harbor Assault—North Africa, 8 November 1942.* AuthorsDen.com, 2011

Index